Whispered Memories

To Caroline

I hope you enjoy it)

Love Nicola x

Whispered Memories

Nicola Avery

For Charlie, Mellie and Harriet.
My past, my present and my future.

'When will you come back?' the young girl asked.

'When it is my time,' he replied.

'Will I recognise you?'

The old man looked down into the face of the child and smiled.

'Look not for me with your eyes,
but with your soul.

'Beneath the beating of your heart you will hear
the faint whispers of memories past
– and know me.'

Chapter 1

She woke on the bedroom floor, the twisted sheets wrapped around her legs and ankles, her whole body trembling. Looking at the jumble of bed linen, she tried to make sense of what had happened, but as usual, any recollection was blocked on her awakening. It normally took some minutes for the shaking to stop. She opened her mouth, but no sound followed and any screaming was done silently. Voluntary movements of her limbs also took time to return. It was always like this – as if she'd returned from some dark place. There would be a feeling of great despair and loss, but hard as she tried, she could never remember any details. Only the state of her body and bed linen bore witness to anything out of the ordinary.

Emma Hart had experienced another one of her night terrors. They came more frequently nowadays, having started shortly after her three-year-old daughter Amelia was born. She had told no one about the violent dreams that played out in her unconscious on some nights. There was little point, as she never remembered anything about them, besides a sense of fear and dread, and without any details, there could be no interpretation or explanation. The dreams, like many other factors in her life, were best kept to herself.

Extracting herself from the debris of linen, she tiptoed to the bathroom and ran the cold water, plunging her hands and wrists into the basin to stop the shaking. With a pounding heart she listened out for Amelia. There was no sound; the cottage remained silent, oblivious to her ordeal.

She crept into her daughter's bedroom to check on her. Amelia lay peacefully on her side, her cheeks a sleep-flushed pink. Looking down at the small shape tucked under the covers, Emma felt the powerful wave of maternal love dissolve any remnants of her night fears. She quietly climbed into the bed and wrapped her slim body around that of her daughter, listening to her every breath and taking comfort from the rhythmic beating of her heart. They lay there together, safe in each other's arms, until the day broke.

'What are you doing in my bed, Mummy?' asked a bemused Amelia, sitting up and looking at her mother. 'Did you mess yours up again?'

Emma smiled at her beautiful daughter, pushing back a long tendril of hair. 'Yes, darling,' she said, gently prodding Amelia's tummy. 'I got all my sheets in a muddle again, and once I got out, I couldn't find my way back in, so I decided to snuggle up with you. You looked so cosy!'

Amelia dropped back into the warm, dented mattress, wrapping her arms around her mother's neck and kissing her.

'Now what do you want for breakfast?' Emma asked.

'We want runny eggs and soldiers,' Amelia replied, leaping out of bed and landing on the bedroom floor on all fours. 'We're hungry.'

What a pair we are, thought Emma, looking down at her sleep-energised daughter. I'm fighting with unknown terrors in my bed, and my daughter orders food for an imaginary friend.

As Emma and Amelia knelt in the garden digging for worms later that morning, all the bad memories of the previous night evaporated in the sunshine. Beside them on the lawn sat a cardboard box in which a small bird cowered in fright, having recently been grasped from the jaws of their ginger cat, Thomas. Emma was sure that the thrusting of worm pieces through a hole in the box did nothing to alleviate the bird's fear, but Amelia was adamant that worms were the answer.

Strands of honey-coloured hair whipped out from under Amelia's sun hat and caught in her mouth. Emma sat back on her heels and looked at her daughter. There was a strong resemblance between them: the same large green eyes, pale, creamy skin and delicate features; but Amelia's hair with its blunt fringe fell down her back as straight as pump water while Emma's was thicker and darker and worn like a long curtain in waves around her face.

Twisting her own hair back and tying it into a ponytail, Emma wiped her forehead with the back of her hand. Worm digging was warm work, but with her concentration now broken, she stood up, trowel in hand, and stretched her back and legs just as the phone rang.

'Amelia, sweetie, that's Mummy's phone. Stay there with the bird and don't let Thomas into the box.' The ginger tom feigned disinterest but watched Amelia and the boxed bird with one eye open from under the hedge. Emma rushed into the kitchen and grabbed the handset. Aware that part of a worm was lodged under a nail, she teased it out while walking back into the garden, the handset close to her ear. 'Hello?' she answered breathlessly, then broke off the conversation saying, 'Oh no! That wasn't good.'

Her daughter had managed to open the cardboard box and lost both Thomas and the small bird into the hedge.

'Emma! It's Gabby,' a disconnected voice shouted down the phone.

'Sorry Gabs,' replied Emma in muffled tones as she moved into the hedge on all fours in an attempt to prevent Thomas finishing off the worm-splattered bird completely.

Gabby had been Emma's best friend since childhood and was godmother to Amelia. A generously proportioned blonde, overly groomed and fully made up at all times, Gabby owned a recruitment business in town. Straight talking and very practical, she had steered Emma through her ex-husband Joshua's departure, the birth of Amelia and the subsequent divorce. The two had met at primary school. Nervous and new, ponytails and plaits, the girls had been paired at neighbouring desks; from that day on they became firm friends, sharing everything from treats to homework, clothes to make-up, parental gripes to secret crushes. As they matured and followed their own career paths, their friendship never wavered. When Gabby opened her employment agency, it was Emma who helped with the office decor and the creation of the company's logo and sales literature. When Emma's catwalk designs caught the eye of a London fashion house, Gabby had shared her elation. They were always there for one another.

'Where did Joshua tell you he was going when you last spoke to him, Em?' Gabby probed cautiously.

'He said he was going on a business trip for a month and wouldn't be able to see Amelia. Hopefully it's to some war-torn zone with no way out and that the up-herself harpy is with him too.'

Gabby listened to Emma's nonchalant response before replying with some hesitation: 'Er, no Em. He's on his honeymoon.'

Emma sat back on the grass as Amelia chased Thomas up to

the garden gate. She watched him squeeze between the wooden posts and head off into the fields with the small bird in his mouth.

'Joshua got married! My God. Who to? Don't tell me it's the harpy?'

Gabby paused again before continuing. 'Yes ... he married the harpy.'

'But men don't marry their harpies! And we only just finalised our divorce.' As the words left her mouth, Emma realised how lame she must sound. 'I've been *so* stupid, Gabby, haven't I?'

'No, darling. You weren't the stupid one, he was. Shall I come round?'

There was no reply from Emma as she tried to make sense of the emotional punch that had just landed in her solar plexus. He married her! The thought rattled around her head and began to claw at her stomach and heart. The overpowering taste of finality filled her mouth as a small, involuntary cry of humiliation escaped.

'Emma?'

Still no answer.

'Em? I'm on my way.'

Gabby hung up the phone and grabbed her bag and keys from her desk. As she drove to the cottage she prayed that this might make Emma let go and finally get on with her life. Speeding up the unmade track, she drew up outside the gate, and then, jamming her floral stilettos back onto her bare feet, she leaped out of the car. A slight breeze caught on the hem of her pale pink summer suit as she gingerly stepped over a small pile of animal parts that looked oddly to her like a collection of bird bits and worms. Opening the gate, she called out.

'Hello Auntie Gabby. Mummy's sad,' a small, wide-eyed Amelia announced with concern.

'I know, darling. That's why I'm here.'

Emma sat on the grass with both arms wrapped protectively around her petite frame, dressed in a pair of tight blue jeans, silver flip-flops and a simple white T-shirt – by now an ongoing record of the morning's activities. She looked up at her best friend and burst into tears. Although she was thirty-three years old, she still resembled a teenager, with her fine bone structure and enormous, expressive eyes.

Eventually, Emma managed one of her beautiful smiles through her tears and smudged mascara. Aware of her friend's obvious heartbreak, Gabby searched for the right words as her heart squeezed with love for her. 'You're far too good for him,' had been her response when Joshua left Emma. And now, looking at the devastation etched on her face, she knew that for a fact. Dropping to her knees, she gathered Emma and Amelia to her. 'One day there will be someone else for you, Em, someone decent who deserves your love.'

Emma had first met Joshua in a hotel in London's Mayfair. She and Gabby had been staying there after a fashion launch. Flushed with success and too much champagne, Emma had shimmied across the floor to rapturous applause from the milling guests. Wearing one of her own designs – a diaphanous gown of gold chiffon and silk that cupped her breasts and skimmed her curves – and her hair flowing free behind her, Emma had opened her arms wide, tilted her head back and spun on her toes.

'We did it! They loved my dresses,' she cried, unaware of the attention she had attracted.

Joshua had stood nearby, mesmerised by Emma, watching her every move. A half-empty glass of bourbon tilted limply in his hands. As the room swayed he focused on the glimpse of a pearl-painted toenail peeping out from Emma's gold-strapped shoe. Temporarily anchored, he watched as Emma curtsied low to the ground, the layers of chiffon surrounding her like a golden sea. Then she lifted her head and looked straight into his eyes.

The sound of applause had come from a group of Joshua's business associates. Ties askew, their sharp Savile Row jackets discarded in the lobby bar, the men had encouraged Emma and Gabby to join them. Gabby was initially reluctant, but having recognised an old friend waving to her from the group she felt reassured and took Emma over to join the party. Well known for his predatory charm, Joshua had waited as his drink-fuelled colleagues scrambled to introduce themselves, then, nonchalantly, he presented himself to the two women. Tall, with a good muscular body, Joshua wore his dark hair swept back from his forehead. A pair of unfathomable dark blue eyes, framed by thick eyebrows, flashed in Emma's direction.

Later that night in Emma's room, Joshua watched as her evening gown slipped from her slim body. As she emerged from its folds he held his breath. 'My Pocket Venus,' he told her, taking her naked body in his arms. 'I feel as if I've been looking for you all my life.'

So intense was their lovemaking that afterwards Emma found herself crying. Wiping away her tears, Joshua had gently kissed her eyelids. 'I can't let you go now. I'm afraid I might lose you,' he told her. When he pulled her closer, they found themselves trembling in anticipation.

The following morning, Joshua and Emma made no secret of their mutual attraction, saying goodbye to the assembled group and holding hands as they left the hotel together.

'Well that's one for the books!' Percy Bird whispered to Gabby as he helped her into her car. 'Joshua never usually hangs around for breakfast, let alone holds hands.'

Joshua's past was something he kept to himself. It was safer that way. He attributed his competitive spirit to his formative years in foster care and his dark good looks to his mother. He spoke very little about his parents, claiming they'd both died when he was very young. In the City he was headhunted for his abilities, not his family background. And this suited him. Mixing with the cream of the corporate world, moving within their tight circles, he discovered early the benefits of having both charisma and business prowess. As his status grew, so did his reputation with the ladies. And it was during this heady period he discovered that his penchant for older, wealthy women also opened many a corporate door.

When Gabby warned Emma about Joshua's reputation, she had just grinned. 'I know, but I'm helpless, he has these amazing eyes that pull you in and scramble your thoughts,' she confessed. 'I can't explain, but it's as if we were meant to find one another. I feel as if I've always known him.'

And even Gabby was not immune to Joshua's charm. So when he told her one evening that he'd 'rather die than hurt Emma', she had stopped worrying.

Within a month, Emma had moved into Joshua's London flat, where the two of them spent long nights wrapped around one another, planning their future together. When Emma told Joshua one morning that she missed the countryside and wanted to go freelance and design from her own home, Joshua appeared delighted.

'You'll need space. We could buy a cottage in the country, with a cat,' he suggested.

Emma had laughed excitedly. 'I could cook you homemade meals from real food grown in the garden. No cardboard-wrapped pizzas or foil dishes,' she added, pointing to the remains of their curry takeaway.

'And I suppose I'll be wearing green wellingtons and attending church fetes?' Joshua had quipped.

'Only at weekends,' she had replied. 'I rather like you in your business suits,' she had whispered, undoing his tie as she smiled knowingly into his dark blue eyes.

Emma's parents were cautiously optimistic when she finally introduced Joshua to them. 'You're so special to us my darling,' her father had told her. 'Your mother and I are thrilled for you; we just want you to be happy.'

'I am happy!' Emma said. 'Do you like him?'

'Of course we like him,' her mother said hastily. 'It's just you're such an ethereal creature, Emma, a gentle soul that loves unconditionally. Your world is creative designs and couture. His is so …' she paused, waving her hands for the answer.

'What your mother is trying to say,' interrupted her father, 'is that you are both so different from one another. Joshua's a self-made man. While you design and sew, he hunts the floors of trading rooms, mixing with speculators and strategists, hedge funders and risk takers. What do you know of his way of life? Will he understand yours?'

Emma had looked serenely at her parents, patting her father's arm. 'Don't worry, Daddy, we have all the time in the world to get to know one another.'

Six months later they married in Antigua. There were no family members on the beach that day, just a few random locals acting as witnesses. Despite this, it was one of the happiest days of Emma's life.

After their marriage they bought Rose Cottage in the beautiful Surrey countryside and adopted a tiny ginger cat they called Thomas. Joshua commuted between Surrey and London for business and Emma worked from the cottage. Their existence appeared to be a heady but harmonious mix of business, travel, and social and domestic events.

Using her design talents, Emma transformed the interior of the cottage as well as the garden to create a beautiful home. Happily absorbed with paints and fabrics, she visited garden centres and mowed lawns. Every day for her was fulfilling. She designed, cooked, cleaned and planted her growing garden, loving every minute of what she called her perfect life.

'Emma, you have become a domestic goddess,' crooned Gabby as she bit into a warm jam sponge cake. 'This is to die for and I love what you've done to the dining room.'

For Joshua, however, the novelty of the cottage wore off quickly. As he walked the surrounding fields in his welling-ton boots, he began to see only the mud and soggy grass and not the breathtaking views. The low beams in the sitting room became a hazard, not a ducking novelty, and the endless vases of freshly picked flowers made it difficult for him to find a clear space to put his things down. He began to miss the expensive leather furniture that didn't dent when sat upon, the tidy order of well-chosen magazines on his dust-free glass tables. As Emma excitedly displayed her new purchases for their home, he found himself unable to relate to her enthusiasm. Nodding, he would smile to appease, all the while viewing each new purchase as potential clutter or a dust trap. The stillness and sounds of nature at the cottage made him uncomfortable and he began to crave the nightly display of city lights, the rush of traffic and the hum of air conditioning. Even Emma's home-cooked dinners began to irritate him and he felt restless when in the cottage.

'Couldn't we just have a pizza tonight?' he asked one Friday evening, returning home late.

'It's not London, darling. Not sure where I can rustle up a

decent pizza out here at short notice. Anyway, I've cooked you braised lamb shank for dinner – your favourite.'

'Freeze it. Let's go out!' he had said.

Emma never saw the writing on the wall. As Joshua's business commitments began to keep him later and later in London, he made a suggestion. 'Why don't I stay in the London flat during the week and come home at weekends? You can come up there with me during the week sometimes if you want to.'

'What about my work? And Thomas?'

'Ah, I forgot about him. Perhaps you could get a neighbour to feed him?'

Emma had to agree that Joshua's suggestion made sense. So during the week she shopped and baked, gardened and designed, looking forward to weekends with Joshua. They constantly kept in contact via mobile phones and emails, and when Joshua was unavailable Emma would leave a message on his voicemail; he always got back to her. To Emma, her life was still perfect.

Within six months Joshua had created two wardrobes: the first for London, comprised of business suits, expensive shirts and cashmere coats; the second a more relaxed tailoring style for his life with Emma. But in that time he'd also created two lives, including a relationship in London with the stunning Annette Barrett, a business associate and past lover. Joshua's two lives interchanged seamlessly until Emma became pregnant.

On the evening chosen to celebrate her pregnancy, Emma had laid the dining table beautifully with a white linen cloth and her best china. On the sideboard opposite stood an elaborate and oversized bouquet of mixed lilies which perfumed the air. Conscious that Joshua might be held up, Emma had chosen a meal that could remain in the oven without spoiling. As she waited with excitement, fussing around the table, the phone rang. Her shoulders dropped and her face crumpled as she listened to the voice on the other end of the line.

'Of course I understand. I know how sensitive this merger is … yes, obviously we can celebrate another evening. I'll speak to you tomorrow. Oh – thank you for the flowers,' she added, turning towards the extravagant arrangement as a tear slipped down her cheek. 'They're beautiful.'

The merger had obviously been Annette, the harpy.

Joshua left Emma in the second trimester of her pregnancy, assuring her he would take financial responsibility for his child. His words – 'marriage doesn't suit me and I'm not ready for a baby' – changed the pattern of her world forever, like a single twist of a kaleidoscope. He moved into his luxury apartment in the City full-time, leaving Emma the cottage and cat. His life resumed without much anguish; hers was shattered.

First came the shock and then the denial. After this, the constant tears. Gabby watched as Emma tried to piece her life back together again, all for the sake of her growing baby. Throughout this period Gabby was always there, supporting her friend through the emotional unravelling, the angry outbursts, the hysteria and the depression. Gently but firmly, she coaxed Emma back to work and onwards towards happier days.

Emma was twenty-nine when she'd discovered she was pregnant, and in her excitement she'd turned her talents to designing outrageous but exquisite baby wear. Gabby had encouraged her to show them to a few of her fashion contacts, and the take-up of her tiny clothes from exclusive babywear shops had surprised Emma. 'Heart Seeds' came into full production just prior to the birth of Amelia. Gabby knew that Emma's pregnancy was her lifesaver. Still, she never forgave Joshua for the pain he caused her friend.

Emma and Gabby remained in the garden as the sun began to set. Gabby watched as a small group of ants hurriedly crawled over her discarded shoes towards their nest in the adjacent rockery. She had put Amelia to bed earlier, allowing them an opportunity to talk, but very little had been said.

Emma sat in an oversized wicker chair, her arms tucked around her slim legs, and, as night fell, the hurt closed like a fist around her heart. She poured herself another drink as memories of her short time with Joshua clawed at her emotional scars, teasing her for a reaction. 'What's wrong with me? Why does he still have the power to hurt me?' Then, lifting her head, she caught her friend's eye. 'I need to move on, don't I?'

Gabby nodded her head in agreement.

'I suppose I always thought he might come back. Stupid, I know. Each day part of you hopes that they will come back to you ... even though you know they won't. Some part of you just can't let go – not completely.'

Swinging around in the chair, Emma uncrossed her slight body. 'I'm going to take Amelia swimming tomorrow. Do you want to come with us and do the godmother bit?'

'I'd love to. Call me when you're up and about,' Gabby said, and after kissing Emma on the cheek she saw herself out.

Emma remained seated in the moonlight for a while, a relaxed and sated Thomas collapsed at her feet. The evening was warm and still, and she could hear the lapwings call out in the dark as she finally retired for the night.

The morning sun lit the countryside, bouncing off the wheat in the adjoining field. Gabby drove them to the swimming baths, arriving in time for the mother-and-toddler group.

'I can't join in,' Gabby protested as she wandered into the fray of mothers in her black Speedo swimming suit. 'I'm not her mother.'

'You can be honorary mother for the day. Give me a chance to actually swim in water deeper than a paddling pool,' Emma insisted.

'Ok, it's splash time,' Gabby shouted, noisily entering the toddlers' pool and displacing a great deal of water as her solid, Lycra-encased body hit the surface.

Both Emma and Amelia burst out laughing. Then, having lowered her giggling daughter into Gabby's arms, Emma set off for the main pool, gingerly slipping herself into the shallow end. As she waded deeper into the water, she looked over at her daughter with her bright red armbands, happily splashing with Gabby. A whistle blew, the class started and the children began to kick in unison.

Emma closed her eyes, enjoying the sensation of the warm water supporting her body until a sudden sense of fear swept through her. Instinctively, she again looked across to the toddler pool for Amelia and Gabby. Reassured by their smiles and laughter, she lowered her shoulders back under the water and began to swim. But with each stroke her sense of unease continued to grow, and looking around she realised that the pool and the surrounding area had disappeared and a mass of dark water now stretched endlessly around her. It was as if she had been transported into a wide expanse of ocean. The flat surface had turned choppy and the distant noise of gentle splashing and laughter had been replaced by a haunting sobbing. The water tasted salty and she smelled the acrid odour of burning oil. As she looked around in confusion, a white face with an open mouth appeared to rise up from the depths. Emma watched in horror as a clawed hand, black and scorched, broke through the dark surface before sinking back below. Unable to move, she found herself slipping under, the shrill blast of a whistle filling her head as she sank lower. Opening her eyes, she watched helplessly as bodies with blank faces and flowing hair drifted past her. A vice-like pain clawed at her chest and her head felt as if it would explode from the lack of air. Her lungs folded under the pressure. She opened her mouth in a silent scream, then, drawing in the water with a gasp, she surrendered to the inevitable.

Emma saw a light through the blanket of grey that surrounded her. It shone like a beacon drawing her into its brightness. She felt it enter her very being, and with it came a sense of peace. Waves of an emotion so divinely beautiful washed over her as she felt herself dissolve into the light.

Gabby never understood what made her look over in Emma's direction, but as she did she knew something was wrong. Unceremoniously thrusting Amelia into the arms of a nearby mother, she shouted for assistance, climbing hastily out of one pool, then diving into the other. Whistles blew as a lifeguard followed her into the water. Moments later she surfaced, gasping for breath, the lifeguard beside her holding a limp Emma in his arms. Pressing her fist to her mouth, Gabby stifled a cry. A row of stunned mothers and small children watched as Emma was lifted from the water.

Emma lay still in a puddle of chlorine water. Amelia watched wide-eyed as a stranger covered her mother's mouth with his own, pumping her chest and pinching her nose. She searched for reassurance from Gabby as her mother's slight body moved violently under the hands of this unknown man. As the lifeguard turned Emma onto her side, she retched water onto the concrete. A frightened Gabby held Amelia close to her while the pool attendants called for an ambulance.

Emma lay unnaturally still, her face drained of all colour. Her eyes were closed, but she was breathing, and her long, dark hair, tangled from the water, lay twisted and knotted under her head. The ambulance crew laid her on a stretcher, wrapping her in blankets, and as they carried her towards their vehicle, a shivering Gabby, still holding Amelia tightly, gave them the necessary details on her friend.

'I'll follow you,' Gabby told the paramedics, rushing back with Amelia towards the changing rooms. Hurriedly, and with some difficulty, she tried to make light of the situation for Amelia's sake as she struggled to put clothes onto their damp bodies. Then, dressed as best as she could manage, dishevelled and with damp hair, Gabby drove to the hospital, ringing Emma's parents from her car.

Chapter 2

Caroline Stockwell stroked her daughter's head, teasing out the chlorine-scented hair onto the pillow.

'Sorry I worried you all,' said Emma. 'I still don't understand what happened. I must have fainted, lost my footing and slipped under. How's Amelia?'

'She's fine, Emma,' her mother assured her. 'Gabby's been looking after her. You gave us all quite a fright.'

'Sorry,' Emma whispered again.

'What have the doctors told you?' Caroline asked, linking her arm in her husband's.

'Oh they talked medical jargon, Mummy; something about water blackouts, hyperventilating, lack of oxygen to the brain – all suggestions on why I could have lost consciousness.'

'Have you been examined properly, Emma? What about any lasting damage? You did have to be resuscitated, after all.'

'Emma's fine, dear. Don't pressurise her,' said Stephen Stockwell, patting his wife's hand to calm her while returning his daughter's sheepish and embarrassed grin.

'Thanks, Dad. Yes, they initially mentioned possible damage to my lungs or other organs, but they've run tests and everything's ok. I feel fine, just very confused as to what happened.'

Emma was frightened, though. She had no intention of telling anyone about what she'd seen. To explain how the pool had disappeared and been replaced by endless stretches of ice-cold water would be a step too far. To mention the fact that she had also seen floating bodies around her could result in certification.

A nurse arrived at Emma's bedside. She elevated her head and made her more comfortable. Caroline took the opportunity to whisper to her husband, 'I'm worried, Stephen. What did they tell you?'

Taking his wife's hand in his, Stephen Stockwell looked back at his daughter lying under the white sheets and the beige hospital blanket. 'They told me she'll be fine. They don't believe there's any permanent damage as she wasn't under the water for long and breathed on her own immediately afterwards. They said they've been monitoring her and, because she hasn't developed any additional symptoms and her blood-sugar levels are good, they're happy to release her.'

'Thank God she's all right, but is that it? They'll just send her home?'

'Yes, but she'll have to visit her own doctor for a follow-up evaluation.'

'Well, I still don't think that's enough, Stephen,' said Caroline, shaking her head with concern. 'Why did she collapse like that in the first place?'

Stephen nodded. 'Leave it with me. I'll speak to Emma later about getting some more tests done, just to put our minds at rest.'

'Thank you,' Caroline murmured, releasing her husband's hand. 'I'll go and phone Helen now – she's been worried sick.'

Emma's sister Helen had carved out a successful career for herself as a freelance journalist. Single, stunning and very bright, she had recently published an article in *Time* magazine, a copy of which had been proudly sent to all the Stockwells. Her work of late had been so frantic that she had spent little time with her family, but as she asked her mother to send Emma her love, she made a mental note to change that, relieved at the news that her sister would be ok.

As she hung up the phone, Caroline caught a glimpse of Gabby at the end of the ward.

Arriving at Emma's bedside, Gabby kissed Stephen and threw her arms around Caroline. 'How's our patient?' she asked, smiling in Emma's direction.

With a thermometer stuck under her tongue, Emma could only manage a grimace.

'Before you ask, I've left Amelia with Auntie Hetty next door, and when I last saw her she was standing on a large wooden chair up to the elbows in cake mixture. They're making chocolate brownies for your return. But judging by the state of your daughter I would recommend you avoid them ... heavens knows what she's been putting in that bowl!'

When the hospital discharged Emma, Gabby drove her back to Rose Cottage. As the car pulled up the track, Amelia and Hetty were ready and waiting for them. A short, stout lady in her early seventies, Hetty lived in one of the surrounding cottages. She had white, unruly hair that she attempted to tame into a loose bun, and her pink, round face featured a pair of pale blue sparkling eyes and a smile that stretched from ear to ear. Most importantly, Hetty adored Amelia who, clasping a misshapen chocolate brownie in one hand, now ran towards her mother with open arms. 'We've been feeding Thomas, Mummy,' she announced in excitement as the cat wandered up the path to greet them, slowly flicking his ginger tail. 'He doesn't like brownies. Look,' she said, pushing the remnants into his face before he turned tail and bolted. 'See!'

Emma collected Amelia into her arms and squeezed her tightly. 'Mummy missed you,' she whispered, snuggling into her body.

'I love you, Mummy. You won't drink the water again, will you?'

Leaning back to look at her daughter, Emma replied, 'No. I promise.'

'I've put the kettle on,' Hetty interjected. 'What you need is a nice cup of tea.'

Gabby smiled as Hetty's plump and bumbling form negotiated the path back into the cottage. 'Will you be all right, Em?' she asked quietly, helping her with her bag.

'It was just a funny few moments, Gabs. Don't worry about me, I'll be fine.'

But Gabby had noted the dark smudges under the sockets of Emma's eyes. 'I'd like to stay over with you two tonight in the cottage, if that's ok?' she said. 'More for my sake … you gave me quite a scare.'

Holding Amelia's sticky hand in hers, Emma nodded in agreement. 'Thanks, Gabby,' she said. 'I'd like that.'

In fact, Gabby stayed longer than one night. During the week, she left Emma and Amelia to go to work, returning in the evenings for dinner and to sleep over. The arrangement for the weekends was more relaxed, and this quality time was special for both women. Over this period Gabby noted how Emma's face was beginning to regain its vitality again, and with Gabby there, Emma found that her nightmares were becoming less frequent. Although Emma never mentioned the dreams, Gabby was aware there must be some issue troubling her friend, having found her shaking and sweat-drenched in the bathroom early one morning. 'Just a bad night,' had been Emma's explanation. But when Gabby saw the mess of bedclothes on Emma's floor, she thought it must have been an interesting night to say the least.

Three weeks after the swimming pool incident, as Emma and Gabby were attempting to barbecue threaded tiger prawn and chillies on wooden skewers without incinerating the sticks or dropping their contents onto the hot coals, the house phone rang. Emma rushed back inside to answer it, salad bowl and servers in one hand, and grabbed the receiver with the other. 'Hello,' she answered breathlessly.

'Hello, Emma. It's Joshua. How are you?'

Emma's hand paused, the salad bowl suspended in mid-air.

'I'm fine, thank you, Joshua,' she answered. Then, in a slightly clipped voice, she added, 'How was your wedding?' As the words spilled out of her mouth, Emma wished she could retract them. She had promised herself that she would not ask that question. It was up to him to tell her.

'Ah, the jungle drums beat fast. I'm sorry, Emma. I was going to tell you after we got back. Annette and I wanted it to be a quiet and unassuming affair,' he explained, noting how dry and chalky his mouth suddenly felt.

Emma's silence on the other end of the phone made Joshua feel uncomfortable as the familiar sense of guilt washed over him. She had the unique ability to make him feel culpable for his actions – something he never experienced with anyone else.

The introduction of Emma into his life had not been in the plan. It was as if he had inadvertently slipped through to a parallel universe. She was so beautifully fragile, a delicate fairy nymph amongst his world of hornets. He had looked at Emma and found himself temporarily lost, and their marriage had been a surprise even to him. In reality, their union was a weakening in his game plan, like placing a butterfly on a boxer's glove. And Emma's pregnancy had threatened the rules: he could no longer pull his punches; the butterfly would have to go. But now, with her on the other end of the phone, he found himself unconsciously recalling times they'd had together and something within him began to surface. Her voice interrupted his thoughts and brought him back to the moment.

'Congratulations,' she said graciously, putting down the salad bowl to ensure she didn't drop it.

'Thank you, Emma. Can I speak to Amelia?'

'She's in the garden with Gabby. Hold on, I'll call her.' Walking towards the kitchen door, Emma called out for her daughter.

'It's your daddy; he wants to speak to you,' Emma said

'Daddy ... Mummy's been sick,' began Amelia, taking the handset. 'She went under the water and swallowed lots of it, then she sicked it up, so they took her to hospital.' There was a break in Amelia's excited banter as she looked up at her mother with wide eyes. 'He wants to speak to you.'

'What happened?' Joshua asked with unnatural concern as the vague image of a shape under water flashed in his mind.

'Oh nothing really. I went swimming and they think I must have passed out as I went under the water. I am fine though. Nothing to worry about.'

'Was Amelia with you?'

'Yes ...' Emma started, then added, '... she was with Gabby in the children's pool.'

'Did she see you go under the water?'

'No ... I don't think so.'

'But she said you sicked it up.'

Emma paused, feeling cautious about her answers. 'She saw me as they brought me out of the pool.' Emma found herself reluctant to recall the event and even more reluctant to admit to Joshua that her small daughter had witnessed her having mouth-to-mouth resuscitation. 'She's fine. Amelia's very matter of fact regarding the whole incident. I've explained what happened and she has no fear of water. She's perfectly happy to splash about in the bath and she still wants to go swimming.'

Just the previous night Emma had found the perfect opportunity to bring up her resuscitation episode. Amelia had been happily playing in the bath, pushing her plastic doll under the soap bubbles then pulling it out and kissing its face. Realising that Amelia was re-enacting the pool incident, Emma had explained in simple terms what had happened to her. Amelia had listened, then, tipping her doll upside down, she shook the water from its eyes, mouth and neck before adding that Charlie had told her that if you sicked up the water, you'd be all right. Charlie was the name Amelia had given to her imaginary friend and, as usual, Emma had been impressed with his grasp on matters.

'Well, I'm sure you are aware,' Joshua continued, 'that children can become traumatised later in life by such events.' Joshua's voice sounded authoritarian and Emma felt her hackles rise.

'No – she's fine, not traumatised at all,' she answered abruptly, wanting so badly to make reference to his abandonment before Amelia's birth and the trauma *that* could cause in later life.

'Sorry, Emma, I don't mean to tell you what to do. I'm just naturally concerned about what Amelia saw. Are you ok now?'

Emma listened to the change in Joshua's tone. 'Yes, I'm fine,' she answered.

'Nothing to worry about and no lasting effects from a chlorine dunking.'

As she put her head around the kitchen door, Gabby realised that the conversation with Joshua must be fairly one-sided. Emma's answers were brief, followed by lengthy silences, during which she would raise her eyebrows and roll her eyes for Gabby's benefit. Grinning, Gabby signalled she would be outside with

Amelia. She knew Emma's performance was for her benefit; the news of Joshua's marriage to Annette had hurt her badly and she wondered if that could have had something to do with her accident in the pool.

'So are we still on for Amelia to stay overnight and, if so, when can I arrange to pick her up?' Joshua asked.

Emma felt her stomach knot. Previously, when they'd discussed Amelia spending a night with her father, she'd been happy with the idea. But that was before his marriage to Annette. Now as Joshua raised the matter again, Emma found herself reluctant to agree to anything definite. She knew that to deny him access now, after trying so hard to promote it, would be churlish, but a rogue thought popped into her head. What would happen if he and Annette wanted greater access on a more permanent basis? Emma shivered involuntarily. 'Where are you living now?' she asked.

'I've moved into Annette's home in Epsom. Amelia will love it – huge and spacious, masses of room to run around in!'

'That sounds lovely for her. Hopefully it's not too big, though – she needs to know someone is close by at night time.'

'Oh, she won't worry when she sees where she's sleeping.'

After confirming a pick-up time for Amelia, Joshua put the phone down. He was not happy with Emma's explanations about the pool incident and made a mental note to cross-examine the staff at the swimming pool. He knew there would be a full record of the episode for health-and-safety purposes.

As Emma hung up she brushed her hair back from her face with her hands. Joining the others outside, she threw a half-hearted smile in Gabby's direction, although a small trace of a frown between her eyebrows betrayed her emotions, and her eyes glistened with the faint glimmer of tears.

'How did it go?' Gabby asked.

'I have a feeling that Joshua is going to make an issue of the pool incident,' Emma whispered, watching her daughter tease Thomas with a prawn stick on the grass. 'He always did make me feel like a child. All those questions about the water, the depth, the temperature. I nearly told him about the bodies ...'

No sooner were the words out of her mouth than Emma regretted saying them, seeing the look of incredulity on Gabby's face.

'I think you need to tell me the whole story when Amelia's in bed,' said Gabby. 'And I mean the whole story.'

'Ok,' Emma replied with a sniff, wiping her eyes with the back of her hand.

That night, Emma explained to Gabby how the pool had changed into an endless stretch of dark, choppy water; how the temperature had dropped so low she had been unable to make her limbs work, and it was then that she thought she saw something in the water that looked like a woman's body.

Gabby listened quietly to her friend's account, unaware that it had been censored. 'I'm not qualified to comment,' she said, 'but was there an incident in your childhood where you may have got into trouble in some water?'

'No. I asked Mummy and Daddy the same question and they said no. I do have nightmares though.'

'About what? Drowning?'

'That's the problem, I don't know. I wake up in a terrible state but never remember anything about them.'

'How often do these happen?'

'Before your stay they'd been a frequent occurrence.'

'Did you have one the other night?' Gabby asked, remembering seeing Emma in the bathroom and the chaotic bed linen on the floor.

'Yes.'

'And you can't remember anything about them?'

'No.' Emma went on to explain that she always woke up terrified on the bedroom floor with the bed linen normally wrapped around her. 'It's as if I've taken part in a struggle of some kind but with no recollection of the dream itself. When I wake up, it takes me minutes before I can get my arms and legs to work and my hands always hurt. Before I went under the water in the pool, I remember that my arms and legs felt numb and I couldn't move them. Do you think there's a connection between what happened in the pool and my nightmares?'

Gabby shook her head. 'I don't know, sounds plausible, if a bit scary, Em.'

'What happens if they're not connected? I could have developed a fear of water in addition to my night terrors. I'm in a mess, aren't I?'

Gabby registered the look of fear on her friend's face. 'No you're not. I wish you'd said something about all of this earlier.'

'I couldn't … I was frightened. I thought it might sound as if I had psychological problems. I was scared someone would take Amelia from me.'

Gabby wrapped her arms around her friend.

'They can't take her away from me, can they?'

'No they can't. They're just dreams. Now, do you want me to stay over again tonight?'

'Please. The nightmares don't come all the time, Gabby, but I would like someone with me tonight.'

As the women washed up after dinner, Gabby turned to Emma, her head on one side, and asked, 'While we are alone, who named Charlie and when did he arrive?'

Emma giggled. 'Amelia did. She says he's been with her for

ages, but she only started mentioning him a month back. She won't tell me much about him, says it's a secret, but it's obviously a boy. I don't know his age, but I think he's a child. Supposed to be harmless and very common, especially if there are no siblings – a need for a playmate. Why? What has she told you?'

'Oh nothing, I was just wondering. He's very knowledgeable for a child, don't you think? Amelia gave me chapter and verse regarding ships this evening when I bathed her.'

'But we've never been on a ship. You're the cruise queen.'

'I know …' Gabby paused. 'She said Charlie told her.'

As the night closed in, Emma told herself that she would have everything under control by the weekend. Amelia's overnight stay with Joshua and his new wife would not be a problem.

There were no nightmares that night but she did wake with a sickening feeling in her stomach when she realised she would have to explain Charlie to Joshua.

Chapter 3

Stephen Stockwell persuaded his daughter to have an MRI scan, a CT scan and a raft of blood tests as a precaution, all of which he paid for privately. The results confirmed that Emma did not have a brain tumour or a thyroid problem. The incident in the pool could not be explained medically, but one suggestion was a blackout as a result of an anxiety attack. Emma was referred back to her general practitioner.

Peter West, Emma's doctor, had known her for years and was not comfortable with any anxiety disorder diagnosis. Looking at his patient over his thin wire glasses, he noted the change in her weight since he'd last seen her. The loss emphasised her high cheekbones and made her green eyes look enormous. It was the dark smudges under her eyes in particular that concerned him.

'How are you sleeping?' he asked.

Emma drew in a long and silent breath. She was not prepared to share any of the darker moments and fears.

'Not all that well,' she carefully replied.

'Is Amelia waking you up at night?'

'Not often.'

'Do you wake during the night, Emma?'

'Sometimes,' she replied, raising one eyebrow at Dr West.

'Do you have trouble getting to sleep?'

'Sometimes,' she said, with her infectious smile.

'Do you have trouble getting back to sleep if you are woken?'

Emma grinned.

'I'll take that as a yes, shall I, Emma?'

Dr West liked Emma; she was one of his favourite patients. Explaining that lengthy periods of sleep deprivation could affect the body physically, he suggested a short course of sleeping pills to aid the return of her usual sleeping pattern. They covered the normal relaxation techniques that she could try before going to bed and Emma agreed to avoid caffeine late at night.

Normal sleep pattern, mused Emma as she left the surgery. When did I last have a normal sleep pattern? First it was my pregnancy, then Amelia's arrival and feeding her at night, then her reluctance to stay in her own bed and now, finally, my own night terrors. She laughed quietly to herself as she climbed into her car and, still clasping her prescription in one hand, she decided to give the tablets a go. Sleep would be a start, she thought. Who knows, maybe the tablets could prevent the night terrors. As she started the car she wished she could have told Dr West everything about that day at the pool: how the water's temperature changed, how her body locked up in terror and what she saw in the water. But Emma had read somewhere that hallucinations were a symptom of psychotic behaviour and had made the decision not to tell for fear of being labelled. She smiled to herself as she imagined her medical notes: *hallucinations in the water, feelings of overwhelming panic, heart palpitations with night terrors*. And then the diagnosis: *symptoms normally attributed to anxiety disorder*. Following that, there would be a visit from social services who were wary of single parents with small children and anxiety disorders. Amelia was the most precious thing in her life and she was not prepared to risk losing her. It was also obvious to her that Joshua wanted more contact with Amelia. A label of an anxiety disorder or neurosis would play straight into his hands.

Emma knew this was something she had to handle outside of

the normal medical channels. She had already started researching. Trawling the internet for articles and books related to dreams and sleep problems, she discovered an endless cache of theories. Curled up on the settee one evening she began with one that looked promising. Amelia lay beside her, cocooned in her pink teddy duvet. She watched the fingers on her daughter's left hand rhythmically pull at the worn ribbon around the neck of her toy rabbit, Buddy, her small mouth twitching as she dreamed. Smiling down at her, Emma gently blew away the tiny duvet feather that had settled on her cheek.

Emma had recently received her copy of *Time* magazine, featuring the article written by her sister Helen. It was an interview with a Dr Michael Warner, an internationally renowned psychologist and hypnotherapist who had also published a number of books on sleep. Helen referred to him in her article as the 'Dream Man'. Emma had already found his name on the internet and had read up on most of his studies on sleep disturbances, including details of a stage referred to as 'slow-wave sleep'. According to Dr Warner, sleepwalking, night terrors and sleep-talking all occurred during the slow-wave sleep stage, and if a person was woken at that point they usually had no recollection of their dreams. He also suggested that clinical hypnotherapy could be beneficial for those suffering from dream disturbances.

Emma was convinced that there must be a link between her night terrors and what happened in the pool, and she knew it was vitally important that she remembered the contents of her dreams. If the Dream Man was prepared to hypnotise her, she felt she should give it a try. Unless she understood what had triggered the pool incident, she would always be afraid that something or someone could do it again. The more she thought about it, the more certain she became that Dr Warner could help her. She would speak to her sister first, but she would be very careful about what she actually told her.

Having called Helen and agreed a date for dinner, Emma lay back on the settee. Instinctively, she knew she was on the right track. Closing her eyes, she dozed, allowing her mind to drift as she sank back into the cushions. When she woke up, the night had rolled in and it was pitch black and turning chilly. Shivering, she wrapped Amelia and Buddy tighter within the duvet. 'Time for bed, little one,' she whispered, dropping a kiss on her daughter's warm forehead as she carried the quilted bundle upstairs.

The small brown bottle of sleeping pills stood beside her lamp. She had not yet started the course of tablets. Before turning off the bedside light, she set the alarm for seven-thirty. Joshua was due early the next day and she still had to pack Amelia's things.

Emma closed her eyes only to wake once again on the floor, her body damp with perspiration. The clock showed three a.m. as she climbed back into her untidy bed. Remembering that Joshua was picking up Amelia in six hours, she turned into her pillow and forced her eyes closed.

Chapter 4

The day of Amelia's visit to her father had arrived. Up early, Emma wandered into her daughter's room where she found her sitting up in bed and holding a one-sided conversation with Charlie. *This is really going to impress Joshua,* she thought.

'Do you want to do some snail picking, darling?'

'Ooh, yes please!' Amelia yelped in delight as she threw her little legs off the bed.

Emma didn't like the snails or slugs eating her plants, but she didn't like killing them either. Her humane solution was to collect up as many as she could and deposit them down the lower end of the adjoining field. They called it 'snail picking'. Amelia, fascinated with the thought that snails carried their houses on their backs, would periodically turn the luckless creatures upside down and shake them, hoping to make their furniture fall out. Also, convinced that slugs were, in fact, snails looking for new homes, she would collect any empty snail shells and line them up in a row; then, referring to the slugs as 'house hunters', she would encourage them to wriggle over the empty shells. Emma had made a mental note to steer Amelia away from a career in property sales.

Opening the heavy cottage door to the sunlight, they wandered out into the bright garden, clad in their nightwear and wellington boots. The heavy night dew still covered everything and Emma reminded Amelia not to sit down on the grass. Following the snails' silvery trail with excitement, Amelia collected various-sized creatures for the bucket. Thomas had broken off from his early-morning hunting to watch them. As the bucket filled, he sauntered over to check the bucket's contents and Amelia shrieked with laughter at the thought of Thomas 'snail picking'.

Emma stood among the different coloured gladioli, her long, tanned legs bare between the hem of her nightshirt and her green wellingtons. Amelia crouched on the lawn, her haunches resting on the heels of her red wellingtons and her long nightdress dragging on the wet grass. A determined slug had hidden between two border stones and Amelia was trying to coax it out with a stick. She held up a slime-covered finger and the stick for Emma to see. 'He's stuck, Mummy! He doesn't want to come out.'

'Let him alone then, darling. Don't hurt him. He'll move when he's ready.'

Wiping her fingers on her nightdress, Amelia bounced off across the grass, her stick waving in the air.

The lawns of the cottage were framed by overspilling flower beds, filled to bursting with an array of blooms and colour. This morning the brazen beauty of the garden was breathtaking. Emma stood and filled her lungs with the fresh air, enjoying the sun on her face and admiring the floral performance. Each plant grew without rivalry, content alongside its bedmate. Emma tilted her head back and, again, breathed in the tranquillity. Amelia's orange marigolds waved gently in the breeze, in perfect timing with the white and yellow daisies. The hot pink begonias, a gash of colour like a garish lipstick, stood out among the pale blooms of the peonies and pinks. Entwined around the wooden fence and through its timber gaps, the unruly jasmine offered up its heady fragrance in forgiveness for its waywardness. A group of flamboyant, self-seeded hollyhocks stood to attention in one corner of the garden while pink climbing roses had wrapped themselves around the cottage's porch, framing the doorway with an explosion of blooms, the scent of which wooed the passing bees. Emma plucked a mint leaf from the herb garden and crushed it under her nose, noting the strong scent of the neighbouring rosemary. She watched, transfixed, as Thomas dived into the mint thicket, rubbing his face and flattening the plants. Clapping her hands, she shooed him away. Amelia looked up from her digging and, seeing Thomas in a run, joined in, chasing him further up the garden with her red plastic fork. In defiance, Thomas stopped and drop rolled into a patch of blue and white lobelia much to Amelia's delight.

With the gentle breeze playing among the garden that morning, the plants moved in unison, like a company of well-disciplined dancers performing their newest moves. As they waved, their signature perfumes diffused into the air, beckoning for applause from the already drunken bees. The high green hedges interlaced with golden honeysuckle, and white jasmine provided privacy, and when Emma looked up at the sky with its pale white brushstrokes and listened to the birds twit and whoop among the old gnarled oak, she knew it was going to be another beautiful day.

'Time for bath and breakfast, young lady. Your father will be here soon.'

Amelia kicked off her wellingtons at the front door and, in an act of bravado, pulled off her damp nightdress in the hallway, scrambling for the stairs as her mother laughed. 'Bath!' she said, clapping her hands.

Emma packed her daughter's overnight bag, trying to make sense of her own jumbled emotions as she did so. She had always hoped that one day Joshua would want to spend more time with his daughter, but she believed his business commitments would delay this until she was older. Now, with the introduction of Annette and his newly acquired marital status, the inevitable had come earlier than she expected. The stepmother was another factor she had not envisaged. She had raised her natural concerns regarding Amelia's age and a night away from home, but Joshua had reassured her that Annette would be there to help him. And Amelia had been so excited at the prospect of spending the night away with her father, so Emma had reluctantly conceded. But now, as she tidied up her daughter's bed and drawers, she thought of Annette and wondered what she made of Joshua's new-found interest in his daughter. From what Emma had heard and seen of Annette, the word 'maternal' would not have been used to describe her.

Emma looked at her daughter and gave her a smile. 'It's only one night, my darling – and if you want me, I'll come and get you,' she told her, though for whose benefit, she wasn't sure.

Unfazed, Amelia replied, 'I won't be lonely, Charlie will be with me.'

Oh dear, Emma thought, adding quickly, 'Perhaps it would be better to leave Charlie behind with me.'

Emma watched her daughter's eyes as she absorbed that comment, smiling when Amelia pulled out Buddy and tucked him into the crook of her arm, tugging at the frayed ribbon with her other hand. Once white, Buddy was now off-white/grey in colour, due to overloving and overwashing. The pale blue ribbon hung loosely around his floppy neck, allowing enough slack for Amelia's constantly exploring fingers to stretch and pull the fibres of the fabric. 'No,' she asserted. 'Charlie wants to come too.'

Emma chose to close the conservation on a positive note, more for herself than her daughter. 'Now darling, you know both your mummy and your daddy love you very much. Thomas and I will be at home waiting for you. We'll miss you when you're away.' She looked lovingly at her daughter who answered by throwing her arms around her.

'It's best to love everyone, isn't it, Mummy?' Amelia asked with innocent clarity.

Her daughter's wisdom never failed to astound and humble Emma. How she wished she could view things more like her daughter.

'Yes, it's best to love everyone, darling,' she replied, feeling guilt over the constant gnawing within her own heart.

Thomas watched Amelia through half-closed eyes from his position on her pink and cream coverlet. Rolling over onto his back he stretched out his body, displaying his soft white underbelly. Amelia dived down onto the bed and kissed the warm fur on his tummy, then pulled away laughing as he tried to wrap his four paws around her head. Emma was always amazed by the patience and good nature of that cat. He never clawed Amelia and appeared to spend the best part of his life making himself available for her attention.

'Can Thomas come?' Amelia asked.

Emma looked back down at the cat, now lying with all four legs in the air, his head cocked to one side and his eyes slanted in a knowing smile. 'No,' she stated with a mock frown. 'Thomas hates the car and he needs to stay here with me to give me cuddles.'

Amelia laughed and plunged back into the cat's soft fur.

Emma and Amelia heard the roar of the silver Mercedes' engine long before the car crunched up the track and reached the cottage.

'Daddy's here,' Amelia cried, and bounced off the bed.

As Joshua opened the garden gate and confidently strode up the garden, Emma watched him from the bedroom window. She could never hate him; it was as if an invisible cord still connected him to her. She breathed out slowly to counteract the feeling of apprehension as a dark, unexplainable sadness washed over her.

Emma had tried dating over the last three years. At one New Year's Eve party she had flirted with Nicholas Page, a local business associate of Gabby's, whose divorce had become final that Christmas. Nicholas was a tall, attractive man in his early forties, with a good body, short, dark hair and a lovely smile. He had a habit of grinning inappropriately at Emma, which she found very amusing, and after a lengthy period of exchanged grins across the room, Gabby had finally interceded and introduced them. 'He's gorgeous,' she had enthused to Emma when she sensed the mutual attraction. 'Gorgeous, newly divorced and solvent!'

'He needs to do something about his taste in clothes though,' Emma had lightheartedly whispered back as she accepted another drink.

'I'd take *him* if he was dressed in a bin bag,' had been Gabby's response.

'Look at mine …' she added, as her own date came into view. '*Mine* looks like he's just stepped out of a body bag.'

The girls had laughed until they cried that night.

Emma had allowed Nicholas Page into her life in small amounts, but despite encouragement from Gabby and her family, she had found his attentions too overbearing. He was not at ease with a small child in the house and had developed an allergy to cats. There had been some mildly satisfactory fumbling, but her heart was not in it. And despite the antihistamine tablets, the cat proved too much. Nicholas Page went on to marry his secretary within six months of Emma suggesting that they call it a day. Now, shutting down the memories, she turned from the window.

'Shall we go down and meet Daddy, then?' Emma asked, offering her outstretched hand to her daughter. Hand in hand they descended the stairs.

Joshua glanced around as he walked up the path. On the lawn a red watering can lay on its side and a brown bird hopped around its spout with interest. He noticed a large garden fork standing up against the wall, and beside it on the ground lay a child's set of plastic garden tools – a bucket, a green spade and a red fork. The bucket stood upright half covered with a red plastic lid. He looked inside and saw a collection of snails and slugs, all climbing at different levels, a layer of pierced cling film stretched over the bucket top, preventing their escape. He smiled to himself. Like mother, like daughter, he thought.

Reaching the porch, Joshua looked up at the climbing roses and their heavy, overblown blooms. The scent was almost overpowering. Wary of the hovering bees, he pushed back a bough, accidentally pricking his finger on the thorns. The sound of the gathering bees threatened to drown out the sound of the doorbell.

As Emma opened the door, Joshua greeted her with a muffled 'hello', a nod and a finger in his mouth.

Acknowledging the probable cause of the injury, Emma apologised. 'Sorry about that. I need to cut the roses back, but I love the smell and I hate to destroy such beauty.'

'It's like Sleeping Beauty's castle,' Amelia added in complete seriousness, and Joshua laughed, sucking the blood from his finger as he entered the cottage.

'I've packed Buddy,' Emma told Joshua, her voice sounding breathless as her heart hammered inside her chest. Hastily, she rummaged in the bag to buy herself some time to control her voice. 'And I've packed two pairs of pyjamas just in case and because she does like to have a choice. Please call me if she doesn't settle,' she added as she zipped up Amelia's bag, aware that she was avoiding Joshua's eyes, her uncharacteristically brisk manner hiding the deeper emotions that were building within her. *Why am I so scared to let him have Amelia?* she questioned herself.

'She'll be fine. But I'll call you if there's a problem,' Joshua assured her as Amelia hugged her mother goodbye. Emma's stomach crawled into unexplainable knots. Her daughter's hand looked so tiny in Joshua's as they walked towards the car, and a slight sigh caught in Emma's throat as she watched them leaving.

As if she realised her mother's reluctance, Amelia turned back. 'Bye bye, Mummy. Love you,' she called.

'Bye bye, darling. Love you too. Be good,' Emma sounded slightly hoarse and scratchy even to herself as she watched Joshua strap Amelia into her car seat. And as the silver car disappeared from view, she stood for a moment longer, staring down the empty track. It was as if some vital part of her had just been taken away.

Thomas had ventured out to watch the departure and now demanded attention by rolling among the dust and dirt on the track. Lying on his back, his dusty paws in the air, he looked long and hard at Emma.

'Come on, Tom, you dirty boy – look at the state of you! Time for me to get on with some work.' Thomas rolled over once more, then shot off into a hole in the nearby hedge.

Emma had a number of new designs to finish for Heart

Seeds. Throwing herself into work mode, she used the free time to work without interruption. She normally created her designs in the evening, when Amelia had gone to bed. Now, taking advantage of the daylight, she spread her work out on the conservatory table and immersed herself. Each garment she designed was fashioned with the image of Amelia as a baby and Emma found herself smiling and humming to herself as she worked, her compilation of seventies hits providing the background music. The sound of the cat-flap made her glance up and her eyes were drawn to the wooden dresser where a framed photograph of herself with Amelia stood. She grinned as she remembered the day the photo was taken and, wrapping herself in the glow of that memory, she went back to work, the uncertainty of Joshua's real intentions temporarily forgotten.

That evening Helen and Gabby arrived for dinner punctually at seven. The three of them dined simply on fresh pasta with a homemade tomato and basil sauce around the kitchen table. Gabby had brought a rich chocolate dessert and they happily toasted each other with a mixture of wines from the fridge and larder. Laughing together, they put the world to rights. Eventually, the conversation drifted easily towards Emma's swimming pool incident. She used the excuse of a momentary blackout due to overtiredness, which allowed her to bring in the subject of her disturbed sleep patterns and the Dream Man.

Helen listened as she poured herself another glass of wine. 'Well,' she said, 'if you are determined to go down the hypnosis route, then Dr Warner is your man. He's the one person I would trust for hypnosis, and I think if anyone can, he could offer some insight into your sleep disturbances. Do you want me to contact him for you?' Helen lifted her face and looked at her sister. The two of them had the same expressive green eyes.

Emma nodded.

'I'll call him first thing Monday,' Helen said, raising her glass.

'Thanks Helen, I owe you.'

'No you don't … just give me another bowl of that glorious chocolate pudding and let me collapse on your settee for a bit.' Stretching back into the cushions, Helen sighed. 'This is the life, good company, fine wines and chocolate. What more could a woman want?'

'Well, if you really want to know,' said Emma, opening up her dresser cupboard, 'I've more chocolates in here, together with a bottle of Amaretto. My favourite. Who's joining me?'

'As I'm driving, I'll just have the chocolates,' smirked Helen, taking hold of the box and dipping in.

'Gabby?'

'I'll stop on both, thanks. I have an early start tomorrow, so I really should be going. Sorry.'

'Hold on,' said Helen, shovelling another chocolate into her mouth. 'I'll come with you. You'll be ok, won't you, Em?'

'Fine. I'll see you both to your cars.'

The sisters watched Gabby's car bounce off down the track first. 'I'll call you,' said Helen, hugging Emma before climbing into her car and waving as she drove off. Emma watched the car lights disappear from view with a strange sense of anticipation: something was about to happen; of that she was convinced.

Sure enough, that night the nightmares came again. Not that Emma remembered any details. She woke up in her usual state of anxiety and looked down at her hands, one of which was painfully throbbing as two of her nails had been torn back – one bleeding from its rude removal and traces of carpet fibres evident under the other. Looking around, she noted fewer bedclothes on the floor this time. *Well, at least that's an improvement*, she thought, sticking her stinging fingers into her mouth, conscious of the metallic taste of her blood.

Stumbling into the bathroom, Emma looked at herself in the mirror. Her pale skin reflected an unhealthy sheen and there were obvious deep, dark circles etched under her eyes. Good God, I look awful, she thought. 'Sleep. I need sleep,' she muttered as she staggered back to make sense of the bedclothes. The clock by the bedside read three a.m. Remembering the pills Dr West had prescribed for her and justifying taking them with the fact that Amelia was staying with Joshua, she opened the bottle and poured out two tablets into her shaking hand. Sleep, that's the answer, she told herself, as she climbed back into bed and allowed the medication to take effect.

Joshua stood outside the cottage ringing the doorbell. He had been there for some minutes. There was no reply. Annette tried the house phone on her mobile, but there was still no answer. Joshua was annoyed. Emma's car was in the driveway and the bedroom window was wide open – what was she playing at? He tried her mobile as Annette stood watching Thomas play with Amelia's dragging rucksack strap. Chasing Thomas around to the back door, Amelia crouched down and called for her mother through the cat-flap.

The sleeping pills had worked. Emma had slept. She had, in fact, overslept, losing all sense of time or day. She had forgotten that Amelia was being dropped back Sunday lunchtime. Now, grappling with the heavy bolts, she finally opened the old oak door while, still groggy from the sleeping pills, she tried to focus on the group in the doorway. Joshua stood silently on the doormat, his perfect mouth set in an unimpressed grimace. Behind him was the statuesque Annette.

Emma still wore her creased pink pyjamas, her tangled hair was sleep-glued to one side of her head and her teeth were unbrushed. 'I'm so sorry,' she began, stopping as she saw Joshua pick up Amelia, restraining her in his arms. Emma's eyes locked onto the dark hairs on his forearm and the bulging curve of his bicep. For a moment she recognised the eyes looking at her, but the nose and mouth belonged to someone else. Somewhere in her distant memory something stirred and then was gone. 'No,' she pleaded, grabbing onto Joshua's arm and staring into his face, the features of which appeared to shift and change as she did so. As he stepped towards her, she pulled back with a small cry, then, blinking, she let go of his arm, the ground under her feet shifting as a noise like the rushing of the sea filled her head. She fumbled for the doorframe, her knees buckling under her as she folded unconscious to the floor.

Chapter 5

Joshua passed Amelia to Annette and scooped up the unconscious Emma. He carried her into the sitting room, Annette following behind with a white-faced Amelia.

For a moment, as Joshua looked down at Emma's pyjama-clad form lying in his arms, guilt seeped through a small crack in his impassive veneer. The hidden truth, corrosive in nature, left an unpleasant taste in his mouth. With unexpressed emotions dangerously close to the surface, Joshua quickly deposited Emma onto the settee. Standing back from her fragile form, he looked over at Annette. One glimpse of her uncompromising expression and a shutter slammed down on his past.

Annette kept her distance, carefully reading her husband's face. She believed that only she could get Joshua what he needed. Her current objective was greater access to his daughter, on her terms, and then their lives would be perfect. Emma's performance today was a gift.

Dragging herself back from a state of semi-consciousness, Emma realised that the crying in her head came from somewhere outside of her own body. Opening her eyes slowly, she waited until the room settled back into focus. She could see Amelia struggling in the arms of Annette. Once free of her constraints, she rushed over to her mother, cupping her face with her two small hands. 'Hello, Mummy,' she whispered.

'Hello, darling,' Emma answered as she placed her own hands over those of her daughter. 'I'm fine now,' she said, her mouth dry, as if she had been sucking chalk. Looking up at Joshua, she requested a glass of water.

'Annette, please take Amelia into the kitchen and get Emma some water.'

Looking around the room with poorly disguised contempt, Annette asked, 'Where's the kitchen?'

'I'll show you,' said Amelia, jumping up in eagerness to help.

Emma knew Joshua was going to demand some sort of an explanation, and for that she was glad both Annette and Amelia were out of the room.

'We need to talk …' he started.

Emma's heart was beating far too quickly and the familiar sense of dread and panic began to build again within her body. Flashes of traumatised faces filled her head and with them came the fear and confusion. Closing her eyes, she tried to shut the images out.

'I'm very sorry …' she interrupted. 'My fault – I took a couple of sleeping pills last night and obviously overslept. I must have got up too quickly when I heard you arrive, which is why I felt woozy just now.'

Joshua watched her closely, his mind calculating. 'That was more than woozy. You passed out in front of me,' he told her, a snarl of amused criticism playing on his lips. 'Why are you taking sleeping pills, anyway? Surely that's dangerous with Amelia in the house? You might not hear her when she calls.'

Joshua's tone was inescapable, making Emma cringe.

'I don't make a habit of pills at night. Last night was the first time and only because Amelia was away,' she defended, looking up to meet his eyes in an attempt at defiance just as Amelia burst back into the room. Annette followed, her tall, lithe body swaying purposefully. In her hand she carried a cut-glass tumbler filled with water. It was one of a set given to Emma and Joshua as a wedding present. As she took the glass from Annette, she realised the absurdity of that thought.

Joshua pulled his mobile from out of his jacket pocket and made a call.

'Stephen, it's Joshua …' he started.

Emma recoiled in horror when she realised he was speaking to her father.

'… Emma has had some kind of relapse and I don't think she should be here on her own. I'm going to take Amelia back with me and I think you need to come over and look after your daughter.'

'No!' Emma cried out, scrambling to her feet and grabbing the mobile from Joshua's hand as Annette watched the exchange.

'Daddy, it's me … No, I'm fine. I'll explain later … No, I'm not sick – I took a sleeping tablet and overslept, that's all … No, I don't need you to come over.' Emma looked back at Joshua. 'Trust me. I'll call and explain later.' With that she ended the call and passed the phone back, beckoning Amelia into her arms, her face flushed with indignation.

Annette stood beside Joshua looking down at her old adversary. She raised a perfectly pencilled eyebrow, observing Emma from behind a mask of flawless make-up, her geometrically cut dark hair skimming the tops of her finely chiselled shoulders and dropping like black shimmering silk over her collarbone. Annette loathed Emma – couldn't bear that Joshua had been married to her, but worse, that she had produced his child. Annette's own inability to conceive made her hatred all the more consuming.

Annette Barrett was three years older than Joshua. Born in Chichester to a French mother and a British father, she had married Maximilian Barrett, a semi-retired self-made millionaire, when she was twenty-two. She had a long history of liaisons with a number of his business associates and rivals; intelligent, ruthlessly determined and very aware of her own sexuality, she was attracted to powerful men. Max Barrett knew how much his wife enjoyed the life he provided for her, so he overlooked her dalliances, but he did demand discretion.

Joshua had been the last in a long line of conquests. Annette's relationship with him in the beginning had been mutually convenient, allowing for non-exclusivity. That was until he met and married Emma, shortly after which Max Barrett had died unexpectedly and tragically. On his death, Annette inherited not only her husband's considerable wealth but also the controlling shares in his vast business empire: the Barrett organisation. Now she had both the money and the power. She was also single again. And it was then that she changed the rules: she wanted Joshua, exclusively.

Annette knew Joshua; she understood his weaknesses. After Max's death he was offered a position within the Barrett organisation that she knew he would never turn down; however, with this promotion came conditions. The heady combination of power and wealth was like an addiction to Joshua.

Now, as Annette observed Emma, taking in every aspect of her dishevelled appearance and agitated manner, it was the perfect time to whisper to Joshua her misgivings regarding Emma's ability to cope with his daughter. It was time to play the 'not-fit-to-be-a-mother' hand. The thought of taking something so precious away from Emma felt deeply gratifying and Annette stifled a smile as a plan began to formulate in her mind.

The sound of the house phone in the cottage cut through the tension.

'Hello?' Emma answered. It was her father. 'No, he's still here.' Emma listened, looking directly at Joshua.

'Ok, Dad, I'll see you in an hour.' Emma hung up the phone. 'My parents are on their way over now, so any suggestion of Amelia returning with you will not be necessary.'

'I want to stay with you, Mummy,' Amelia cried, tucking herself into Emma's side.

Emma felt the weight of Joshua's gaze as she stood proud, all five foot two inches of her in her bare feet and pink pyjamas. 'Thanks for bringing Amelia home,' she continued, pulling down her top in an effort to regain control of the situation. It took all of her strength to look into the faces of both Joshua and Annette. 'I'll show you out,' she said, moving quickly towards the door and opening it wide in an act of bravado.

'Say bye-bye to your father, Amelia. Joshua, I'll speak to you regarding access on another day.'

Joshua realised he had lost this round and, kissing Amelia on the cheek, told her he would see her soon. Emma watched as the pair left through the garden gate. Her last image was of the back of Annette's head, her perfectly cut, black hair reflecting hues of blue and green in the sunlight. A distant memory made her shudder.

Closing the door behind them, Emma drew the heavy bolts shut. 'Bastard,' she whispered in angry frustration, leaning her back and full weight against the old wooden door as if to block further entry. 'Who does he think he is? How dare he suggest taking Amelia?' Shaking from the encounter, and still propped against the door, she felt her knees begin to buckle. Closing her eyes, she slid down until she was seated on the cold flagstone tiles. Then, putting her head in her hands, she shut out the moment.

Amelia sat on the settee with Thomas on her lap. She wore

her hair in a tight plait that pulled at her hairline and the delicate flesh around her temples and above her ears. 'Mummy!' she cried out in a small voice.

Rising from the cold floor, Emma moved back into the sitting room. Smiling at her daughter, she sat down beside her and calmly undid the plait, upset at the severe manner in which her hair had been scraped back off her face. 'Better?' she asked as she gently combed out her daughter's hair with her fingers.

'Thanks, Mummy, my hair hurt,' Amelia answered, pushing Thomas off her lap and wrapping her arms around her mother. 'I had a nice time, but I missed you, Mummy.'

Emma planted a kiss on the top of Amelia's head and sat for a moment, enjoying the closeness of her small daughter. 'I missed you too.'

After her parents had left, later that evening, and with Amelia tucked up in bed, Emma avoided sleep by tuning in to any television programme that provided noise and laughter. Thomas assumed most of her lap, but even his warmth and comfortable purring couldn't dispel her sense of unease.

Back in Epsom, Annette watched as Joshua paced the carpeted floor, a glass of scotch in his hand, his mood desperate. The weekend could not have been more perfect. She knew Joshua wanted greater access to his daughter and when he wanted something badly enough, he usually got it; he was so like her. Of course, she knew that having Amelia on a more permanent basis would require some adjustments, but she also recognised the benefits. And once she had regained control of all parties, she would look into the prospect of boarding school. Amelia would be no trouble.

That evening, encouraged by Annette, Joshua instructed his solicitor Giles Manning of James, Proctor and Proctor to apply for full custody of Amelia.

'I'm in a position to provide my daughter with a secure and safe family environment, which I feel she needs,' he advised Giles. The image of a desperate woman in pyjamas floated into his head, but he blocked the thought immediately, banishing it to a deep, dark place within his mind. Amelia would live with him. Joshua's base needs began to resurface, crushing any compassion or morality.

'I suggest you cite threats to Amelia's safety when in Emma's care. Ask for medical reports on Emma's current state of health. No ... make that reports on both her mental and physical health. You can embellish the business in the pool and the collapse we witnessed in the cottage. I have an accident report from the local swimming pool, including names of lifeguards present – I'm sure we can put some pressure on one of them. You know the angle: danger to Amelia ... that sort of thing. I'll leave the legal jargon to you. Play up the psychological and emotional stress on my daughter and make sure you emphasise Emma's inability to care for the child on her own.'

That night, as Annette straddled Joshua's body, running her sharp nails across his chest and down the sides of his torso, she smiled at the thought of Joshua's call to Giles Manning. The removal of Amelia would crush Emma. As Joshua groaned under her, she pushed his arms back onto the mattress. She could smell his need. Trapping the palms of his hands flat on the bed, she lowered herself onto him, her tongue exploring his open mouth. Quickening the pace, she mercilessly rode him until he cried out. The control was delicious.

Chapter 6

Dr Michael Warner, alias the Dream Man, greeted Emma at his door. He stood six foot tall in a pair of burgundy leather mules. Dressed in dark trousers and a black cashmere sweater, he was clean-shaven with a shiny bald head and immaculately trimmed dark eyebrows. His piercing dark brown eyes were framed by oversized tortoiseshell spectacles, while a paisley silk cravat did its best to hide an obviously scraggy neck. Emma guessed he was in his early sixties and concerned with the process of aging. On his fingers he wore a number of large rings, the finest of which was a yellow gold signet featuring a large blue lapis stone. Smiling one of her largest and most beautiful smiles, Emma took the doctor's outstretched hand. He looked so different from what she had imagined. Gabby is going to love my description of this man, she thought as they shook hands.

'Come in, my dear, come in,' Dr Warner said, waving her theatrically towards his sitting room door. The room had two large, overstuffed settees, an abundance of cushions, voluminous drapes and outsized table lamps. Along the walls stood two magnificent mahogany bookcases bursting with books.

Emma and Dr Warner had already spent time chatting on the phone and he had been looking forward to meeting her. He had been very impressed by her sister Helen and was intrigued by the challenge Emma presented. Confident that he could remove the memory blocks and enthused by the idea of more dream case material for future studies and books, he had agreed to see her.

'Please, take a seat and make yourself comfortable.'

Emma allowed herself to collapse into one of the large burgundy brocade settees. 'I have to confess, I'm feeling a little apprehensive about all of this,' she began.

'It's to be expected, but I can assure you there is nothing to fear.'

Shuffling over the green carpet, the Dream Man took the seat opposite Emma. 'Now I need you to relax,' he said, encouraging her to lean back on the cushions and close her eyes. She was aware of the background music flowing from the sound system in the therapy room.

The descriptions Emma had given the doctor of her physical state on waking and her inability to remember anything about the bad dreams themselves were of great interest to him. He had worked on similar cases in which memory blocks had been successfully removed through clinical hypnosis. He explained that his intention was to create through guided imagery a 'safe place' for her, where she could totally relax. From this place of security, she would be encouraged to remove her memory blocks and allow herself to understand the nature or subject of her nightmares. He warned her that there could be something in her childhood that she unconsciously perceived as a 'trauma'. This, he explained, could hold the key to her nightmares. Aware of the emotional risks, Emma had agreed that he could take her back to scenes of her childhood if necessary.

As Dr Warner began the relaxation process, Emma found her senses heightening. At first she was overly aware of all sounds in the room – the ticking clock, the soft background music and the rhythmic tapping of the doctor's fingers. Conscious of her thumping heart, she focused on her breathing as instructed and listened to his voice. As his syrupy tone flowed over her, the rhythm of her heartbeat settled, as did her breath. Breathing in and out deeply, she found her shoulders dropping as the tension drifted away. Systematically, Dr Warner drew Emma's attention to different parts of her body, instructing her to focus on each one and then to relax it. Starting with her feet, he moved up to her chest, by which time her entire body felt heavy and comfortably relaxed. The music had faded away and even though she knew she could open her eyes at any time, she had no desire to do so. As Dr Warner's voice began to count down from ten to one, Emma found herself floating in a state of complete relaxation.

He described a walk along a sunlit path leading to a beautiful valley with a crystal-clear lake. Emma found the images grew in clarity in her mind's eye as she followed his verbal trail. She paddled in the gentle waterfalls, listening to the sound of the water as it bounced off the coloured pebbles. She saw the rich emerald green grass, the white swans on the lake, the pale blue sky and the dancing rays of the golden sun. The colours and the images floated around her head as she allowed herself to totally relax, safe in the beautiful paradise he had created for her. Emphasising her safety, Dr Warner told Emma she could now recall her dreams without any fears. But despite his encouragement, even in her beautiful and safe haven, she couldn't remember anything about them.

Trying another approach, the Dream Man asked Emma to remember and recount a happy event that she had experienced earlier that day. She described her morning with Amelia in great detail. Working backwards in time, he gently guided her through past days, weeks, months and, finally, years. He steered her through her childhood memories, probing for something that may have triggered her nightmares. Emma had successfully recalled memories back to the age of seven when Dr Warner realised the pitch of her voice was changing. Listening carefully, he knew the voice speaking to him now was not that of a young Emma, but of someone else.

The Dream Man watched as Emma slipped back further than he had anticipated. He suspected she was now experiencing a past life, which was not what he had expected, and the challenge she presented suddenly became more interesting. Adjusting his position, he turned on his tape recorder.

'Can you tell me your name?'

'Charlotte,' she answered.

'How old are you?'

'Seven.'

'Can you describe where you are?'

There was a pause as Emma lay still on the settee, then her eyes began to move quickly beneath her closed lids and her head moved a fraction to one side, as if looking at something visible only to her.

'A nursery,' she answered, a ghost of a smile dancing on her lips as her cheeks flushed pink.

'Describe it to me, Charlotte.'

'It's a warm room. There's a fire in the hearth and a bell rope above the mantelpiece. There's a washstand with a white and blue jug in a bowl.' Emma stopped speaking, remaining quiet against the cushions, still smiling at the images she alone saw.

'Can you tell me the month or year, Charlotte?'

Again, Emma took her time to respond. *'It's Christmastime.'*

'Now look around the nursery, what else can you see?'

'A crib.'

'Is this a nativity crib?'

'No.'

'Is it a crib for a baby?'

'Yes.'

'Is there a baby in there? Walk towards the crib and have a look.'

Emma remained motionless on the settee, her eyes moving frantically behind their closed lids. After a while she resumed talking. *It's my baby brother.*

'What's your brother's name?'

'Charlie.'

Dr Warner breathed deeply, realising that this past-life recall could hold the key to Emma's nightmares. Looking down at his client, he knew the next stage was critical and could cause her distress as it unfolded.

Emma lay back in her own world of soft, grey, hazy images, distant sounds and remembered smells. Once again, she found herself able to pierce through the haze and suddenly all she viewed appeared perfectly in focus. As she relaxed more deeply, the colours intensified. She could hear Dr Warner's voice.

'I want you now to move on in that life as Charlotte – on to the next significant period in that life. If something makes you feel uncomfortable or frightens you, you can pause the memory or fast-forward it to another period. You will be in control and safe. My voice will travel alongside you at all times.'

Dr Warner knew this was Emma's past and only hers to see. He could build a scenario from the words she spoke, but that would only be a loose skeleton. The detailed flesh was in her head. He also knew that for the more sensitive individual, the colours, the sounds, the senses and the emotions were all intensified during a past-life recall, death of a loved one caused pain and, in each life, there was always loss. Understanding this was part of the journey. Slowly, aware of the fragility of his mission, he needed to encourage Emma to explore her past uninterrupted, but he required her to tell him what she saw and felt. His skill lay in asking specific questions, the answers to which would provide him with greater detail. But Emma would choose her direction. This way she could remove herself from a painful memory should she feel it necessary. In his experience most individuals created their own blocks during a regression and an inbuilt censor would come into effect when needed. For his part, as the emotional anaesthetist, he could only watch and listen. His role was to undertake spiritual and emotional keyhole surgery – with a blindfold.

Chapter 7

Charlotte lifted her boot-clad feet carefully as she stepped onto the deck. Behind her, her father held her baby brother in his arms. Today they were finally going home. The excitement was intense and she felt a knot building in her stomach as various stewards and porters disappeared with their boxes and luggage. She looked around at the magnificent ship and its beautiful passengers and again felt a sense of wonderment.

Glancing down at her hands, she pulled her soft, cream, kid-leather gloves over her little fingers. She watched as her mother, sporting a large beige and black hat, scooped her brother out of her father's arms and followed the steward towards their suite of cabins. Charlotte's father had just completed a business deal, and although she understood little about the politics, she knew it was significant for all of them and for his company. Her father and grandfather dealt in wool and textiles. Charlotte loved the textures and feel of the materials. When she grew up she wanted to use them to create beautiful clothes. She looked again at her parents. They seemed happy now. She felt happy too. Turning back, she took one final glimpse of the quayside.

Sitting on the bed in their suite, Charlotte held her baby bother in her arms. She watched as a man gave her father a note. He opened it. She looked up at her parents as they exchanged a look. She'd seen that sad look on her mother's face before.

They took a walk out on the deck. A lady came to speak to them. Charlotte recognised her. The lady stood taller than her mother and had an accent. She wore her thick, dark chestnut hair piled high *and her clothes were beautifully cut in the latest style. Her skin was white and perfect. Charlotte thought her quite handsome; she reminded her of one of her porcelain dolls. She smelled of perfume – her mother told her it was lily of the valley. And as the woman put her gloved hand on her father's arm and smiled, she noticed how her mother shuddered …*

Dr Warner's voice interrupted Emma's train of memories: 'Can you tell me where you are, Charlotte, and what you can see around you?' he asked, using her past-life name.

Emma still lay on Dr Warner's settee, but her face and flickering eyelids betrayed the fact that her unconscious was somewhere else.

'I'm on a ship. A big, beautiful ship filled with elegant people …' she answered.

'Who are you with and how old are you now?'

'I'm with my parents and brother. I'm eight.'

'What are your parents' names?'

'Henry and Anne.'

'What is your brother called and how old is he?' asked Dr Warner, checking that the baby she had referred to previously had survived and that this wasn't another sibling.

'Charles … Charlie … he's nearly two.'

'I want you to describe to me everything you can see and everything you can sense and feel. Remember that at all times you are safe and can rewind or stop any scene should you need to. My voice will continue to travel alongside you. Nod if you understand me.'

Emma nodded and let her unconscious take over again.

'… I'm walking on the deck with my parents and Charlie. The air is crisp out here. I feel better, I was feeling sick down in the cabin. My brother is laughing in Mother's arms. People are nodding

at us. We've stopped to talk to a group of ladies and they are patting my head. The lady with the accent has joined us; she smells of lily of the valley perfume. I don't like her hat. It has black feathers on it that shimmer blue and green in the light. It reminds me of a bird that flew into the conservatory window last autumn and broke its neck. Father told me it was a raven. Father is talking to someone. They have a funny accent too … like the lady's …

There was a pause in Emma's narrative. Dr Warner gently prompted her to continue.

'*We are walking around the ship – there is a café with wicker chairs and potted palms. I'm now in the dining room, it's so beautiful. It's like a white wedding cake: it has two levels with a balcony. Above me is a huge dome with carved plasterwork in gold. I can see a painting; it looks like a cherub with angels. The chairs are dark wood covered in red material. The tablecloth is pure white and the table is laid for dinner. Father said we would come back later.*

'*We are moving towards another room. It's the writing room. Mother is here. She looks up at us and smiles … there are palm plants in here too …*

'*Now I'm walking along a deck with my father. He has Charlie in his arms. Mother is with us, her eyes are red; she looks as if she's been crying. She leaves us. Father looks worried. I take his hand. He's wearing gloves. He smiles down at me. I'm not worried anymore.*

'*I'm now walking with Mother and Charlie … I can see Father ahead. The lady with the bird hat is with him. Something is wrong. I start to run towards him … Mother stops me. My father and the lady move away together. Mother has stopped … I'm looking at my mother – she looks unhappy.*

'*We're entering my parents' suite. There is a smell of lily of the valley in the air.*

'Now Mother is whispering. I'm pretending to be asleep: my eyes are half open and I can see my father holding my mother's hand to his lips. He is kissing her neck and she is stroking his face and head. I feel safe now …

'We are leaving the dining room. Father has brought our coats. We're walking on the deck again. It's foggy across the water, and I can't see much. I feel excited though – we are close to home …'

'I'm holding my father's hand. Charlie is in his arms. Father is laughing … then there is a loud noise like a firework explosion. I hear another noise – not as loud as the first … more muffled. I'm frightened. Everyone is running and shouting around me: the ship is tilting … we are running along the deck.

'There's a funny smell in the air. Father is shouting at me to get into the boat. I don't want to go. There are too many people crowded around me … the boats are too far up in the air … I'm frightened. Charlie is crying … so much screaming. I can't see my mother.

'I'm being lifted up. I can feel myself dangling over the railings. My father's arms are stretched out. I can see the muscles in his arms bulging and tensing. I'm struggling … I can see his eyes … so frightened. He is throwing me towards a boat. I'm screaming … below me is dark water. A man has caught me. I'm in a small boat. We are rocking. I'm screaming for my father … so much noise around me – everyone is crying and screaming. I can't see Father or Charlie. I'm crying … so frightened … so frightened …

'I can see my father with Charlie now. He is shouting something to me. We are still rocking. Something has dropped on one side. I'm tipping out … falling … I'm in the water. It's cold, so cold … I can see white faces in the water … I can feel tugging … I can see a face and a hat – wet bird feathers. Something is pulling at me … my

60

chest hurts ... I can't breathe.

'I'm being lifted out of the water ... I can see feet and knees. I'm wet, cold ... I'm so cold I hurt. And I'm so frightened ... I'm looking around for my father and Charlie. I can't see them ...'

Emma gasped for air, her head shaking from side to side. *'They've left me,'* she whispered, resting against the cushions, her face now damp with tears.

Not wishing to prolong her distress, Dr Warner made the decision to move the regression on to its natural and inevitable close. Leaning forward in his seat, he watched Emma closely, gently instructing her to move on to the last day in the life of Charlotte.

Emma stirred and gasped for air again. Holding her breath for a moment, she paused. Dr Warner found himself doing likewise. Was she going to recount a death at sea? As she exhaled and began to speak, he listened with genuine relief as she described herself lying in a large bed.

'I'm in my bed. I'm very tired now, but happy ... I'm not afraid. I have had a wonderful life. I'm ready to join my husband now.'

'Is there anyone with you, Charlotte?'

'Yes. All my children.'

'How many children do you have, Charlotte?'

'Four.'

'What was the name of your husband?'

'Adam.'

'How old were you when you married Adam?'

'Twenty-five.'

'Where did you meet?'

Emma paused and smiled, remembering something special that only she was privy to.

'Liberty – the statue.'

'How old are you now, Charlotte?'

'Seventy-two.'

Dr Warner knew that the next question he would ask would be a cliché, but clichéd or not, he asked it each time, and he was always impressed by the answers.

'What lessons did you learn in your life as Charlotte?'

There was a long pause, then: *'Understand the weakness of man and the power of forgiveness – forgiveness brings understanding. Love is the answer.'*

'Are you ready to leave this life as Charlotte?' he asked.

'Yes,' she replied.

Any ties to memories of unhappiness and loss in a past life now had to be cut. Guiding Emma through the final moments in Charlotte's life, Dr Warner encouraged her to symbolically cut the ties to Henry and the bad memories from that lifetime. He created the image of golden scissors for her to use and a metal safe in which to lock the cords away forever. Her last image was of an intense bright light that drew her towards it, filling her with a sense of peace and understanding. She described an emotion so intense and beautiful that, at that moment in her mind, she claimed she understood everything. As she looked towards the bright light she could make out the faint outline of someone coming towards her. The image was not clear at first, but as she found herself drifting towards the brightness, she smiled.

'My mother's here.'

Happy that the regression was closed, Dr Warner brought Emma back to her safe place. Using words and imagery designed to repair emotions and strengthen the ego, he created a magical setting filled with natural beauty, warm sunlight and cloudless skies; a short respite for Emma. He knew that once she woke there would be many questions. For some people, a past-life regression tore down walls of preconceived belief, plunging an individual into a whirlpool of doubt and uncertainty. For others, it was simply a journey of discovery, providing them with answers. It was their quest.

Counting up from one to ten, the Dream Man brought Emma back to the present. A hesitant smile played on her lips. Whatever had taken place in that life as Charlotte, no matter how devastating, had been acknowledged and released. He watched as she opened her eyes. Blinking several times, she shivered. The expression on her face said more than words ever could.

'Hello, Emma,' said Dr Warner.

Emma knew that something quite extraordinary had taken place. She was overwhelmed with the emotions she had experienced and found the concept of a previous life surprisingly easy to comprehend. But her discovery of her life as Charlotte was personal, and she didn't want to share it. Hugging the images of passing into the light to herself, she closed her eyes again, the scenes still fresh in her mind.

'How are you feeling?' Dr Warner's voice interrupted her thoughts.

'Cold … I'm emotionally drained, yet I have this feeling that I've found some sort of peace at last. Is it normal to think like this?' she asked, as tears began to fall down her face. She rummaged in her leather bag, pulling out car keys and a packet of mints wrapped around a shredded white tissue. 'Damn!'

'Here, take these,' Dr Warner said, pushing a box of man-sized tissues in her direction, allowing her to compose herself. 'Believe me, your emotions are a normal response to a regression.'

Emma blew her nose quietly.

'Was there anyone in that life of Charlotte's you think you recognised? They don't have to look the same, just feel familiar.'

'Yes,' Emma paused for a moment before continuing. 'Henry, my father. I know it sounds rather creepy, but there was a resemblance to Joshua, my ex-husband – not in the features, but something behind his eyes and the way he carried himself. Is that possible?'

Dr Warner smiled wisely, nodding his head.

'Then there was Adam.' Emma closed her eyes and tried to remember more, but that particular memory refused to expand. 'I'm sure there's something familiar about Adam, but it's more of an emotion, a feeling. I can't quite place it.'

'I'm sure you will in time,' said the Dream Man.

'I saw my mother when you moved me towards the light. My mother from the ship. She was waiting for me … it was very beautiful.'

'Many people tell me that,' he replied, standing up and stretching his legs.

'Tea?' he asked.

Emma nodded her head and blew her nose again. 'Please.'

Emma's mascara had smudged and the combination of her green eyes and the dark outlines made the doctor think of an exotic Indian princess. He coughed to hide his embarrassment and stepped away from the settee. 'Are you comfortable there or do you want to come into the kitchen for tea? It's a lot brighter and might make you feel warmer,' he suggested as he wandered off down the corridor. 'I've got some biscuits,' he called over his shoulder.

'Tea in the kitchen sounds good,' Emma replied. 'Biscuits sound even better!' Clutching her bag and a soggy tissue, she followed him.

Dr Warner's kitchen was bathed in glorious, natural light, spilling through the glass roof of the adjoining wide, open-plan conservatory. Scattered rugs, leather settees and coffee tables provided an oasis amid a polished grey slate floor that shimmered like water in the sunlight, the surrounding large potted palms emphasising the effect.

Emma gazed in amazement. 'This is incredible,' she remarked, looking up at the glass ceiling.

Dr Warner laughed. He liked this woman. Consulting the labelled drawers of his wooden tea chest, he asked, 'Earl Grey, herbal, ginger, bog standard or strong builder's tea?'

'Bet you don't have liquorice tea?' she teased.

'Well, that's where you are wrong. I have an Egyptian tea with liquorice. It's very good. Do you want to try it? Still goes with my biscuits,' he added, grinning.

Emma sat comfortably, her legs tucked to one side of her body, a large silk-tasselled cushion held tightly to her chest. They had taken their tea and biscuits over to one of the dark-brown leather settees that sprawled under a palm. 'Reminds me of Morocco,' she said, admiring the collection of small inlaid tables and polished brass lamps.

'Have you been there?' he asked.

'Yes. Spent a dirty weekend with a college professor there once, drinking strong, thick coffee and lying around a pool,' Emma replied sheepishly, peering at Dr Warner's face from over her cup.

The Dream Man raised an eyebrow and tried to look suitably shocked.

'No, not *my* college professor. I remember the pool; it felt very still and safe, enclosed by palms,' she added.

'Are you afraid of water?'

Emma took her time to reply. Water had never worried her in the past; but now her past-life recollection and the swimming pool incident made her rethink.

'I think I need to tell you about something that happened to me recently,' she said, looking at Dr Warner across the coffee table. Taking a deep breath she began to describe what happened at the pool.

Dr Warner listened with interest. The idea that Emma had recalled something from her life as Charlotte while in the swimming pool was plausible. What he needed to understand was the trigger that had brought back that memory. Watching Emma sip her tea, asking questions eagerly between mouthfuls of biscuits, he found himself admiring her: the openness, the engaging smile and the laugh that sent shivers down his spine. As Dr Warner encouraged Emma to expand on her experience, remembering the images, he took notes and compared them with those he had already written. A scene-by-scene picture began to develop and the characters took shape.

'So we have a child called Charlotte,' Dr Warner began, 'travelling on board a ship with her father, Henry, who had links to the wool trade.'

Emma nodded.

'There's a brother called Charles or Charlie, a mother called Anne and a mystery woman wearing a hat that clearly troubled you. Then let's not forget the smell of perfume – lily of the valley, wasn't it? The hat and the perfume scent were things you clearly remembered. Tell me, do you like the smell of lily of the valley?'

'No, I hate it,' she replied.

Dr Warner nodded and continued to take notes. 'What sense did you get about this woman in the hat?' he asked.

'I had a sense that her presence was a threat to my family. There was a furtiveness about her.'

'Is there a familiarity with this woman? Is she someone you know today?'

'She didn't feel like a stranger.' Emma thought, and the hat again came to mind. She saw the perfect uniformity of the feathers, the hues of green and blue and realised they reminded her of Annette's hair. 'Yes,' she answered and involuntarily shuddered – a gesture noted by the doctor.

'Who is the woman?'

'My daughter's stepmother.' Emma looked at Dr Warner, a quizzical expression on her face, then asked, 'So were those people really there in that lifetime, or did I create them?'

'Real or associated, they were in your life story of Charlotte. Examine the emotions you experienced as Charlotte. These may be more significant than the characters or events recalled. But remember, some of those emotions you will be experiencing will be through the eyes of an eight-year-old child.'

'There's a strong possibility that I made up the name Charlie.'

Dr Warner looked at Emma, one eyebrow raised in question.

'My daughter has an imaginary friend called Charlie. Perhaps that's why I gave the baby his name?'

Dr Warner adjusted his glasses. 'It's difficult to say with certainty, Emma. Sometimes there is an association with names. Whether or not they were real names in a past life is debatable. Remember, the jury is still out on the prospect of a past life at all, let alone a recollection. The most important point of any regression is finding something that has a bearing on your life at the moment. As I said, it could just be an emotion, a fear. What were the emotions you experienced or sensed in that lifetime, apart from the obvious terror as the ship went down?'

'Love … I do remember such a strong feeling of love for Charlie, the way he felt and smelled in my arms. And shock – the fear and panic when my father deliberately threw me into that boat … then falling out of the boat and into the cold water – the sense of alarm in the water around me seemed so real. I could taste the salt and feel the biting cold. I felt terrified, alone, in danger ... my loving father had discarded and abandoned me.'

'And are those feelings something you could relate to in your present life?'

Emma's expressive eyes looked up at Dr Warner. 'Yes,' she replied. 'All of them.'

The Dream Man continued to scribble in his book.

'So did I experience a past life as Charlotte or did I make it up?' she asked.

'We may never know, Emma.'

'Could I have been recounting scenes from a movie I've seen and forgotten?'

'Have you watched many ship disasters?' Dr Warner asked.

Emma shook her head. 'This all feels so strange. Never has the concept of reincarnation entered my head. At school it was all Heaven and Hell; this is all so ... unbelievable.'

'For some; not everyone.'

'Will my nightmares stop now?'

'As we never discovered the subject of your disturbing dreams, I can't say. But if they are linked to that life as Charlotte, then there's a good chance that they will stop. If only for the reason that you know Charlotte survived the drama at sea.'

'And if not?'

'Ah – then you may need to come back and I'll have to restock on biscuits!'

Chapter 8

Emma's body felt strangely disconnected from her mind as she left Dr Warner's home and looked around vacantly for Gabby's car.

'Well, what was he like?' Gabby asked, giggling. 'What did he do to you? You're as white as a ghost. What did you see?'

'I'm not quite sure what I saw. I think I saw me. But whatever I saw, or experienced, I need to get my head around it.'

'Explain …' Gabby probed, as Emma strapped herself into the passenger seat.

Emma told Gabby that one moment she was remembering scenes of her own childhood, playing with Helen and her parents, when she found herself standing in a child's nursery, leaning over a baby's crib. She described the wallpaper, the white lace and linen, the fireplace, the toys and the oak washstand. 'For one moment Gabs, I felt as if I *was* Charlotte. I could feel the warmth from the fire and I smelled the smell of a baby … and I *saw* myself – no, *felt* myself, stretch to touch the baby's face.'

Emma's expression was animated as she fully described her regression and the life she encountered. 'When I was experiencing that supposed life as Charlotte, everything felt so real. It wasn't like watching Charlotte; it was being her.'

Gabby changed gear, glancing at Emma. 'So does the doctor believe your nightmares are linked to this previous life?'

'He can't say for sure as we didn't discover what they were really about, but he did tell me that if there is a connection, they might stop now that we know that I survived that trauma at sea.

What happened at the swimming pool interested him too – if that's linked to my life as Charlotte it would help explain the visions of floating bodies.'

'But why would you suddenly remember your life as Charlotte on that day in the pool?'

'He doesn't know.'

Gabby turned her face from the road briefly again and looked at Emma's profile. She was shaken by her account. 'Personally, I think all of this is a bit weird. Are we telling anyone about the past-life revelation?'

'Best not,' replied Emma.

'Mummy!' an excited Amelia shouted as she saw her mother and Gabby enter the cottage.

'Hello, my baby girl. Have you been good?'

'Yup.'

Wrapping Amelia in her arms, Emma looked over at Hetty for verification. Hetty grinned and nodded in response. Emma gave her daughter a large and noisy kiss, hoping that the feel of her child in her arms would erase some of the sudden emptiness she felt within her. 'Thanks for looking after her,' she said to Hetty.

'She's been a joy, Emma. She spent a lot of time playing with her new friend Charlie. My nephew Jonathan had an imaginary friend, only his was an elephant.'

Emma and Gabby glanced at one another and smiled as Hetty continued with her story. 'It got awkward at times in the sitting room. You see we had to be careful where we sat – elephant poo, you understand.' Then, laughing loudly, Hetty hugged Amelia and waved goodbye to the women.

Emma stood for a moment looking down at her small daughter. 'Shall we do bath time, then?'

Amelia spun and shot out of the kitchen door into the garden. 'No, Mummy, not yet,' she shouted, running up the garden to her swing.

'Bath time, young lady – now! It's late.'

Amelia hung upside down on her swing, her long hair dragging in the grass. Uprighting her daughter, Emma manoeuvred her towards the house.

'But Charlie doesn't like water,' Amelia giggled.

Emma experienced a momentary shiver. 'Good, then there will be more room in the bath for you.'

As she carried her reluctant daughter up the stairs to the bathroom, Emma saw Gabby pick up a letter from the floor. 'Anything interesting?' she called out over her shoulder, negotiating the bathroom door with her wriggling child.

'Looks official, Em. Has a company stamp on the envelope. Who are James, Proctor and Proctor?'

There was no reply. Gabby climbed the stairs after Emma, the white envelope in her hand. 'Trouble?' she asked, looking at the expression on her friend's face.

'Possibly,' Emma replied. 'It's from Joshua's solicitors.'

Gabby took over the bathing of a squealing Amelia while Emma opened the envelope, giving herself a paper cut in the process. The cut stung and she instinctively raised the injured finger to her mouth. Unfolding the letter, she noticed how her blood had created a crimson heart shape in the crisp folds of the letter. Ironic, she thought, sitting down on the closed lid of the toilet to read.

'It appears Joshua wants to question my rights to full custody of Amelia.'

'On what grounds?' Gabby demanded. 'He can't just threaten to do that; there have to be grounds.'

Emma read on. 'Apparently I may be giving him grounds. What happened in the pool and my embarrassing collapse, in full view of Amelia and Annette, probably count as grounds.'

'I think you need to respond to this quickly. Phone your solicitor now, Em. Don't worry, you'll be fine – he can't just demand that. Courts always favour the mother.'

Emma sat quietly. 'Not if the mother is deemed to have "lost the plot", Gabs.'

With Amelia out of earshot, Emma called her solicitor. His advice was to let him handle all correspondence from Joshua's solicitors and not to get involved. He encouraged her to continue to allow Joshua access to Amelia, provided she felt her daughter was happy with the arrangement, and he didn't appear to be worried by the underlying threats. 'Sabre rattling' had been his terminology. As Emma had been granted full custody of Amelia, any changes to this order would have to be made by a judge in court and only if warranted. 'I'll write to Joshua's solicitors reminding them of the original custody agreement and the reference to "agreed and reasonable access considered appropriate for a three-year-old". Don't worry, everything will be fine,' were her solicitor's final words.

Suitably counselled, but still worried, Emma climbed the stairs back up to the bathroom. Watching Gabby wrap a dancing Amelia in an oversized bath towel, Emma's mind flashed back to the image of herself as Charlotte. The concept of 'fine' suddenly didn't fit the picture.

That night, as Emma attempted to sleep, she found the past-life session replaying in her mind's eye. Safe in her bed, she allowed herself to freeze and rewind the scenes as she journeyed once more on the ship as Charlotte, her hand in her father's and Dr Warner's words still fresh in her head: 'Examine the emotions you experienced …'

With damp eyes, Emma turned over, her pillow scrunched up under her face. Oh how quickly the sense of love and security can be replaced by that of loss and fear, she acknowledged, as she finally gave in to exhausted sleep.

Chapter 9

The following evening Gabby and Amelia were watching a cartoon in the sitting room. Wandering in, Emma smiled at the two of them draped around one another on the sofa. She sat down beside them and watched the screen, dimly aware of movements and colours in front of her, but her mind was elsewhere. The sound of the phone brought her back with a jolt. It was Helen. Taking the phone up into her bedroom, Emma attempted to explain to her sister what had happened with Dr Warner, but the words sounded trite and the story ridiculous.

'Did I make it all up, Helen? That's what is really worrying me.'

'What did the Dream Man say?'

'That the jury is still out on past-life regression theories, but to look for the message within that past life experienced. He talked about repeating patterns and understanding the lessons learned. You didn't tell me he was into past lives.'

Helen was listening attentively, her journalistic mind logging the details.

'Ah … past lives. Well, it didn't come up in my interview with him. Would make sense though; hypnosis could provide a route through to a past life if you could remember one. If it helps, I do know someone who might be able to answer some of your questions. His name is Simon Leighton and he's a child psychologist.'

'I don't want to see a child psychologist, Helen.' Emma's voice sounded tired with frustration.

'No, listen. Simon's been travelling the world investigating claims made by a number of children regarding a past existence. He says the accounts given by children are the best – that's provided they haven't been coached. His case studies have taken him all over the globe, especially India and Sri Lanka. He's just published a book on one child's story. Fascinating stuff.'

'Oh – so you do believe in a previous existence, then?'

'Not sure I believe in it, but it makes for interesting speculation. Simon is great for dinner parties; he can energise a table or clear it. You should meet him. I'm due to catch up with him next week.'

Emma had visions of another colourful character like Dr Warner and shook her head. 'Where do you meet all these strange people, Helen?'

'Oh, here and there through my travels in journalism. And they're not strange, Emma; "learned and brilliant", "colourful and interesting" would be more suitable descriptions.'

'Yeah, right!'

'So, do you want to meet Simon?'

There was a pause on the other end of the phone as Emma thought carefully.

'Ok, I'll say yes. Only because I'd like to ask him some questions, but I'm not having anyone hypnotise me again – on my own or in a group. Is that clear?'

'He won't,' Helen replied, laughing at her sister. 'I'll find out what evening he has free. Oh, by the way, he's single and very attractive. Look him up on the internet. Speak to you later.'

For the next few days, Emma pushed the subject of Charlotte to the back of her mind. She had more important things to deal with. Amelia wanted to stay with her father, leaving her with no option but to make the necessary arrangements. And she was sleeping badly again, the terrors punching their way into her sleep and leaving her emotionally bruised the following morning, but with all details of the dreams still floating tantalisingly out of reach. So much for finding Charlotte, she thought.

The weekend for Amelia's next visit to her father arrived all too quickly, and this time Emma insisted on taking her there herself. Joshua and Annette lived in a large brick town house, set back from the road at the end of a gated drive and surrounded by high hedges. The magnificent house, early Georgian in some parts and Edwardian in others, had been the marital home of Annette and her late husband Maxwell Barrett. It stood three stories high, a labyrinth of connecting structures set among acres of undulating manicured lawns and perfectly tended flower beds.

'Impressive,' Emma mumbled to herself as she removed Amelia from the car. Walking up to the black gloss front door, she prepared herself for some awkwardness as the bell noisily announced their arrival.

Annette opened the door. Joshua stood beside her. Both their faces wore orchestrated smiles. Joshua's unfathomable eyes met Emma's for a brief moment before dropping down to show genuine delight for his daughter. 'Hello, sweetie,' he said, scooping Amelia into his arms and holding her close.

'Hello, Daddy,' Amelia replied, planting a noisy kiss on her father's cheek. Then, repositioning herself in his arms, she drew her face back and looked up at him.

'Daddy, can I show Mummy my new room?'

The request triggered a twitch in Annette's carefully arranged demeanour, but a laugh from Joshua.

Emma looked at the group in embarrassment. 'I don't think so, darling, not today,' she hastily protested, a rude red flush spreading up her neck to her face.

'But I need you to see it, Mummy. Can she come up and see it with me, Daddy?'

'Darling,' Annette purred. 'Let your daughter show her mother her new room. I hope you approve of what I've done, Emma; I've had such fun designing it for Amelia.' Annette's smile grew wider, further adding to Emma's discomfort.

Joshua released his excited daughter from his arms. 'Ok, go and show your mother.'

'Come on, Mummy.'

'Well, if it's all right?' Emma answered, conscious of her scuffed shoes as she tiptoed across the expanse of expensive beige wool carpet.

Amelia scampered towards the stairs, stopping at the foot for assistance. Holding tightly onto her mother's hand, she negotiated the large staircase up onto the first-floor landing. As Emma stepped into her daughter's bedroom, she gasped. Decorated in pastel greens and pinks, the room was breathtaking. Emma touched the heavy floral drapes that dropped from the high windows onto the wool carpeted floor. Italian fabric, she thought, marvelling at the weight – and lined too! A matching coverlet and valance completed the soft-furnishing design. Toys of all description stood around the bedroom in carefully organised groups. It was as if they had just stepped into an expensive toy store.

'I've got a doll's house too, only Annette says I'm too young to play with it at the moment.' Amelia pointed to a delicate white doll's house standing on a raised plinth. Emma wandered over and looked inside the white-framed lattice windows. Each room had been laid out perfectly with appropriate furniture; the master bedroom had even been decorated using offcuts of material from Amelia's own bedroom. A family of four dolls, dressed in Victorian clothes, and a maid and a butler, suitably uniformed, had been positioned carefully within. Emma looked at the details – the tiny knives and forks on the dining table, the bacon slices and fried eggs on the kitchen plates, the soft, glowing lamps in the dining room and the tiny, artificial orchid in the planter standing by the staircase. The last time Emma had seen something so detailed she had been visiting a toy museum with her parents. Small parts, she thought, shaking her head in disbelief.

'Annette doesn't like anything moved in there,' Amelia announced. 'I've got a rocking horse, only I'm not allowed to climb on it without Daddy. I can use the pink princess car, though, but only when the gate is up in my room.'

Emma looked over to the battery car. Too much, she thought. Amelia stood uncharacteristically still. Dropping to her level, Emma knelt beside her. 'That looks fun,' she said, pointing to a wigwam in the corner of the room.

'That's for reading in.'

'Is it?'

'Annette says I need to sit in there and read books.'

'Is that what it's for?' said Emma, her heart hurting with love for Amelia. Everything in this world appeared to have conditions attached.

'I like the wigwam best,' Amelia told her mother, crawling into the safety of the tent and making Emma join her. 'Charlie says I can't break anything in here.'

'Oh, darling,' whispered Emma, pulling her daughter close.

'Annette doesn't like me playing with a lot of the toys in my room. I can look at them, but I'm not to touch them unless she's here with me. She says they're very precious.'

Emma climbed out of the tent and walked towards the bed where a white painted shelf housed an array of soft toys that stood tantalisingly out of reach. She looked up to see Joshua enter the room.

'Annette did this room up especially for Amelia. It was used as a study previously,' he told her.

'It's very lovely, Joshua. Amelia's a lucky little girl.' Emma couldn't help thinking that the room far exceeded anything she could ever create in their cottage. The high ceilings and huge windows allowed for the oversized furniture and voluminous drapes, and despite the abundance of toys and the out-of-bounds doll's house, the room didn't look cluttered. Emma opened up one of the French windows and stepped onto a wide stone balcony with a highly decorative balustrade; a sweeping stone staircase led down to the gardens below. Large pots filled with white and gold lilies stood in rows along the length of the balcony. Beyond the safety of the balustrade she could glimpse the immaculate lawns.

'You will keep this door shut, won't you?' Emma asked in alarm.

'Of course. The housekeeper must have opened it today to air the room; it's not normally unlocked. Amelia knows she mustn't go out here without a grown up.'

Emma stepped back into the bedroom and Joshua locked the door.

'Look, Mummy.'

Emma watched as Amelia climbed up onto the bed, jumping in an attempt to reach the shelf of toys. 'Shoes, Amelia!' she cried, watching in horror as her daughter's dusty red sandals disappeared within the folds of the bed linen.

'But I wanted to show you my fluffy duck,' Amelia grinned at her mother, throwing herself down onto the bed.

'And you can, but we don't bounce on beds with shoes on, do we?'

Joshua, leaning on the doorframe, assessed the situation,

putting his finger to his lips. 'It's all right, Annette hasn't seen you,' he whispered, striding across the room to get the duck. Pulling the toy down, he gave it to an eager Amelia.

As she left, Emma knew Amelia would be fine with her father, although the display of untouchable toys in the bedroom made her uncomfortable. Luckily, she'd packed a few much-loved books and Buddy, of course, for the weekend; Amelia would gravitate to things and people she felt comfortable with – and that would include the inescapable Charlie. Turning the key in the ignition, she shivered involuntarily, experiencing once more that deep sense of sadness and loss. Natural, she thought, putting her foot on the accelerator and moving out of the drive-way, watching as the house grew smaller and smaller in her rear-view mirror.

After waving goodbye to her mother, Amelia played hide and seek with her father among the rhododendron bushes, darting in and out of the foliage in breathless laughter. Screaming with excitement, and chased by an exhausted Joshua, she rushed back into the kitchen where Annette played the perfect step-mother, on hand with expensive, delicatessen-bought biscuits and organic apple juice. Joshua beamed at his new wife with gratitude and Annette smiled inwardly.

After her husband's death, the curtains in his study had been pulled across all the windows, the furniture covered and the room locked up. Annette could not bear to enter it and Joshua respected her feelings, making a study for himself in the den beside the kitchen. All ghosts remained behind those closed doors. So when Annette proposed that they turn Max's old study into a bedroom for Amelia, Joshua thought her suggestion was an act of selfless kindness. But for Annette, there had been no such generosity of spirit in her proposal. For her, it was the perfect solution: it provided a room for Amelia, away from theirs, and gave her an acceptable excuse to rip out Max's much-loved wooden panelling, his specially commissioned office furniture, his self-portrait and those dated drapes. Any associated bad memories were burned, thrown onto a skip or moved up into the attic.

Now, Annette watched as father's and daughter's heads bent easily towards one another at the table. *So far, so good*, she thought. *This is all going to work to my advantage.*

That evening, having tucked Amelia up into her oversized bed, a selection of her new soft toys nestling close to her, Joshua took a final look at his daughter before turning off the main light. Lost among the covers, with Buddy clasped tightly in her hand, Amelia peered out at her father as he blew her one more kiss from the doorway. A white, wrought-iron child gate had been placed across the opening to the bedroom, allowing Amelia to sleep with the door open.

'Where's the picture of the man, Daddy?'

Joshua instinctively looked around the room. 'What picture, Amelia?'

'The big one, the one of the man with the white hair and striped suit.'

'There's no picture of a man in here, darling.'

'But there was. Charlie says so.'

Despite the warmth in the house, Joshua felt chilled. 'There's just a picture of a pretty lady in a field of flowers. Now close your eyes and I'll come up later to check on you. Night night, sleep tight … don't let the bed bugs bite!' Smiling at his daughter, Joshua secured the child gate and turned towards the landing.

The comment about the 'big picture' had unnerved him. There had been a large picture in the room once, a full-length portrait of Max Barrett which used to hang behind his desk. Annette had had it removed and stored in the attic.

The kitchen, basking in the last rays of the sunlight, was a welcome relief for Joshua. He opened the fridge and took out a bottle of wine, watching Annette as she crushed garlic and chopped coriander, the intoxicating smells promising a special feast.

'Glass of wine?' he asked.

'Please. Is she going to sleep?' she asked as he filled her glass.

'Hope so. I'm exhausted. I'll go up and check on her in a few minutes.' He wrapped his arms around his wife's waist and put his head on her shoulder. Max's death was a subject neither wished to discuss. But he worried about the comments Amelia had made earlier and hoped she wouldn't repeat them to Annette. He made a decision not to mention anything about it to her.

'Thanks for the wonderful job you did with the room. Amelia loves it.'

'My pleasure, darling. Things are different now – time for changes, we have your little girl in our house.'

'Thank you. It really means so much to me.'

And don't I know it, thought Annette as she put some water on the stove to boil. 'I'll check on Amelia, darling,' she purred. 'You relax.'

Quietly opening the child's gate, Annette tiptoed over to the bed. The small hump in the bedding stirred and pulled the covers down. A tiny pale face lifted from the pillows and looked directly at her.

'Charlie says you should have given the man his medicine.'

Annette froze. 'What man?' she whispered.

'The man who fell …'

Annette stood rigid. Her mouth felt dry and her heart banged within her rib cage.

'Charlie says the man's ok now and he's forgiven you.'

'Oh … That's good. Shall we go to sleep now?'

'Ok. Night night.'

Replacing the child gate and turning towards the landing, Annette felt uneasy; there were things that only she knew about Max's accident.

In the morning Joshua brought Amelia into their room. As she climbed up onto their bed and tucked herself in among the covers it was as if nothing had happened the previous night. Both Joshua and Annette breathed sighs of relief, neither having mentioned their conversations with Amelia to the other.

It was bright and sunny as Joshua played with Amelia in the garden later on. He'd pumped up a small plastic paddling pool and filled it with shallow water. Floating orange and silver rubber goldfish with large rings on the ends of their mouths bobbed about while father and daughter, dressed in their bathing suits, tried to catch them using plastic hooks on short multicoloured plastic rods. But as Amelia giggled with delight, she lost her footing, rolled over onto the pool's inflatable wall and tipped head first into the water. Instinctively and within seconds Joshua grabbed her, crushing her wet face to his chest. His heart racing, he held her close as a distant memory surfaced.

Chapter 10

Simon Leighton parked his car outside Helen's apartment at around seven. He had been signing books in Winchester all day and craved easy conversation and at least one strong drink. He glanced at his reflection in the car mirror and removed his tie, throwing it onto the back seat with relief. Scraping his tanned hands through his thick hair, he ran his tongue over the front of his teeth. Best I can offer, he thought, tossing a mint into his mouth and retrieving the service station flowers and wine from the car boot.

Helen opened the door to find Simon looking sheepish on her doorstep; the flowers, hastily purchased on the way over, drooped before her eyes. 'Oh my!' she exclaimed with a smile, taking the cellophane-wrapped offering.

'I think the wine's fared better,' Simon told her, kissing her on the cheek.

Helen laughed as she showed him into the living room and poured him a large straight scotch on ice. 'Thought you might need this,' she said.

'A mind reader,' he replied. 'I can't tell you what a day I've had. I lost count of the number of overweight, over-rouged pensioners who wanted me to sign their books with their 'past-life names' – and that was just the men!'

Helen laughed.

'It was a circus. I know my publisher wants exposure, but today I was reminded of why I don't do book signings.'

'Now, be nice, Simon. Exposure sells books. No pain, no gain!'

'I know, but I can still loathe the ridiculous performance, can't I?'

Helen smiled, looking again at the sad bouquet. 'I'll see if I can resurrect these in some water. You haven't forgotten Emma's joining us for dinner, have you?'

Simon watched Helen walk towards the kitchen. He had forgotten, not that he'd admit it. 'Looking forward to meeting her at last,' he offered, secretly hoping Emma would be as attractive as her sister.

Helen spun and looked back at Simon with a knowing glint in her eye.

'You'll like her, I promise.'

Born in Somerset to a senior general practitioner working within a local medical practice and a paediatrician for the district hospital and baby clinic, Simon was the eldest of two, his brother Nathan being three years his junior. Angus Leighton, his father, was a non-practising Catholic while his mother, Camilla, leaned towards a more spiritual and fluid denomination. Together, the couple encouraged their boys to debate freely and noisily on the subjects of faith, life and death. Dinners at the Leighton home were therefore always a lively event.

Simon had shown an interest in religion from an early age. Whereas Nathan rebelled against any religious instruction, choosing psychiatry and calling himself an atheist, Simon chose psychology and referred to himself as a 'searcher', taking a further degree in theology and world religions as he sought the answers. He attributed his deep spiritual awareness to his mother and his need for verification, explanations and proof to his father.

Simon was married for eight years to Anita, a successful London banker. They had met at university, and their divorce five years ago had been both amicable and inevitable. Both parties recognised the gradual disconnection from one another, alluding to conflicting careers and interests, while remaining friends. There were no children. Now, at forty-five years of age, Simon concentrated on the real love of his life: his writing and research work. Despite the demands these entailed, he still ensured that he ate well, slept well and exercised religiously. His mantra – 'We have been given this body for this lifetime; it is our responsibility to care for it' – held him in good stead.

Simon's most recent investigation had involved a five-year-old boy from Inverness who claimed to have lived and drowned previously on a small remote island off Scotland. Working in this highly controversial area, Simon couldn't afford to allow his own emotions to cloud his judgment, so his research always called for a methodical, scrupulous and objective approach; but on this particular investigation, he found himself tested. Bringing both mothers and child together, he witnessed something quite extraordinary take place when the little boy in question finally met up with his 'other' mother. Although the evidence was scant and nothing could be proved, the heart won over the head when the little boy ran open-armed towards the woman. The two mothers now had a lifetime bond through their 'shared child'.

Simon always marvelled at children's ability to accept the concept of a previous life with no question of improbability. For them, it was their truth, surmounting opposing cultures and beliefs. Unfortunately, he had also investigated a number of hoaxes over the years, orchestrated by children, their families or both. It was the search for supporting evidence that both sustained and fascinated Simon. Aware that his findings did not always offer tangible proof and that some of his cases had weaknesses, he continued his search for the answers as the scholars and the sceptics bayed from the sidelines.

Ringing the bell twice to announce her arrival, Emma let herself in through the open door, calling out her sister's name. On the table in the entrance stood an exquisite floral arrangement. She prodded to check it was real, then followed the faint smells of garlic.

'Something smells good,' she called out, as she stepped through the doorway into the main living room. Simon instinctively stood as Emma entered. There was a faint sound of ice cubes clinking as he gripped his scotch glass firmly.

Emma wore a pair of dark jeans that hugged her hips and slim legs, and a turquoise loose-knit sweater over a tight pale blue T-shirt, accentuating her tiny waist and the swell of her breasts. She wore her long hair loose, tumbling over her shoulders in dark waves. Simon had always had a weakness for long, dark hair, and when she smiled, he found himself drawn to her mouth and perfect teeth. Her voice was warm and inviting and as he looked into her laughing green eyes, he felt his breath catch in his throat.

Flustered from the drive over, Emma grappled with her over-sized handbag and collection of keys while extending her hand towards Simon, quite unaware of the effect that she had on him.

'Hello,' she said. 'You must be Simon. Nice to meet you, I'm Emma. Sorry if I'm a bit late, Helen, I got confused in your awful one-way system again. Why do they make it so complicated?' Then, dropping her bag on a settee, she pushed her hair back from her face and smiled in Simon's direction. He smiled back at her, watching the way her mouth curled into a grin as she described her journey. His eyes moved from her animated face to her hands and, out of habit, he looked for a ring on her finger.

'You're not late,' said Helen. 'Simon got here quicker than he thought he would. He's been at his book signing all day. Glass of white?'

'Please ... been an interesting day ... What's your book about?' she asked, sitting down opposite Simon and assessing him.

He was not what she had expected. Standing over six feet tall in a pair of black leather loafers, he wore dark denim jeans that outlined his lean, muscular legs and a pink, open-necked shirt that defined his broad shoulders and body shape. His thick hair, scattered with silver, was worn short and his fringe fell in a slightly foppish manner over one eye. She noted how he brushed it away with his long fingers. He had an attractive face, clean-shaven with engaging brown eyes, and his expressive, lopsided smile – a bit like a mischievous schoolboy's – disarmed her in seconds. As he sat down, she glanced surreptitiously at his stomach – nothing wobbly there, she thought.

'Ah, my book ... It's not to everyone's taste. It's called *A Life in Balance*, and it's an account of one of my investigations. A Sri Lankan child who claimed she'd once lived in a remote village in Pakistan, where she was murdered by her father.'

'Fact or fiction?' Emma asked.

'Could possibly be described as both. It's a factual account of the girl's past-life claim and our research and findings. Of course, we had to change their names to protect individuals; whether or not it's fiction is up to the reader.'

'Didn't you say you found a man in Pakistan who could have been the father?' asked Helen.

'Yes, although we couldn't go around accusing him of filicide, but as we researched and investigated Sarasi's story, we discovered that there was a daughter who had gone "missing". This young woman disappeared before Sarasi was born in Sri Lanka. Sarasi had never travelled out of Sri Lanka, yet she also gave a perfect description of the remote village in Pakistan where the young woman used to live. By the way, I used the name

Sarasi because it means "surrender".'

'So what happened to the young woman – his daughter?'

'The family and village closed ranks on us. All we could establish was her existence and the fact she had gone missing. We weren't allowed to speak to either the mother or sisters.'

'Did Sarasi meet any of them?' asked Emma.

'Not possible, although we did film an interview with the father and three of his sons. But because of the sensitive nature of her allegation, we couldn't put any parties together. In truth, although we felt she was credible, there was no tangible proof to substantiate anything.'

'Was it an honour killing?' asked Helen.

'According to Sarasi, yes. The family in question lived in one of the rural areas of the southern province of Sindh. It helps if you understand a little of their culture, their religion and customs, but also their strong sense of honour. More importantly, their belief that the women are the property of the males within the family.'

There was a sound of inhaled breath. Simon smiled. 'Their view of women as "commodities" to be bought, exchanged or sold is deeply entrenched within the very fabric of Pakistan. The male has the right to determine a woman's fate, as his property.' Simon watched as the two women shuffled uncomfortably. 'It's not my intention to judge in this book, but it does highlight the practice of honour killings and the collaboration of the community in covering up these— '

Helen interjected, 'Atrocities.'

'Sadly, yes,' Simon concluded.

'No man has the right to determine the fate of any woman,' said Emma, her voice stiffening with indignation.

'I know,' said Simon. 'For me it was a difficult case to remain detached from and one of the most haunting I've ever investigated. I experienced so many conflicting emotions. You have to understand, the practice of honour killings is widespread in many parts of the world. There's also reluctance among the authorities to prevent or punish perpetrators of these crimes. I found that difficult to comprehend. The little girl's description of her own murder showed me the darker side of human nature. But however distressing it was in its finality, as Sarasi narrated her tragic end at the hands of her father, she did so with not just a sense of great sadness but with dignified compassion and understanding.' Simon paused, looking away in thought for a brief moment before continuing. 'It was as if she was aware of something that I, the investigator, was not. I can only describe it as "forgiveness". To listen to a small child talk about such a tragic event without any sense of hatred or fear shook me to the core. "Generosity of spirit" is what I call it in the book. For a seven-year-old girl, she was the most mature soul I've ever met.'

Emma found herself shivering. 'Do you hypnotise any of these children?' she asked.

'No. Children speak freely when they want to.'

'Did the Sri Lankan parents accept her past-life claims?' asked Helen.

'We started investigating Sarasi's claims *because* of her parents. Her journey was as much theirs as her own. Sarasi's ability, despite her age, to understand and forgive such a crime was astonishing to all of us. It was almost as if she understood the faults and failings of man.'

Listening to Simon, Emma found herself remembering Charlotte's words from her session with Dr Warner: *Understand the weakness of man and the power of forgiveness – forgiveness brings understanding. Love is the answer.*

'A truly humbling experience,' Simon continued. 'I only hope that's conveyed in my book.'

'Will she remember that previous life as she gets older?' Emma asked.

'Yes, I think she will always remember, because she wants to. Physically she carries a violent pink birthmark on her chest, corresponding with her description of her fatal injury in that previous life in Pakistan. Her past-life memories may fade, but not that mark. Sarasi believes she has returned to teach others about forgiveness.'

'Do physical wounds always carry over, then?' asked Emma with concern.

Simon nodded. 'There's a suggestion they do.'

Helen looked at her sister. 'You've recently discovered your own past life, haven't you?' she said.

Simon studied Emma as she took a second glass of wine from her sister. A faint pink flush had risen to her cheeks and he noted how she bit her bottom lip as she gave her sister a look of exasperation.

'Thanks, Helen! Yes, it wasn't what I expected to discover.'

Simon looked on with interest. 'How did you "discover" this past life then, Emma?'

Emma looked at Helen for support. 'I visited a hypnotherapist, on Helen's recommendation, hoping he could unlock a memory block. The past-life recollection was an accident, really, and now I'm not sure what to believe. In all honesty, I'm finding it all quite ...'

As Emma spoke she noted how Simon's eyes never left her face. 'Uncomfortable?' he probed.

Emma nodded.

'Man needs to believe there is something more to life than

just death at the end. The concepts of past existences, reincarnations or rebirths are widely accepted by many cultures and faiths,' Simon told them.

'Like Hinduism and Buddhism?' asked Emma.

Simon looked over at Emma and Helen and swigged his drink. *This is going to kill the evening,* he thought. *I wasn't expecting to be giving a religious lecture tonight.* Then, taking a deep breath, he answered: 'Hinduism and Buddhism have parallel beliefs, but they differ in practice and theory. One is a more metaphysical teaching where a soul is reborn into another body. This is central to most Indian religions such as Hinduism, Jainism and Sikhism. Buddhism, although referring to reincarnation, refers to "energies" and "the stream of consciousness" that link with all life. Rebirth is more of a moral teaching.' Simon looked over at the two women. 'Religious history lessons can get boring – shall I stop?'

'No. You're not boring us. Carry on, but layman's terms, please,' laughed Helen.

'So does a belief in reincarnation and past lives depend on where you're born and live – geography? Those religions you mentioned aren't the prevailing norm here in the West,' said Emma.

'No. Surprisingly the idea of returning in some other form is a more common belief than realised. Obviously, the majority of people within Judaism, Christianity and Islam don't believe that individuals reincarnate. But there are groups within all of these religions that do refer to reincarnation or rebirth.'

'Really?' Helen exclaimed.

'Like who?' Emma asked.

'Let's see,' Simon continued, 'Well the Hassidim, the Kabbalists, the Cathars, the Druze and the Rosicrucians, for example. And there are many others under different names practising throughout America and Australasia.'

'So reincarnation, rebirth or a past-life existence is more widely accepted than I thought. What about you, Simon? Do you believe in past lives?' Emma asked.

Simon stretched his long legs out in front of him. 'I'm always asked that.'

'Well, you are the investigator,' prompted Helen.

'I'd like to believe that death is not the end – more another beginning. I try to remain as impartial as I can to ensure an unbiased approach to my work.'

'But you haven't answered my question,' Emma said.

Simon grinned at her. 'I want to believe. That's why I study and investigate. The idea that we can reincarnate across countries, genders, nationalities and faiths, if adequately proven, would alter the concept that people worldwide have of one another.'

'How?' Helen asked.

'We'd understand one another. Half the world's problems come about through our own ignorance. Countries and cultures fight over ways to worship and ways to live. We all think our way is the only way,' added Simon.

'So why, if it's true and we have all lived before, don't we remember our past lives? Wouldn't that help?' asked Helen.

'Sometimes people do remember – flashes of unexplained familiarity.'

'You mean déjà vu?'

Simon nodded. 'But most people find acceptable explanations for those moments. There's a suggestion that all children remember their previous lives, but as they're normally unable to communicate this intelligently until they're about three, and by then they have evolved in their current lives, they choose simply to absorb or forget these memories. For those who do remember, past memories can be confusing and, in most cases, any mention of a previous existence is termed childish nonsense. These children quickly learn to say nothing, as there is usually little or no benefit, and it's easier to forget. Of course, there are always exceptions. Some children never forget.'

'How old are the children you've investigated?' Emma asked.

'They've all been older than three and not only remembered their previous life but wanted to communicate the facts.'

'So why must we forget, then?' asked Emma.

'Some people hold that it's vital we forget our past lives to ensure a successful life in the present. How would we learn to walk if we only remembered our stumbles and falls?'

'So how do you know the children aren't just making it up?' Emma asked. 'Surely you must have studied hundreds of hoaxes or planted memories.'

'Well I don't know for sure at the time. I can only investigate the evidence and find an acceptable explanation. And yes, I have uncovered a hoax or two.' Simon watched as Emma lowered her head. 'If you're interested, I have a copy of my book here. I brought it for Helen, but I'm sure she wouldn't mind me giving it to you if you'd like to read it. I can get another for her,' he added, passing the hardback over to Emma.

'With regard to your own personal experience of a past life, you have two choices: forget about it or investigate it. If you choose to investigate, look at it as a detective challenge; view the images and collect the facts. Prod and poke at it. There'll be something there that can be substantiated or else will have a similarity to some emotion or situation in your current life. Challenge yourself; it can be quite therapeutic. Remember, nothing can be taken at face value. If you want some help, you can call me. I can act as a sounding board.'

Emma looked up at her sister for an acknowledgment and placed the book in her bag. 'Thanks,' she said.

Dinner was a far more light-hearted affair, punctuated with laughter and amusing banter. As Simon left for the evening he kissed both girls goodnight, giving Emma his business card with contact numbers in case she needed his help. As the door closed behind him, Emma found herself clasping the card to her chest with both hands.

Helen saw this and laughed. 'So you like my friends now. Not so weird, eh?'

Emma smiled. 'No, not so weird,' she said. There was something about Simon she couldn't place, something so familiar and reassuring.

'Are you going to call him, then?'

Emma looked at her sister and pursed her lips together. 'Maybe,' she said elusively.

That night Emma's dreams were vivid, but there were no nightmares. She recognised faces of people appearing in them, although she couldn't put names to them. And, surprisingly, there was no reference to water. *Maybe something* is *changing*, she thought, punching her pillows and curling up to go back to sleep.

Chapter 11

Joshua arrived back with Amelia who ran to her mother and hugged her tightly before being sidetracked by Thomas who was skulking around the rockery. She threw down her pink rucksack and called out to him in delight, chasing him into the cottage.

Joshua watched until Amelia was out of sight before turning to Emma. 'So what's the story with this "Charlie" and when did it start?' he asked.

Emma groaned inwardly. She had been expecting this. 'Oh, her imaginary friend Charlie – he's a new addition and quite harmless, we're all getting used to him.'

'I'm not worried about whether or not *you* are used to him, I want to know when it all started – and when it's going to stop? It can't be normal for children to talk to imaginary friends.'

Emma found herself bristling at his tone. Carefully, she controlled her response. 'Oh, but it *is* normal, apparently. As to when it will stop – I have no idea.'

Joshua cleared his throat, his face scowling with a look of irritation as he watched her closely, waiting for more information.

Emma continued, 'Charlie hasn't been around long. I've been told to let it run its course, as it is not harming anyone. She'll drop Charlie when she's ready.'

'Well Annette and I don't think it's healthy to encourage this any longer. We're concerned that it will lead to bigger behavioural issues in the future.'

Emma noted the look he gave her with this comment and winced.

'Does she talk to you about the things Charlie tells her?' he continued.

'Yes, sometimes. Charlie appears to be very learned and wise,' Emma replied with a smile, hoping to break the tension, as she could see Amelia watching them from the open kitchen door.

'Well, the things she mentioned this weekend were not wise and could have been very damaging.'

Emma had been watching Amelia with one eye, and for a split second her concentration had wavered. Joshua's comment brought her back instantly. 'Damaging in what way? What did she tell you?'

Joshua looked towards the kitchen to ensure Amelia was out of earshot. 'She asked me where the big picture of Max in her bedroom had gone.'

'Max? She used his name?'

Joshua corrected himself. 'No. She asked where the picture of "the man" had gone.'

Emma breathed a sigh of relief. 'She must be remembering some other picture. Maybe Annette has changed one since her last visit.'

Joshua paused. 'She hasn't. But there was a picture of Max in that room when he was alive.'

Emma's face paled in disbelief as she registered his words.

'It was a full-sized portrait and hung in his study. Annette had it removed and put in the attic. Amelia claimed Charlie told her about the man in the picture.'

Emma looked at Joshua. There was no possible explanation for what she was hearing. 'Sounds like coincidence or childish imagination to me,' she ventured, nevertheless. She swallowed; her mouth felt dry.

'Apparently, Charlie told her that the man in the big picture had white hair and wore a striped suit,' Joshua went on.

'Oh my God!' said Emma, her hand flying to her mouth.

Joshua looked accusingly at Emma. 'Did you ever tell Amelia anything about Max or how he died?'

Emma's mouth opened in horror at what he was suggesting. 'I don't know anything about Max, or his death – and why would I tell Amelia? What sort of mother do you think I am?' Emma looked at her ex-husband. She knew what his response would be.

'Well you're going to have to speak to her,' Joshua continued. 'The last thing I want is for Amelia to mention that tragic part of Annette's life. If you have in some way been instrumental in filling her head with any of this, I will take action. Is that clear?'

Emma gritted her teeth; the meaning behind that last remark was not lost. 'I'll try and find out what's going on in her head,' she said. 'But you have to remember, Joshua, she's not even four yet and doesn't always realise what she's saying.'

'Then speak to "Charlie". He appears to be the most influential spokesperson around here at the moment!' And turning on his heels, Joshua left, forgetting to say goodbye to his daughter. Emma listened to his car drive away as she considered the latest revelations.

'Has Daddy gone?' Amelia asked, looking at the empty track outside.

'Yup. Had to rush. Busy day. He said to say bye-bye.' Emma looked at Amelia's small face which looked forlorn. 'Here, give Mummy a big hug. I missed you.'

Amelia threw herself into the security of her mother's arms and kissed her noisily. Then, linking hands, the two of them wandered back into the kitchen together.

As Amelia watched cartoons later on, Emma paced. Catching

sight of Simon's business card propped up on the dresser, she moved towards it and picked it up. Perhaps Simon could throw some light on the arrival of Charlie. She'd run out of answers and Joshua's reaction was beginning to frighten her.

Simon was delighted to receive Emma's call. He'd managed to get her address and telephone number from Helen, and although he'd been hoping she might phone him first, he hadn't expected her call to be regarding her daughter. He listened carefully as Emma tried to explain the latest developments; her attempt at humour only badly disguised her anxiety. Simon told Emma he would need to meet Amelia before he could make any judgment, and conscious of her mounting distress he agreed to meet her the following morning at the cottage.

Still holding Simon's card in her hands, Emma felt a mix of trepidation and excitement. *I know involving him is a risk,* she thought. *But I need to talk to someone who will understand and someone I can trust. If he listens and I never see him again, then I'll be no worse off than I am now.*

The following morning, Emma nervously tidied up, wiping down the kitchen worktops at least twice. Amelia, aware that someone of import was about to arrive, helped by moving the cushions from one settee to another, finally settling for a large pile on the floor. Despite her initial anxiety, as soon as Simon stepped into the cottage Emma knew she'd made the right decision. Amelia connected with him instantly, happily chatting to her new-found friend, showing him her favourite toys, introducing him to Thomas and taking him to where she and Charlie liked to hide in the garden. According to Amelia, Charlie liked Simon too.

When Amelia went for a late-morning nap Emma had a chance to ask Simon the burning question: 'Well … is she a normal child of nearly four?'

'She's perfectly delightful, very bright and remarkably well adjusted to the idea of a father and mother living separate lives.'

'What about the Charlie situation?'

'Many children have imaginary friends – some human and others animal. I don't think Charlie is an issue to be worried about. She may just be using him as her way of getting answers to thoughts that worry her. In my view, she'll drop references to Charlie when she is ready.'

'Joshua thinks I'm feeding Amelia information about his wife's dead husband, Max.'

'Why, what has Amelia said to him?'

'Oh it all revolves around a picture Amelia asked about. She claimed Charlie told her about it. Apparently, she asked Joshua where it had gone.'

'Was there ever such a picture?' Simon asked.

'Yes. When Max was alive. It was a full-length portrait of him and it hung in the room where Amelia now sleeps. Whatever she said to Joshua must have hit a nerve.'

'Could she have seen it in another room?'

'No, never. According to Joshua, Annette had it moved into the attic before she changed the study into a bedroom for Amelia.'

Simon picked up his tea and drank slowly. Over the rim of the mug he could see Emma's hands, pressed firmly together as if in prayer, the tips of her fingers brushing her upper lip.

'I think Joshua believes I'm orchestrating something sinister against Annette and using Amelia in the process.'

'Too extreme; Amelia is too young to be played in that

manner,' Simon told her. 'It sounds like Joshua's overreacting. There's probably a simple explanation to it all. Did you ask Amelia about the picture?'

'Not directly. She volunteered information about her weekend with her father on the night he brought her home. She told me that Charlie liked her room but was sad that they'd taken away the picture of the white-haired man. I didn't want to push her further. She seemed quite matter of fact about it all.'

Simon raised an eyebrow.

'You see my problem. Charlie is creating issues where I don't need them.'

Simon noticed the slight lift in Emma's shoulders and tone. 'Do you mind me asking – out of interest, what are the arrangements for Amelia? Who has custody?'

'I do. Although, Joshua has rights to see her, at my discretion.'

'Is he happy with that?'

Emma looked into Simon's kind face. 'No. Not now,' she whispered.

Fully aware that she had only just met him, she wondered how much detail she should disclose about her private life.

'Do you think Joshua could be looking for an excuse to change the arrangements?'

Clutching a cushion to her chest, Emma nodded. 'And I haven't helped the situation, either.'

'Why is that?'

With a deep sigh Emma continued, briefly outlining the original custody arrangements, Joshua's recent marriage, his new-found interest in his daughter, and the letters from his solicitors.

Simon listened without comment as Emma then touched on her family, Joshua's affair with Annette, her marriage break-up, her business life and work, her friends and hopes for the future.

He had been taking mental notes and had gleaned enough of her background to give him an insight into what made her 'tick'. And the more he listened to her, the more attractive he found her.

Emma spoke honestly with humour and passion; despite her physical fragility, her emotional strength was obvious. She described her near-drowning incident in the public pool and the 'visions' she had seen in the water with detached clarity, laughing in embarrassment when she made reference to her fainting on the doorstep in front of Joshua and Annette. Throughout, she spoke calmly and coherently, displaying a wry, apologetic smile when she mentioned points that made her uncomfortable. 'My fear is …' Emma paused and looked directly at Simon. 'I'm afraid I'm becoming unglued and that would be exactly what Joshua needs to take Amelia away from me. I saw Dr Warner in the hope that he could remove the memory blocks to my night-mares. I had thought that by remembering and understanding my dream terrors, I could perhaps make sense of my recent col-lapses; and if I knew *why* they happened, I could prevent them from happening again. But instead of removing the blocks, I've now created another person called Charlotte from a tragic past life on board a ship that sank.' Emma shook her head in mock frustration. 'Plus, on top of all that, I have Amelia's invisible friend Charlie to contend with.'

Simon smiled back at Emma. 'As I said, everything can have a plausible explanation. I'm obviously interested in your past life as Charlotte though. Would you mind telling me something about it?'

Emma gazed at Simon's face and the look he returned was gentle and reassuring.

'That's only if you want to,' he added.

Emma had no difficulty in recounting every detail from

that past-life recall, noting that the images were now appearing clearer and brighter and that the emotions connected to the recollection no longer felt so intense, allowing her to convey her life as Charlotte objectively. When she'd finished she leaned back into the settee with a sigh. 'Well that was then; this is now,' she quipped.

'I'm sure Dr Warner told you about the similar themes and links with your current life,' said Simon.

'He did. And I also understand that a "past-life experience" could just be my subconscious telling me something about my current life. I've looked at the possible links.'

'Interesting ones?'

'Sounded plausible to me.'

'Can I ask you a few questions and see if I can impartially find the links?'

'Sure.'

'Ok, let's try this approach. Use your imagination and give me a suggested scenario,' Simon coaxed. 'For example, the woman on the ship – the one you felt you didn't like – what do you think her relationship was to Charlotte or her parents?'

Emma paused and dug deep into the memories.

'Just use your emotions and guess,' Simon told her. 'You can never know the truth. Tell me what you think and feel when reviewing those particular images.'

'Ok,' Emma paused and closed her eyes. 'Gut feeling ... I'd say there was some sort of liaison with my father.'

'So we put affair down against Henry in that life and affair against Joshua in this one.'

'But Charlotte was Henry's daughter, not his wife. Surely that's different from Joshua's infidelity to me?'

'Affairs and their aftermath can have an emotional effect on more than just the individuals directly involved. I'm sure you understand that, especially with Amelia.'

'Ok, but aren't we reaching here?' Emma asked, sitting herself bolt upright.

'Yes, slightly. But these are purely scenarios,' said Simon. 'Now describe the emotions experienced by Charlotte on the ship.'

'I felt happiness and security and love; then fear and loss and a sense of abandonment.'

'Familiar emotions in your current life?' he asked.

Emma paused, 'Yes. All of them.'

'Ok, we'll put that down and you can expand on it later. Now, what else feels important that you remember?'

'There's an image that I keep replaying. It's of my father as he held me over the side of the ship. I can see the muscles in his arms tensing under the strain. I remember the terrified look in his eyes and how he kept mouthing the words, "I'm sorry".' Emma closed her eyes for a moment. 'That day Joshua came to drop off Amelia – the day I collapsed ...'

'Go on,' prompted Simon.

'I remember the expression on Joshua's face as he held Amelia. It didn't appear to belong to him ... it looked superimposed. I can see the way his muscles tensed as she tried to pull free.' Emma sat up in her seat and looked at Simon, suddenly incredulous.

'That was the image that made me collapse! I'd seen it before. No, I remember *feeling* that before.'

'Good, we're getting somewhere. Can you think of anything else from that life as Charlotte that's carried over?'

'Yes, my dislike of lily of the valley; I hate that scent.'

'Who wore it?'

'The woman on the ship – the lady in the hat. The one I

think was having a liaison with Henry, my father in that life.'

'Do you know anyone who uses that scent?'

Emma paused. 'I won a bottle of it at a church fete as a child. I remember spraying it on myself on the way home and feeling so nauseous that my father had to stop the car. I was violently sick and my mother threw the perfume away.'

'Interesting, isn't it?' said Simon. 'It's possible that past-life memories associated with that scent triggered your sickness, or that you've linked the unpleasantness of car sickness with it. Smells are powerful and can be connected with places, things or people. In aromatherapy the scents from plant material and oils can affect a person both psychologically and physically. But whether we're talking past or present, it's obvious that you don't like lily of the valley.'

Emma nodded. 'What about Charlie being the name of my baby brother on the ship as well as Amelia's imaginary friend? Could I have been subconsciously influenced by the events in my current situation and transferred them into a life as Charlotte?'

'It's possible.'

'Maybe the name Charlotte was influenced by Amelia's Charlie too. Isn't it odd to have a family with a Charlotte and Charles together?'

'Not necessarily ... male and female versions – child mortality could have been an issue then. Charles could have been an important name in their family.'

Drawing up more similarities, Emma found herself laughing with Simon as they wandered into the kitchen. 'Surely some of these links are a bit woolly?' she asked, refilling the kettle.

'Maybe,' said Simon, 'but fun to try and match.'

'So why do you think I "froze" in the swimming pool that day?'

'It could be that the incident in the pool was triggered by

something Joshua said or did that you found stressful. It could have been a subconscious memory from your current life, or even from a previous one. We call it a trauma trigger.'

'I like that. It sounds credible – and treatable.' Walking back to the settee with fresh tea, Emma found herself enjoying the comfortable exchange with Simon. The subject of a past-life existence was not something that was easy to think about, let alone talk about, yet Simon made it feel relatively believable.

Simon smiled at her. 'Had you ever had a near-drowning experience as a child or adult before this?'

'No, that was the first thing I checked with my parents.'

'Ok, so what else from that past-life recall is worth noting?'

'The hat.'

'The hat?'

'Yes. The woman on the ship – I hated her hat. It was decorated with bird feathers – like a pair of black wings shimmering with blue and green reflections.' Emma laughed.

'What's so funny?'

'Annette – Joshua's new wife's … she has this perfect geometrical hairstyle with sharp, pointed layers; it hangs lower in the front when she tilts her head, like the drooping wing of an injured bird. It's jet black with shades of blue and green that reflect in some lights.' Emma shuddered.

'You don't like Annette, do you?'

'No. I think it's possible I made up the hat up in my regression because of my dislike for her.'

'Maybe. The similarity of distaste is interesting though, isn't it?'

'Ooh, the gloves, they were kid gloves with tiny cream buttons … wait, I had buttons on my boots too. And the scent of lily of the valley was in the cabin.' Emma's green eyes grew wide now. 'That woman was in my parents' cabin,' she said indignantly as Simon chuckled. 'I keep remembering more bits,' she went on. 'I'm so glad you are here, you make it all sound so acceptable. I'm not frightened by what I remember from the session any more.'

'Good, but your reference to "acceptable" is far off the mark. What we are discussing and doing here is still viewed as unconventional by many.'

'Yes I know. Would be perfect ammunition for Joshua.'

Simon noted Emma's sparkling eyes. 'Then I suggest you don't tell him.'

'Enough,' cried Emma, laughing and clapping her hands. 'I'm exhausted and I'm sure you must be. Let's change the subject.'

Just then they heard Amelia call out.

'Do you want to come with me?' Emma asked Simon, who followed her dutifully up the stairs.

Amelia was sitting quietly on her quilt, surrounded by her favourite toys and with Buddy tucked up right beside her. Thomas had obviously hidden under the bed earlier and Emma could see the white tip of his ginger tail swinging under the coverlet.

'Hello, my little girl. Did you think Mummy had forgotten you?'

'No, Charlie and I have been reading.'

Simon sat down beside Amelia. 'Can I sit here?'

Amelia nodded, making room for him.

'What have you been reading?' he asked.

Amelia showed him a beautiful children's book of weather scenes. It was open on the storm page and the illustration depicted a crashing sea lit up with thunder and lightning. 'Charlie says the moon drives the sea,' said Amelia, looking up at Simon with a perplexed expression. 'Are those the sea's wheels?' she asked, pointing to the turbulent, froth-covered waves.

'They do look a bit like wheels, don't they,' replied Simon. 'I wouldn't want to travel far on those though, would you? Looks a bit too dangerous and wet for me.'

Amelia smiled, turning the page to a scene of sunshine over a field of barley.

'That's more my style; perfect weather for a picnic,' said Simon.

'I like picnics,' said Amelia, closing the book and clambering out of bed. 'Can we have one in the garden?'

Emma's eyes met Simon's. 'Do you have time?' she asked.

Simon nodded with a grin. 'I think that's a perfect idea.'

'I'll go do the sandwiches while you, Amelia, can take Simon outside.'

Amelia duly took Simon's hand in hers and walked him towards the stairs. 'Come on,' she said. 'We need to find a good spot.'

Soon after, having eaten a quick 'picnic' with Emma and Amelia, Simon excused himself. As he left the cottage he took Emma's hand gently in his own. 'All that has happened to you can be explained. I need you to stop worrying and to relax. Your daughter is safe. No one can take Amelia away from you without your consent. She is not at risk; she is a delightful, intelligent, well-adjusted three-year-old.'

'Who talks to imaginary friends.'

'That's normal for some children.'

'And me?'

'I believe you to be a level-headed and responsible woman, and there is nothing I have seen or that we have discussed today that makes me think otherwise.'

Emma looked at Simon and found her eyes filling with tears at his kindness.

'You might find yourself remembering more about your regression. Don't worry, it's very common; write it all down, and any emotions felt too,' he added.

'Do you think I'll remember any details from my nightmares?' she asked.

'I don't know, Emma. It depends on what the nightmares are about and if your unconscious feels you can cope with all that's been hidden. The unconscious is a powerful tool and it will protect us if necessary. Don't force anything; it will come in its own time.'

'Could I potentially experience another trigger? I'm frightened of collapsing again or blacking out.'

'If something does make you panic, just tell yourself you're experiencing a trigger response or a flashback. Remind yourself that the emotions or feelings are memories of the past – an event you've experienced and survived. Another useful exercise is to ground yourself.'

'How do you do that?'

'Feel the ground below your feet, touch something around you, have a drink of water, try stamping your feet on the floor and breathe deeply. If this doesn't calm you down and you still feel panic, call me.'

Emma smiled.

'Relax. You have nothing to worry about. I'm on the end of the phone … and I'd like to see you again.'

Chapter 12

The sun was beating through the open window as Amelia burst into Emma's room with Thomas in tow.

'Breakfast, Mummy! We're hungry.'

Emma opened her eyes and leaned over to look at her alarm clock. Nine o'clock, no nightmares and she hadn't taken any sleeping tablets. Falling back onto the pillows, she allowed Amelia and Thomas to climb all over her. She felt happier and more relaxed than she had for a long while. Sleep – what a wonderful medicine, she thought to herself. That and the fact she had met Simon Leighton.

Kissing both her daughter and the cat, Emma bounced out of bed. She grabbed her dressing gown, tucked Amelia onto her hip and scurried down the stairs with Thomas following behind them.

Having wandered from the kitchen, Amelia sat proudly on the toilet in the downstairs cloakroom, her pink frog pyjamas wrapped around her ankles. When her mother called her for breakfast, Amelia leaped off, kicking her pyjama bottoms to one side and ran out into the garden, a tumbling Thomas in pursuit.

The garden smelled of cut grass and summer. Emma stood surveying her home and the surrounding fields as a bare-bottomed vision ran past her, giggling with delight. Could there be a more perfect day, thought Emma, re-entering the kitchen and picking up her mobile. There was a missed call from Joshua. She erased the message. 'Nothing is going to spoil my day,' she said aloud. Then her phone rudely rang and, with a groan, she checked the number. It was Gabby.

'Well? How did you get on?' she asked breathlessly. 'What did he tell you? I'd like to try regression. I'm sure I must have been a queen – possibly Cleopatra. Do you think he'd do me?'

'Not if he has any sense!' Emma replied, laughing. 'Thought you said it was all too weird for you.'

'A girl can change her mind, can't she?' Gabby whined. 'Tell me, what was he like? Didn't rate the last one you described.'

Emma smiled as she thought of Simon Leighton in her kitchen helping her make tea. 'He was very pleasant. And he wants to see me again.'

'Professionally or unprofessionally?'

'Gabby! He is a perfect gentleman and "professionally" doesn't come into it. He is a friend. And no, before you ask, he didn't hypnotise me.'

'So he is hoping for "unprofessionally" then,' Gabby said, giggling down the phone. 'What are you doing for lunch? Can I treat you and Amelia?'

'Why don't you come over here? It's a lovely day; we can have a barbecue in the garden. I've got some steaks and sausages. I fancy celebrating.'

'What are we celebrating?' asked Gabby.

'I think we may have found an explanation for my strange behaviour. I'll fill you in later.'

'I take it you discussed the Charlotte thing again?'

'Yes, and it's not a "thing", Gabby.'

'It's all a "thing" unless it can be explained. What about Charlie and the picture ... thing?'

Emma had mentioned Joshua's reaction to Amelia asking him about the portrait of Maxwell Barrett. It had all sounded innocent enough until she admitted that Amelia would never have seen the picture, yet she had been able to describe Max and point out the wall where the painting had hung, claiming that Charlie had told her about it. Gabby had been disturbed, referring to the incident as one of those Charlie 'things'.

'Ah … the picture "thing". Haven't got to the bottom of that one yet. He doesn't appear to think either of us is nuts though.'

'Ooh, lots to catch up on. Sounds exciting. You'll have to fill me in on everything. See you around twelve. Kiss to Amelia.'

Emma hung up the phone and cleared away the breakfast things before moving back out into the garden. Standing there in her dressing gown with her long hair tumbling over her shoulders, she absorbed the fresh summer air again. The grass in the shade was still damp from the morning dew and there was a faint essence of crushed roses on the breeze. How she loved this cottage.

Back inside, she called out to Amelia for her bath and deliberately left all the post on the mat untouched. 'Today is my day; nothing is going to spoil it,' she announced again, this time to the overgrown potted anthurium that was threatening to take over the hallway.

As she laid the table for lunch outside, Emma saw a white van drive up the track and park outside the gate. A figure hidden by a bouquet of flowers grappled with the latch.

'Here, I'll help you,' she said, opening the gate.

'Are you Ms Emma Hart?'

'I am.'

'Then I think these must be for you,' the deliveryman said, thrusting the enormous bouquet into her arms.

'How lovely, thank you.' Balancing the flowers, she pulled out the small white envelope hidden in the top of the display. 'To a lovely and wonderful woman,' it read.

'Ooh, what have you been up to?' Gabby asked as she burst through the gate just behind the deliveryman. 'Are they from him?'

'Don't know. There's no name.'

'What's the message?' Gabby asked, taking the small white card from Emma.

'To a lovely and wonderful woman,' she read out loud. 'Well we can safely rule out Joshua. This one sounds keen. Any guesses?'

'No, just hoping,' replied Emma, and she carried her flowers into the kitchen to arrange them. The smell was intoxicating and she felt her spirits lift even higher than they had been earlier. When her mobile rang with an unknown number, she was still laughing with Gabby.

'Someone sounds happy,' a voice said.

Emma's stomach jolted. 'Simon,' she answered. 'Yes, I'm very happy.'

'Oh. Why's that?'

'Well, it's a beautiful day, the sun is shining and someone has sent me a gorgeous arrangement of flowers.'

'Did that someone give their name?' he asked.

'No,' she replied, grinning at Gabby and Amelia who were hovering near by.

'Then he must think you're a "lovely and wonderful woman",' said Simon.

'It *was* you! Oh, thank you, Simon. They are so beautiful.'

'I meant what I wrote, Emma.'

Emma moved away from Gabby and Amelia, catching a glimpse of her bright eyes and flushed cheeks in the hall mirror as she passed.

'Can I see you again?' Simon asked. 'I could make the

excuse that I want to help you further, but the truth is, I want to see you.'

With a fluttering stomach and a wide smile she replied: 'I'd love that.'

When Emma rejoined them, Gabby noticed how relaxed her friend appeared. It had been a long time since she had seen her so at ease. Whatever had happened the previous day was obviously just what she needed.

'So was Simon the mysterious admirer – and when are you meeting him again?' Gabby asked.

'Tomorrow night,' replied Emma, her face lighting up as she did so.

'And I suppose you want me to babysit?' Gabby asked, tongue in cheek, looking sheepishly in her friend's direction.

'Oh please, Gabs – if you could.'

'Anything to keep that look on your face.'

Simon arrived at the cottage promptly at eight the following evening. Amelia was in bed so Gabby was free to judge. As he walked through the door, she noted the expression on his face as he saw Emma. This one will do, she thought, ushering them out for the night. Looks like the 'Joshua spell' may finally be broken.

Simon had made a booking at a local bistro close to his home and practice, and Emma noticed the familiar manner in which the maître d' greeted him. She followed him, walking elegantly towards the dining table, then sat herself down, tucking her legs under the white tablecloth. Simon positioned himself in the seat opposite her and ordered drinks for them both. Emma felt relaxed, enjoying the easy connection as they watched one another over the intimate, lighted candle.

Emma was wearing a fitted blue and green silk dress that clung to her breasts and skimmed her stomach and slim hips, fanning out at her knees. A pair of high, strappy shoes displayed her pretty toes, and her shapely legs were bare and tanned from the summer sun. Dangling from her ears and dropping to her jawline hung a pair of emerald earrings. As she moved her head, the reflections from the candlelight bounced off the green stones, competing with the colour of her eyes. She had clipped back her normally tumbling hair into a loose chignon that highlighted her cheekbones and neckline, and when she turned to acknowledge a waiter, Simon saw her face in profile and held his breath. *What timeless beauty,* he thought, imagining her as an elderly woman, the dark, wavy hair turned snow white and her glowing skin etched with fine lines. *She will always be beautiful to me*, he thought, as he sat transfixed.

'You look stunning tonight, Emma.'

'Thank you,' Emma replied, her face blushing prettily.

As if on cue, the waiter arrived and the moment was lost.

'Do you eat here often?' Emma whispered over the top of her menu, increasingly aware of the familiarity between Simon and the restaurant owner and staff.

'Yes, I do. It's become a favourite haunt of mine over the years. When I'm in the country I tend to come here a little too often, I'm afraid. They understand my need for good, clean cooking, fresh fish and crisp vegetables or salads. I always intend to eat sensibly at home, but I sometimes get caught up with something and lose track of time and the fact that I need to buy food. They have even been known to open the kitchen here just for me, and they always give me this table as it is away from the main hub. I think they're surprised to see me with someone quite so glamorous. It's usually just me and some notes for company, or a crusty old colleague professor.'

Cheeks flushed with contentment, Emma sat and looked at Simon, a twist of a smile playing on her mouth. This was perfect – too perfect. She was almost frightened to blink in case she altered the moment.

'To a brighter tomorrow,' Simon said, lifting his glass in Emma's direction.

'To now,' she replied, touching his glass with her own.

From that evening on, Simon became a permanent fixture in the lives of both Emma and Amelia. Even Gabby, protective to the last, knew Simon was the answer. Amelia adored his attention and gentle manner; he called her 'enchanting' and 'princess' and played patiently with her for hours. And for Thomas, Simon provided the perfect lap, large enough to curl up in and a safe refuge from the constant prodding fingers of Amelia. He would purr in contentment, trembling with happiness at Simon's patient stroking. And Emma would watch the three of them sitting together on the settee – Simon, her daughter and the cat, all so vital to her own happiness – knowing that at last she had found the love she needed.

Chapter 13

Late one Sunday afternoon, Gabby, Simon and Emma were enjoying the last of the day's heat in the garden when Joshua arrived to drop Amelia back home. Walking around to the back of the cottage, he found Emma and Simon sitting close together on one of the sun loungers.

'Who's that with Mummy?' he asked Amelia.

'That's Simon. I told you about him,' she answered, calling out as she ran towards the couple.

Hugging her daughter with both arms, Emma laughed. 'You're back! I missed you.'

Amelia unwrapped herself from her mother's embrace and bounced in front of Simon expectantly.

'Don't I get a kiss?' he asked.

Amelia beamed as she kissed him gently on the cheek.

Emma laughed again; she found she did that a lot these days. Then, looking up, she saw Joshua watching them. 'Thanks for bringing her home,' she said. 'Oh, I don't think you've been introduced. This is Dr Simon Leighton, a friend of mine. Simon, this is Joshua, Amelia's father.'

Leaping up from the sun lounger, Simon greeted Joshua with a warm smile and a firm handshake.

'Pleased to meet you,' Joshua said, registering the doctor title, his eyes flickering from Emma's face to Simon's.

As Joshua left, Emma watched him drive away down the track with detached emotions. Gone were the tense and muddled knots she once felt in his presence. Standing quietly she sensed that the old ties that had once held Joshua and herself together were finally disconnecting. *'Understand the weakness of man and the power of forgiveness – forgiveness brings understanding. Love is the answer.'* With the memory of Charlotte's haunting words once again playing in her head, Emma was beginning to see Joshua in a different light. 'We can both love her,' she thought, walking back towards the laughter, making a mental note to talk to him without the lawyers.

That evening after supper Gabby left and Simon stayed. They waited until Amelia was safely tucked up in bed and then adjourned to Emma's bedroom. Simon held her face in his hands and looked at her with such tenderness that she felt the final emotional barrier tumbling down around her. She tried hard not to cry, but as Simon whispered endearments and stroked her hair away from her face, she felt the tears falling. Experiencing stirrings she'd thought long lost, she found her body trembling with anticipation. The kiss had been exploratory, his mouth gently nibbling, but as she tasted his lips and felt his firm body on top of hers, something within her began to answer. Lifting her hips she pushed her body up to meet his. There was an accidental clash of teeth as the nibble became a bite. The heady mix of his male scent and the taste of salt and wine on his tongue crashed any remaining barrier, allowing the torrent of sheer need to burst through. As she shuddered, his mouth silenced her cries of ecstasy, his body trembling with the intensity of their passion.

When Amelia burst into her mother's room the next morning there was barely a trace of Simon, the only suggestion that he had been there being the dent in his pillow and the ripple of a smile on Emma's lips as she slept.

Three days later, despite Emma's attempt to contact Joshua directly, a letter arrived from James, Proctor and Proctor. She took it out into the sunshine, hoping that the bright light might evaporate some of the darkness that seemed to envelop it. Remembering Simon's advice, she started the 'grounding' exercises, breathing deeply and stamping her feet.

'Well, Joshua has really surpassed himself,' Emma told her father as she reported the contents of the letter over the phone. 'His lawyers have requested medical reports verifying my state of mind. He's asking for custody of Amelia on the grounds of diminished responsibility. He's citing concerns for Amelia's physical and mental welfare and wait for it … there's even a suggestion of unprofessional conduct with Amelia's child psychologist, a Dr Simon Leighton.'

Stephen Stockwell listened to his daughter carefully as she told him of the innocent meeting with Simon in the garden and the comments regarding Amelia's invisible friend Charlie. He thought the whole situation was becoming ridiculous.

'Joshua's rattled, Emma. He probably realises he's made some big mistakes and unfortunately it's you that's bearing the brunt of his frustration and anger.'

'But for God's sake, why?' Emma asked. 'He's moved on and married Annette. I'm letting him build a relationship with his daughter. What's his problem?'

'Maybe there are other issues behind the scenes we're not aware of.'

'But to suggest I'm psychologically unbalanced, or that Amelia is under threat from me … and why the attack on Simon?'

Stephen Stockwell could hear the strain in his daughter's voice and felt sad. She had been so happy of late. 'I hear you, Emma. I've no explanations for Joshua's behaviour. Maybe it's time you and your lawyers ramped up your fight, showed your teeth. Obviously his claims are ridiculous and wouldn't stand up in a court of law, but do you want it to go that far? I think it's all got to stop. What does Simon say?'

'I daren't tell him,' she answered. 'I'm too embarrassed.'

'Talk to him. If anyone can understand, he will.'

Emma put the phone down to her father feeling a great deal stronger. *How did this all become so destructive,* she thought, *and how strange that love can produce so many faces?* Grabbing her mobile, she called Simon and told him the latest.

'Don't worry, Emma. It's normal dirty tactics – laughable really. Your father's right. Speak to your lawyers and, if necessary, we'll answer Joshua's claims together. Don't worry. No one's taking Amelia away from you. Not on my watch.'

Simon arrived back later than Emma expected that evening, so he missed saying goodnight to Amelia. Creeping up the stairs to check on her, he looked in through the open door. She lay on her side, Buddy clasped in her left hand, the fingers of her right hand pulling at his ribbon. He watched her tiny rosebud mouth twitch as she breathed in the scented night air blowing in from the surrounding fields. So innocent and trusting, thought Simon, as he quietly backed away so as not to wake her.

'You have a beautiful daughter,' he told Emma in the kitchen as he folded her into his arms and smelled her hair.

'I know,' she replied smugly. 'Takes after me!' Detaching herself, she bent down to open the oven door.

'Hmm, that looks good.'

Emma turned her face to look up at him, pulling an

120

unimpressed look. Playfully, Simon tossed the oven cloth in her direction, hitting her on the bottom.

'Smells good, I meant to say.'

After dinner, with the television quietly on in the background, Simon looked down at Emma as she sat curled beside him on the settee. 'Are you still worried about Joshua's threats?'

She nodded.

'It'll be fine. We'll work this one out together,' he reassured her, holding her to him and brushing the dark waves of hair off her face. 'As your lawyers told you, Joshua will never be able to take Amelia, so you have no fears on that count. Trust me, time will resolve this. Now let's forget this for tonight, I have something here that I think you may find interesting.'

Standing, Simon collected a large book and brought it back over to the settee.

'I found it tucked away in an old bookshop I rummage in. It's not a good copy – it's mould-mottled in parts, but the prints aren't too badly affected. I remember you said you were interested in designing swimwear as your next venture. Well, this was published in New York and appears to be a swimsuit gospel for the nineteenth and twentieth centuries.'

'Oh, thank you, Simon,' Emma said, opening the book carefully. A faint musty smell filled her nostrils. 'It's wonderful … look here, that's the American illustrator Charles Dana Gibson and here are his famous illustrations of the Gibson Girl.'

Simon looked at the pen-and-ink representation of the beautiful and independent American woman at the turn of the twentieth century – tall and slender, with ample bosoms and curvaceous hips and buttocks.

'Just look at the exaggerated S-curve torsos. Back then in the 1890s they wore the swan-bill corset to get that effect.'

'Think of all the damage those corsets must have done to them,' commented Simon, enthralled by the drawings. 'Were they real women?' he asked.

'No, idealised figures, but based on real women. Look how he draws their necks, elegantly long and thin, with all their hair pinned up on their heads.' Emma loved the inspired hourglass figures of the period and hungrily devoured the images.

'Thought you'd enjoy it,' Simon said, happy to see a smile back on her face.

'Look, that's the classic maillot – short sleeves. See how they abandoned the bloomers and hose,' she excitedly pointed out.

'What's a maillot?'

Emma looked up from the book. 'It's an early one-piece bathing costume,' she explained.

'Oh, silly me, I should have remembered. What were the early bikinis called?'

Ignoring Simon, Emma continued to turn the pages. 'Look at these …'

Simon peered over at the drawings.

'These postcards are quite risqué for the period. Notice the décolletage, the bare legs and the string straps on this one.'

Simon laughed. 'Sort of early "page-three" modelling.'

'Most of the models were unnamed actresses. They're quite beautiful, aren't they, even by today's standards?'

'Too meaty for me. And the swimsuits have too much material for my taste.'

Emma laughed and continued to scan the pages, sharing her knowledge of the period and fashion with Simon until one particular sepia image caught her eye. It depicted an unusually handsome and statuesque woman with thick, dark, wavy hair piled high on her head. She posed with her face turned slightly

122

to the camera. Emma caught her breath and leaned in closer.

'What is it?' a bemused Simon asked as Emma studied the grainy photograph.

Passing the open book carefully to Simon, she walked over to her bureau.

Simon looked at the postcard print. The caption read, 'Unknown actress'. Rummaging through her desk, Emma looked for the notes on her regression that Simon had encouraged her to keep and to which she had added memory recalls. Among them was a sketch of a woman. Emma's skills as an artist were good, even in ballpoint pen. She carried the drawing over to Simon and they compared it to the photograph in the book. The angle of the camera had captured the woman's bone structure and, despite the quality of the print, her lovely features were distinguishable. The likeness to Emma's sketch was remarkable.

'The lady with the hat?' he asked.

'The lady with the hat,' she replied.

Chapter 14

Annette pulled into the driveway, parking her convertible next to Joshua's Mercedes. Her shopping and lunch trip had turned into drinks and dinner. As she opened the front door, designer shopping bags dripping from her hands, she called out to Joshua. There was no reply. Carrying her numerous purchases, she trod the length of the hallway, strode up the magnificent central staircase and entered the master bedroom. Dumping the bags on the bed and kicking off her Jimmy Choos, she noticed the open French windows. Her heart missed a beat as one of the doors banged shut in the night breeze.

'Joshua,' she called. There was no answer.

Hand on heart, she pushed open the glass door and turned on the outside light. Since Max's accident, she had altered the lighting system for the patio and the staircase leading to the garden. The soft, angled lights now complemented the old stonework, highlighting the darker recesses and the opening to the sweeping steps. She looked down to the garden below. An orange glow from the light in Joshua's study fell on a small patch of the surrounding grass and flower beds. As she peered down, she involuntarily shuddered and a piercing pain shot through her head, leaving her right temple throbbing. Reaching out with her right hand, she steadied herself against the stone balustrade as ghostly fingers dug deep and painfully into her buried memories. For a moment she felt a sense of fear and panic and called out Joshua's name again. The night owl hooting in a tree startled her. Turning back into the bedroom, she switched on every light as if the brightness would dispel her unease.

Annette found her husband downstairs in his den. Joshua sat stiffly behind his dark mahogany desk, a pile of discarded papers scattered across the polished wood. As Annette entered, Joshua clenched his jaw and looked at her long and hard through narrowed eyes.

'Oh, there you are. Didn't you hear me call?' she asked.

'Have you any idea what you've done?' The venom in his voice was chilling. Annette stood silently, watching the expression on his face as with one angry swipe of his arm he pushed the papers across the desk towards her. She watched as they slid onto the carpet below. 'How long have you and John Buckley been involved in this?'

John Buckley was the Chief Executive Officer for a number of large financial institutions and had been both a business associate and close friend of Max Barrett. When Joshua joined the Barrett Empire, John Buckley had been one of the first to congratulate him. He'd persuaded Joshua to join a circle of useful and powerful contacts, all of who had proved to be invaluable business and investment sources. After Max's death, it was John Buckley who had rallied around, helping with the lawyers, funeral arrangements and Max's personal matters, his affection towards Annette being obvious then. And it was John who had diplomatically rebuffed rumours regarding Joshua's relationship with Annette before and after Max's death. Grateful for his help, Joshua had forged a close bond with Buckley over the following eighteen months, trusting his advice and his friendship – a bond that was now Joshua's undoing, it seemed. 'Do you realise the consequences of this?'

Annette said nothing, experiencing a sense of déjà vu.

'If this becomes public knowledge, there will be a legal

investigation. We will not survive that, Annette, personally or professionally.'

Annette watched as Joshua, normally so controlled and restrained, appeared to collapse in front of her eyes. Like a puppet with the strings cut, he hunched his shoulders and dropped his head down towards his chest, raking his fingers through his uncharacteristically dishevelled hair. As he raised his head, she saw a look of fear in his dark eyes. 'I've put a call in to someone I know for advice, off the record, and I bloody well hope he can tell me how to cover the tracks, distance ourselves or dig ourselves out. We potentially have a case of information theft, insider dealing and arbitrage. How the hell did you two manage to carry this off? There must have been a whole raft of others involved.'

Annette had been playing the insider trading game for many years. It was, to her, an exciting and lucrative game with fringe benefits, John Buckley being one.

Damn him, she thought now, realising that it was her physical need to control him that had probably been their downfall. Sex and power were a heady mix but never made sensible bedfellows. John needed her too much. He had obviously become careless, greedy or both with their portfolio.

'I suppose you've been screwing him too?' Joshua threw the question at her, holding up his hand and adding quickly, 'No, don't answer that. I'll pack a few of my things and move into the London flat.' Lifting his head he regained some of his composure. 'We'll be in touch, I can assure you. This mess has to be cleared up fast before it unravels. You have done some despicable things in your life, Annette, but this? The risks to us, to the company – I don't understand … why? Surely it can't be for money? You want for nothing.'

Joshua stood, moving away from his desk towards the hallway. He knew that he would be investigated and implicated. It had been his responsibility to generate the lists of acquisition targets. Many times he had used John Buckley as a sounding board regarding rumours within the City. His detailed profiles and investment valuations on a number of priority targets, together with his plans for approaching those chosen, would have been accessible on his personal computer at home; Annette knew the passwords. He remembered the number of sensitive meetings she had encouraged him to hold privately in their home, after hours, and the papers he would leave on the desk in his study. Joshua now realised his mistakes. Opening the front door, he turned back and shouted to Annette, his voice filled with contained fury, 'What the hell would Max have said about your stupid games?'

Annette listened to the door slam before moving into the dining room where she stood motionless on the green carpet and looked out through the large draped windows. *He didn't like it either,* she thought, remembering the night of Max's death and the argument.

Despite his reputation as a ruthless businessman, Max Barrett was always honourable. And he expected the same of others. Any suggestion that sensitive business information was being shared with a third party would put his reputation and that of his company at risk. That evening, he had been waiting upstairs in his study. A pile of documents lay face up on his desk. He needed to speak to Annette. Pushing the papers aside, he frowned; if he had uncovered the trail, then others could too. He knew these papers implicated his wife.

Damn, Annette had thought as she heard him call out to her. She had been looking forward to a long, scented bath. Her evening with her latest lover had been an adventurous one, and although she enjoyed the rush of the sex, she loathed the smell of stale male afterwards. She fixed her smile in the hall mirror, touched up a smudge to her lipstick and shook her perfectly cut hair into place. The thought that Max might recognise the lingering scent of another man amused her. Entering the study, she gave her husband a winning look. She listened to his angry accusations without any response or reaction. Checking her nail varnish for chips, she avoided his eyes.

Normally a controlled man, Max was finding the desire to wrap his fingers around his wife's throat overpowering. It was her blatant lack of remorse that drove him to fill his glass with straight whisky and down the warm liquid, despite his doctor's warnings. Draining the glass, he moved from behind his desk and threw open the French windows onto the patio. Stepping out, he took a number of deep breaths to calm himself, aware that the beating of his heart had intensified and his chest felt constricted. Recognising the familiar signs of stress, he walked along the stone patio and breathed slowly and deeply. The air smelled sweet, but he found it difficult to swallow, the realisation of what his wife had done playing in his head. He paused at the top of the stone staircase and watched the moths dance around the feature lights. Closing his eyes for a moment, he willed his heart to silence its thunderous beating. The pain came suddenly. Out of habit Max reached for his tablets. Patting his shirt pocket he found nothing. The pills stood beside the whisky decanter in his study, he remembered.

Annette Barrett did not kill her husband – well, not in cold blood; but her lack of action could be described as cold-blooded and it did hasten his untimely demise. As Max struggled with the pain in his chest, his body spun and stumbled. He had drunk two large whiskies, and the combination of alcohol and pain caused him to tilt and stagger to his right, tipping him into the opening of the steps. Had he been at any other point on the patio, the balustrade would have blocked his fall.

One could argue that his fall was again not Annette's fault, but as Max rolled down the steps and called out to her, she heard but chose not to respond. Instead, she waited for the silence then walked out onto the patio and peered down the partially lit staircase to the garden below. Max lay awkwardly at the base of the steps, his twisted body partly in the flower bed and partly on the grass. Removing her shoes, she gingerly descended to the last step and peered closely at her husband. There was a large red gash across his forehead, his eyes were closed and his left arm lay at an unnatural angle. She held her breath as she watched his chest move, then she carefully retraced her steps back up to the patio, through the French doors and into the study.

On the desk lay a number of documents. Recognising the names of the companies and the dates of acquisitions, she scooped them up for disposal later, then calmly closed and locked the patio doors, pulling the heavy drapes shut. In the morning she would claim that she had assumed her husband had already retired for the evening and forgotten to lock up. The fact that they had separate bedrooms and bathrooms made her story all the more plausible.

Running the bath in her beige and gold bathroom later that night, Annette had allowed herself to relax in the scented warm water as all traces of her latest devotee were washed away.

The gardener discovered Max Barrett the following morning. His death was listed as a tragic accident brought on by his heart condition and the fall. Annette milked the sympathy, expressing how generous Max had been to her in life and even in death.

Her husband's passing had secured Annette's future; her position within the company ensured her crimes went undetected. The path had also been cleared for Joshua. All Annette needed to do was reel him in.

Now, as she picked up a glass and a decanter of brandy from the drinks cabinet, she smiled cruelly at the memories. 'You never really left, did you?' she spoke aloud to the house, wandering from the dining room into the hallway. She half expected a reply as she swallowed the burning liquid, refilling her glass immediately.

'What is it you want?' she shouted. 'Surely you're not surprised? You of all people understood me. I didn't mean you to die like that. I just got frightened and your fall provided me with the solution to a problem.' Draining her glass she raised it to the room before refilling again. 'You were too honourable!' she shouted, spinning around as if she heard an answer. 'I wouldn't have settled for a divorce and you knew that.'

The house suddenly felt overwhelmingly large. Despite the bright lights firing in most rooms, Annette felt a darkness and, for the first time, fear. She dialled a well-used number and left a message. 'Joshua's left me,' she said. 'He knows enough and I'm not taking responsibility alone. We need to talk.'

Then, pouring herself yet another large brandy, Annette raised her glass and acknowledged her ghosts.

Chapter 15

Joshua drove around for hours into the night. He'd needed to clear his head and think. Fully aware of his own vulnerability, he also felt a sense of responsibility towards the Barrett Company and Max. He needed answers.

'Annette!' he shouted, opening the front door. 'I don't care what the time is, we need to talk.' There was no response. Joshua stood for a moment, his tense body turned towards the main stairs. 'Now!' he continued. 'Where are you?'

There was a muffled noise from above. Joshua's long legs took the stairs two at a time.

Annette stood in her dressing gown. Devoid of make-up, her face looked pale and blotchy. She was unsteady on her feet and used the doorframe as a crutch, leaning into the cream paintwork to support herself, the top of her dark hair static from the contact.

Joshua had never seen her in such a state. 'Have you been drinking?'

'Yes,' she answered, her eyes focusing in his direction. 'Anyway, what's it to you?' Her voice sounded slurred. 'Such a pity you've found me out …' She looked to Joshua for a reaction. 'Max found me out too, you know, only he fell and died before he could do anything. My poor Max. I covered my tracks back then; must have made a mistake this time.'

Joshua stood quietly, her words pouring over him like ice water.

Annette laughed at his obvious shock and discomfort.

'Don't look at me like that. You're just as guilty. You justified our relationship while he was alive. His death was advantageous to the both of us.' Annette waved her empty glass at Joshua as she crossed the room. 'Admit it. You never *really* questioned me regarding his death, even though you must have had some suspicions.'

'What are you saying?' Joshua whispered, a feeling of dread adding to his state of despair.

'Your little wife Emma – she wasn't going to give you all that I could. You knew that. Max knew how ruthless you were too. We're as bad as one another Joshua; we both want things. Max understood.'

'What suspicions?' he asked, feeling sick to his stomach as he realised he was about to hear another truth he didn't want to know about. 'What suspicions?' he asked again, his voice rising.

'Max knew about our affair. He wanted you to work for him; he encouraged it, although I didn't need much encouraging. He was lame in the bedroom stakes; I needed more and you gave it to me. Max understood.' Annette watched Joshua for a reaction before continuing. 'Remember how I told you on the night Max died that I found correspondence on his desk from a private investigator about our affair? Well I lied. It wasn't a report about us; it was an exposé on my dealings. We rowed that night over insider dealing. He didn't care a toss about our affair.'

'So he knew what you and John Buckley were doing?'

'He uncovered some of it, yes, but not all. But then he died. Poor Max. He was always so generous to me.'

'You bitch! So all those years when you made me feel guilty about Max's heart attack, you were lying.'

'Yes,' she answered, moving back towards the door. Joshua grabbed her and spun her around to face him.

'You always claimed that you went to bed and then went in later to close the patio door and curtains. Please tell me you weren't with him when he died. Please tell me that you couldn't have saved him?'

'Why the guilt now, Joshua? It suited you back then to have me – and everything that went with me. You didn't have to make too many sacrifices.' Annette went limp in Joshua's arms. He sat her in a chair and moved away, waiting for her to continue.

'I need another drink,' she said waving her glass in his direction again.

'No. You've had enough.'

Annette hurled the empty glass across the room and fixed her eyes on Joshua before describing every detail of that night. The pitiless manner in which she relayed the truth about Max's death sickened Joshua. He shuddered at the image of her deliberately walking away from his broken body and calmly locking the patio doors. What sort of woman had the ability to do something so terrible? But the knowledge that he may also have been culpable in some way only sickened him all the more. The position he now found himself in and the potential legal investigation could be described by some as divine retribution. *Perhaps Max is having the last laugh,* he thought.

Exhaling slowly through his nose, Joshua reflected on all the damage he and Annette had caused to Max and Emma. An image of Amelia formed in his mind's eye and he blinked to lose it. The realisation of what he'd attempted to do tasted unpleasant; he was no better than Annette. He too was capable of being cold-blooded, especially in his determination to take his daughter away from her mother. Now, looking down at his spent wife with a sense of disgust, he asked the question he already knew the answer to. 'Did you ever really want Amelia?'

'No, she was a way to hurt Emma.'

'Why?'

'I knew how much you loved her. Oh, you loved the life we shared in London – all that excitement, the sex, the money and the adrenalin rush from the intoxicating power. But I knew how dangerous Emma was. My world made you hungry for more, but Emma's gave you unconditional love. When Amelia was born I thought you might weaken. I hated Emma all the more. I wanted a child, your child, but I couldn't have one. So I waited, ensuring you left Emma before the baby was born and filling your head with the dark and heavy weights of parenthood. Once Amelia was old enough, I encouraged you to take her away from Emma. Why else do you think I married you? We offered a stable environment for a child. Amelia was going to be my way of holding you forever and destroying Emma. You were so easy to play, Joshua. Through your own inadequacies, you destroyed your marriage.'

Joshua knew Annette was right. As he drove away in the early hours of the morning, her words playing around in his head, he understood that he'd failed both Emma and himself. He knew now that he had to find a way to undo, or at least lessen, the damage he'd done – for everyone's sake.

Chapter 16

Emma reluctantly listened to the voicemail message left by Joshua. Noting the strained tone in his voice, she chose to ignore it. The last thing she needed was a conversation with him and a day ruined. But later that evening, snuggled up on the settee against Simon's warm body, she remembered Joshua's request for her to call him urgently. Looking at her watch she realised it was now too late to call, but resolved to speak to him the next day. Then, closing her eyes, she settled back against Simon.

That night Emma had a vivid and terrifying dream in which she was struggling against the forces of a violent storm. In her arms she held a small baby tightly to her chest, a torrent of ice-cold water threatening to drag the baby from her grasp. Fighting against this wall of water, she watched in horror as the riverbanks on either side of her appeared to collapse, trapping her among the floating debris. As the water rose higher and threatened to engulf her and the baby, she screamed and woke herself up. The last disturbing vision, caught in her mind like a frozen movie frame, was that of a pair of terrified eyes and a mouth, open and screaming to the wind.

Her nightmare had woken Simon, who held her tightly in his arms, stroking her head as she tried desperately to control her shaking. 'Well that must have been some dream,' he said. 'I thought you were going to hit me when I tried to calm you down. Look at the state of the bedcovers.'

Emma surveyed the mess she had created, then realised

that for the first time she could remember all the details of her nightmare. 'I remember, Simon! I remember what it was that frightened me.'

'Tell me?' he gently coaxed.

'It's not completely clear,' she began, waiting for the thumping in her chest to settle and her voice to stop shaking.

'That's normal. Just start with the main points that were the most powerful. The rest will follow.'

'It was raining,' she said. 'I was trapped between two steep walls of earth. I was fighting to stay afloat in fast-running water that swirled around me. There was debris in the water, and as I fought to stay afloat I could feel myself being dragged down. In my arms I was holding a baby and I was terrified that I would let it go. Then I saw a man in the water with me. He put his hands out and I could see his eyes; they looked bloodshot and his mouth opened as he screamed. He was so close to my face,' Emma shuddered. 'I reached out, but all I could feel was slippery, wet earth. Then I was lifted up out of the water.'

'That's quite a nightmare,' said Simon, pushing back the damp hair from her forehead. 'How do you feel now?'

Emma lifted her pale face to look at Simon. 'Drained.'

'Come here, closer.'

They lay wrapped together among the tangled sheets, whispering.

'Do you think this could be the end of my nightmares?' she asked.

'Well you seem to have remembered the details this time and that alone makes them less terrifying.'

Emma nodded. She had remembered this time. The dreams couldn't hurt her any more and the realisation brought tears of relief. 'Simon?' she whispered.

'Mmm,' he replied, turning towards her and laying his arm protectively over her stomach in readiness to go back to sleep.

'Do we experience things in this life that we got wrong in another?' she asked.

There was no answer. Wriggling from under his arm, Emma leaned up on one elbow and, looking down at him, she repeated the question.

Begrudgingly, he opened one eye and grunted.

'And if that is the case ... will I have to live another life with Joshua, in some form or another ... until I, or he, get it right?'

'Slow down, Em. It's still the middle of the night and I haven't got my "past-life therapist" head on.'

Emma looked down at Simon's tousled head against the pillows and smiled.

'Sorry, it's just I can't stop thinking,' she justified, as she stroked his thick hair back from his face. 'I love you,' she crooned.

'I know. And I love you too, but I'd love you a lot more if you'd let me get back to sleep.'

Snuggling back down into the safety of Simon's arms, Emma allowed herself to think of nothing but that moment and drifted off to sleep.

Chapter 17

Emma said very little while she dressed the next morning, her mind preoccupied with countless unanswered questions.

Simon watched her as she dropped her head and towel dried her hair. 'I'm sorry Emma, but I don't have all the answers you want. Yes, I know I've investigated many previous-life claims and I know I've written books on them, but it's always through the eyes of a psychologist. I'm the guy looking for the minutiae of detail that will either verify or destroy their claims.'

Emma looked up into Simon's eyes.

'I'm programmed to look for proof,' he went on. 'I have to prove the facts, not make up answers that could fit. I'm an investigative journalist, Em, not a fiction writer.'

The disappointment on her face was clear.

'My problem is I'm a psychologist first. I've never personally experienced a past life nor felt the intense emotions that can go with it. I'm sorry.'

Emma drew away, turned on her hairdryer and waved it through her damp hair.

Simon waited until the noise had stopped. 'I do know someone who could help answer your questions though.'

'Who's that?' Emma asked.

'My mother.'

'Your mother?' Emma paused, hairbrush in hand, looking into Simon's intense brown eyes and catching the flicker of light that flashed back at her. 'Now why doesn't that surprise me?'

Simon grinned and took the hairbrush away from Emma, watching her look of annoyance as he blocked the mirror and scraped the brush through his own hair. Passing the hairbrush back to her, he flashed another of his infectious smiles. 'Yes, my mother. She's a wonderfully wise woman. She was a paediatrician for many years in her local hospital, and she has views on life and death and the various journeys we each undertake. But not just from a clinical viewpoint. It's as if she's privy to some higher consciousness. You'll love her – and she's dying to meet you and Amelia.' Simon paused and looked at Emma, shrugging his shoulders. 'Even if you don't like her views, I guarantee you'll find her fascinating; she's a great sounding board. Nathan and I have sparred with her many times over the years about the meaning of life and what happens next.'

'Who wins?'

'Debatable. Depends who has the last word.'

'What does she think of your line of work?'

'She finds it "intriguing". She's always been supportive of my studies and research. She taught me that blind faith was as prejudicial as blind denial and that I must always search for the answers to the questions myself. She used to tell me the truth I sought couldn't be taught or read about; it had to be found and felt. I'm still searching, Emma.'

'I think I'd like to meet her,' Emma said, a warm smile back on her lips.

'Good, because I've accepted an invitation to stay for a long weekend with my parents. I so wanted to introduce you and Amelia to them. What do you think? Will you both come away with me tomorrow and spend the weekend with them?'

Emma looked hard at Simon's face as he held her hands in his. His eyes shone with the warmth of encouragement. *No question,* she thought. 'I'd love to.'

'Good. Tomorrow it is, then. We'll leave around eight-thirty so we can be there in time for a late lunch. You'll love the house; it's an old rectory. Mother can help Amelia feed the ducks and Father can bore you with the wonders in his greenhouse.'

Emma watched Simon's face; he was as excited as a child, grabbing her around the waist and kissing her hard on the mouth.

'See you tonight, then, you gorgeous woman. I've got to go and do some work. Justify my publisher's advance!'

Simon rushed out of the cottage, leaving a bemused Emma to organise the weekend trip with Amelia. She watched from the back bedroom as his silver Toyota drove down the track, then she called out to Amelia, 'Come on, we have to speak to Auntie Hetty about feeding Thomas and sort out our things for the weekend.'

'Why?'

'We're off on a little holiday tomorrow.'

'Is Simon coming?'

Emma smiled at her daughter, nodding her head. 'We're going to meet his mummy and daddy.'

'Ooh, will we like them?'

Emma looked at Amelia. 'Do you like Simon?' she asked.

'Oh yes.'

'Then we'll like them too,' Emma assured her daughter. *But let's hope they like us,* she thought to herself.

'Will Charlie like them?' Amelia asked then, before pushing something into Emma's hands and adding, 'Buddy has to come too!'

'Of course he does. But it's a bit early to pack him – you'll need him tonight.'

Amelia stood quietly, a questioning frown forming between

her eyebrows as she examined a small yellow plastic duck in one hand. 'Will I need my duck?' she asked.

'I think they have ducks down there, but we'll pack it just in case.'

Amelia's face lit up as she clapped her hands and ran into her bedroom for more goodies.

That afternoon there was a text message from Joshua on Emma's mobile asking her to call. She stared at it feeling that familiar knot in her stomach before the tension transferred to her neck and shoulders. Aware that she couldn't avoid this call any longer, she rang his number. His phone went immediately to voicemail. Emma didn't leave a message. Dropping the phone on the bed she carried on with her packing.

Joshua called her back that evening. His voice sounded strained on the other end of the line. Apologising for the lateness of the call he explained he was going away for a couple of weeks and wouldn't be able to see Amelia as arranged, adding that he'd like to meet up and talk to Emma on his return.

'Will I need to bring a lawyer with me?' Emma asked, her tone flat and weary from the effort of controlled politeness.

'I've dismissed those lawyers,' was the simple reply.

Chapter 18

Joshua lay still, his bruised body lightly covered by the thin hospital blanket. 'Thank you,' he said, passing his phone back to the attentive blonde nurse. They'd found it still switched on and undamaged in his shirt pocket. The last call he had made before the accident had been to John Buckley's voice-mail on which, his anger and frustration boiling over, he had left a damning message about final reckonings.

Both his hands and his face bore superficial cuts, and the livid mark across his chest from the safety belt had already turned dark mauve in colour.

'You're a bit of a miracle,' the nurse told him as she administered his painkillers. 'The paramedics are still talking about you in the canteen. They say you must have made a pact with God or the Devil as, by rights, you shouldn't be here.'

Joshua tried a faint smile in response.

'Now, do you want to sit up or lie flat?' she asked as she plumped up the pillows.

'Up, please.' Joshua's voice sounded weak and reedy to his ears, but with the pills beginning to take effect and the gnawing pain in his head and body subsiding, he allowed his mind to drift back. *Something was definitely out there that night*, he agreed.

He had been driving recklessly, desperate to get away from Annette and her sick revelations. Images of a broken Max crying out for help, and Annette, drunk and dishevelled shouting her spiteful admissions, played relentlessly in his head. Fuelled by adrenalin, rage and self-loathing, he'd pressed his foot down hard on the accelerator in a bid to outrun his demons. With both hands firmly grasping the steering wheel, Joshua had pitted the car against the undulating countryside and the wet, winding roads. Throwing it into a blind bend, he felt the back wheels catch and lock as the road in front of him dropped away into a steep descent.

'Oh no! Please – no!' he'd cried at the unresponsive steering wheel. He stamped on the footbrake and engaged the handbrake as the car spun spectacularly out of control, rebounding off the verge before falling down the embankment. 'Shit!' he'd screamed when the car flipped over in mid-air, then crashed sideways through the sparse shrubbery and finally righted itself as it came to rest on a deserted golf course.

Joshua had stood outside the car surveying the damage; there was no pain, no shock and no fear – just a sense of weightlessness. He could see his own body still harnessed in his seat, limbs flopping like a spent puppet, face pushed to one side by the airbag. Both eyes were closed and there was a dramatic flesh tear to one cheek where a shrub had taken a swipe at him through the open window. Joshua looked at his lifeless body without compassion; if this was his death, then it was better than he deserved. He watched as a small drop of blood dripped from one nostril and joined the red pool already collected between the airbag and his upper lip.

'Joshua.' He heard a voice call out, but when he looked around, he saw just the darkness and the wreckage of the car. His limbs felt unnaturally light as he bent towards his trapped body. A large chunk of the surrounding hedgerow had forced itself through the smashed windscreen into the passenger seat, its thorns gouging the blue leather upholstery. One of the wing mirrors, amputated during the accident, lay on the ground beside the car, its glass scattered in the long, wet grass, the sharp shiny shards reflecting the moonlight. Looking down, Joshua could see his own shattered reflection in the gleaming debris and that of a shadowy figure standing behind him.

Joshua had felt no fear, just an overpowering sense of confusion. And it was then that he saw him: a young man – tall, lean and dressed in blue and yellow cycling shorts and a matching top. In his gloved hand he clasped the strap of his cycle helmet. Turning silently, he walked slowly away from Joshua, moving up the grass bank towards the road and a soft, glowing light on the horizon.

'Wait!' he shouted at the young man. 'Please, wait. Can you see me?'

The cyclist kept on walking.

'Stop! I'm here! Can you see me? I'm frightened. Please don't leave me now. I want to come with you,' he implored.

The young man turned, looking back at Joshua, his eyes filled with compassion. 'No, Joshua,' he said softly. 'It's not your time. Go back … you still have much to do.' And with that, he turned again and melted away.

Joshua had cried out, desperate to follow the voice into the light as unseen hands gently pushed him back towards the trapped body in the car. He felt a sudden jolt and then a sharp pain in his lungs. He gasped for breath, exhaling and inhaling deeply, then reconnected with his self as tiny, pale pink bubbles formed around his nostrils. Above him, a light grew bigger and brighter and then split into two as a camper wagon's headlights dropped down the hill, panning the golf course and lighting on Joshua's car wreck.

'You have visitors,' the nurse in the pale blue uniform announced with a girlish grin. 'These are the two young men who found you.'

Still dozy and barely awake, Joshua lifted himself back up the pillows. Dazed, he looked up to see two lanky youths moving towards the bed. Both were dressed in the uniform of the travelling student: faded jeans, grubby T-shirts emblazoned with the names of affiliations or bands, neither of which Joshua recognised, and stained trainers.

The taller of the two smiled. 'Hi. It's Joshua, isn't it? Great to see you free of all that metal, mate,' he began in an Australian drawl. 'You're one lucky driver. That car was a mess. I'm Chris, by the way, and that's Jim,' he waved one hand in the direction of his friend.

'Hi,' said Jim, outstretching his hand, his trainers squeaking loudly on the highly polished hospital floor.

Joshua looked into the fresh faces of the two young men and smiled hesitantly, the stitches on his face not allowing much movement on one side. 'Thank you both. I'm lucky you were on that road.'

'More than lucky,' added Jim. 'We'd taken the wrong road. If we'd not come off the main stretch and onto the golf course for a pee, it could have been a very different story.'

'Yeah, you must have good connections upstairs,' Chris said, pointing his finger towards the ceiling. 'Nobody does that to a car and walks away. You looked very uncomfortable with your face in the airbag. How are the ribs?' he asked, shaking his head in disbelief. 'Man, that safety strap was locked tight.'

Joshua looked down at his strapped ribs.

'The face looks impressive too,' Jim said, admiring the large square piece of gauze firmly attached to Joshua's cheek.

Joshua lifted his hand and touched the bandage. 'Seven stitches. It looks worse than it is, or so the doctor told me. And the nurse assures me I'll still be handsome,' he added, giving a tentative, lopsided smirk. 'Tell me – when you found me, was I conscious? I can't remember much; it's a bit strange and hazy in places. Was I talking rubbish?'

Jim replied, glancing briefly back at Chris first before doing so. 'You didn't make much sense at the beginning. Kept mumbling something about staying and another chance, and referring to someone called Henry. We thought that was your name until the paramedics found your wallet.'

'Henry? I don't know anyone called Henry. Was there anyone else involved in the accident or at the scene?'

The two boys shook their heads. 'Nope, only your car and you,' said Jim. 'They said you must have dropped off the road above and flipped onto the golf course.'

'I don't remember. I must have been very confused when you found me,' Joshua admitted.

'Not surprising. You were trapped in a mangled car. Think anyone would have been confused in that state,' said Chris. 'Glad we found you, mate, and that you're going to be all right.'

'Very glad you did. And thank you,' said Joshua, relaxing back into the pillows again as the boys shook his hand gently and then waved goodbye.

On his discharge, Joshua took a taxi to the house in Epsom. The driveway was void of cars and the garage empty. Turning the key in the lock, he let himself in.

The house felt eerily cold, and as he wandered through the rooms he found himself thinking of Max and shivering. Annette had taken most of the smaller valuable pieces from the house, including the set of antique French miniature paintings from over the mantelpiece. The dining-room cabinet had been plundered and the two dark mahogany wood drawers that housed the silver cutlery gaped open and empty, while two small rings in the dust betrayed the last positions of the solid silver candelabras. Joshua smiled to himself as he wandered into the kitchen and looked at the wine fridge; she'd even taken the cold champagne from the lower racks. And his valuable collection of red wine had also disappeared.

Joshua opened the fridge door, pulled out a plastic bottle of semi-skimmed milk and twisted off the top, sniffing it before putting it to his lips. Taking a large swig directly from the bottle, he remembered how she hated him doing that. Then he belched, wiped his mouth on his stained sleeve and picked up an apple that had been carelessly thrown onto the table. *The bitch even took the fruit bowl*, thought Joshua. 'That wasn't hers,' he chuckled, biting into the apple.

He went upstairs next and opened the door to Amelia's room, the handle of the plastic milk bottle still hooked over one finger. Annette had clearly vented most of her anger here. She had used a thick, glossy lipstick to draw a sticky red line across his daughter's bedroom wall. The lipstick had obviously broken under the force and the tacky red remains, including the Lancôme case, lay trodden into the carpet. *Never liked that colour,* thought Joshua, taking another swig from the milk.

Amelia's pretty bed linen had been dragged off the bed and now lay in a pile on the floor. Teddies, toys and books lay scattered haphazardly around the room. Her doll's house, also a casualty of Annette's temper, stood minus its chimneys, lattice windows and front door. The tiny flower boxes that Joshua and Amelia had created one wet afternoon had been prised off, and her porcelain doll, its face smashed beyond repair, lay spreadeagled over the pitched roof.

Joshua carefully closed the door to his daughter's room, keen to shut out the evidence of his wife's hatred. Moving into Annette's dressing room, he checked her main closets; they, as well as her drawers, had been emptied. Signs that she had left in a hurry were obvious from the unmatched underwear and make-up that lay scattered on the bedroom floor. Joshua picked up a pair of her black lacy panties and turned them over in his hand. *Such a price for so little material,* he thought, as he casually dropped them into the bin. The bathroom cabinets had been cleared out too, his personal effects thrown into the second basin. His expensive cologne and aftershave bottles, all gifts from Annette, had been smashed, their contents mingling to create an interesting scent as the bottles bled out onto the dark blue shower tiles.

Joshua found that the safe in his study had been opened and left ajar. There was no sign of Annette's passport or her jewellery; even the cash, together with some sensitive paperwork, had been removed. *Thorough job,* thought Joshua. *You must have had help.*

Collecting the few pieces of clothing and personal effects that had survived his wife's wrath, he stuffed what amounted to the remains of his entire life with Annette inside a duvet cover and left the house like a thief.

In the taxi, his swag bag beside him, he was reminded of a night, many years earlier, when he had sat with his brother in a police car, all their worldly belongings stuffed into two pillowcases.

'Where to?' asked the taxi driver, interrupting his thoughts.

'Reading,' Joshua replied, scrolling through his phone numbers before selecting one he had not called for twenty years.

'Hello,' a voice answered.

'Michael? It's Josh.'

There was a moment's silence on the other end. Then, 'Hello, Joshua.'

'I'm in trouble, I need to talk.'

'Where are you now?'

'In a taxi, on my way to you, to Reading. My car's trashed.'

'How far away are you?'

'About two hours.'

'I'll be waiting.' In fact, he had already been waiting for this call – for a very long time.

Chapter 19

Michael Hart was seven when their father was sent to jail on an assault charge. As the older son by two years, he took on the mantle of protector for his mother and younger brother Joshua. He would have done anything for them; he thought his love was all the protection they needed. Then their father came home.

Michael watched as his mother's gentle spirit was crushed under the weight of his father's fist and experienced the fear that made Joshua wet his bed every night. Their lives once more became an exercise in avoidance and survival: avoid his tempers or survive his punishments. All three learned to hide their bruises from one another. But when his mother became pregnant, she unwittingly signed her death warrant. Michael's love was no longer enough.

It happened on a sunny afternoon in early July. Michael and Joshua had walked back from school, their heads buzzing with everything they'd learned, excited at the prospect of sharing their day's news with their mother. Opening the side gate, Michael called out, 'We're home, Mum. What's for tea?'

'I'm starving,' Joshua, chipped in.

Tea was always ready for them. The kitchen would smell of clean, freshly ironed clothes, and the radio would play softly in the background for their yellow and blue budgie Bobbie, who would twitter and dance along with the tunes. Claire Hart loved the way her boys would chatter between mouthfuls, testing one another's knowledge. 'Hungry to eat and hungry to learn,' she used to say proudly. This was their precious time together.

But this day was different.

The place was silent. There was no sound from the kitchen radio or accompanying squawks from the budgie. The boys glanced at one another. As the side gate swung noisily shut behind them, Joshua shuddered, grinding to a sudden halt behind his brother.

Michael saw her first. She lay unconscious on the kitchen floor, her deep blue eyes swollen shut, her long dark hair fanned out around her battered face, now encrusted with congealed blood. There was blood everywhere: the red splatter patterns on the ceramic sink, the surrounding tiles and the kitchen window showed the ferocity of the attack. Michael tried to shield Joshua by blocking his view and pushing him back out of the kitchen, but Joshua had already seen too much. He had seen the crimson pool outlining his mother's head like a demonic halo, but it was the dark spread of foetal blood staining her pale blue maternity dress that would haunt Joshua above all.

The papers claimed that Frederick Hart, unemployed, had come home having spent lunchtime in the local pub and taken out his frustrations on his wife Claire as she scrubbed potatoes for their evening meal. What they didn't write was that he had grabbed his pregnant wife's hair and slammed her face a number of times into the ceramic sink. When he finally let go of her, she had slumped to the floor, both hands clasped protectively around her heaving stomach, where she delivered her baby alone on the kitchen matting. The baby had been a tiny but perfectly formed little girl; they had died within minutes of one another.

The police officers at the scene of the crime, although hardened, found the senseless murder of Claire Hart and her baby sickening. Frederick Hart was arrested back at his local pub and taken into custody. He was later given life imprisonment.

Michael and his brother Joshua were found hiding together in the garden shed. Traumatised by the discovery of their mother, the two boys were taken into care and eventually fostered by separate families. Joshua swore from that day on that he would never allow himself to love anyone again. He had seen how love made you weak and that weakness made you vulnerable. It was Joshua who asked to be fostered without his brother. Michael lost his father, mother, brother and baby sister all on that one fateful night.

As the taxi pulled up outside the modern, red-brick house, Michael was there to greet him. Joshua felt a tightening in his stomach, his bruised ribs hurting as he took in a deep breath to calm his nerves. After paying the taxi driver, Michael opened the door to help Joshua out. The oversized square gauze on Joshua's grey face had lifted on one corner, revealing the fresh stitches.

'Who won?' asked Michael as he took in the partially stuffed duvet cover clutched in his brother's hand.

'Life!'

'Life's a bitch and then we die,' replied Michael with a grin.

'No. My wife's a bitch … and we don't always die when we should.'

Michael led his brother into his home. His wife Elizabeth and their two children had discreetly gone upstairs allowing the brothers space and time. Inviting Joshua to sit, he carefully placed the cotton duvet cover beside him. Joshua looked at his strange luggage and smiled the weak smile of the defeated. Michael's eyes missed nothing; he too remembered.

'I had a car accident,' Joshua began. 'By rights I should be dead, but it looks like I've been given another chance. I've made a mess of things, Michael.'

Michael sat back opposite Joshua and listened. As a professional counsellor he knew how important it was to do this. Joshua gave his brother an abridged version of the more recent part of his life, up to and including the argument with Annette and the accident; Michael made no comment.

'Do you still think about what happened back then?' Joshua asked, looking at his brother, his dark eyes brimming with unshed tears. 'Do you think Mum and the baby suffered?' A fat tear slipped down his cheeks then, catching on the gauze as he recalled the image of his mother that day. 'I ran away!' he cried, as a sob tore from his chest.

'You were only five, Josh, a child.'

'But you would have stayed with her and you weren't much older than me. I made you leave her there and come with me into the shed.' Joshua's face crumpled. 'I so wanted ...' he started, breaking down into heart-wrenching sobs.

'It wasn't your fault, Josh ... you were frightened.'

'If help had come sooner, would she have lived?'

'No ...' Michael paused to allow Joshua to register the answer. 'She was too badly injured.'

'What about the baby?'

'She was born too soon.'

'God, it hurts,' Joshua whispered between sobs. 'It's been eating me up slowly. All these years I thought I had it under control.'

Michael listened, aware of how long he had been carrying the pain of that awful day.

'I was lying to myself, wasn't I?'

Michael nodded, giving his brother time to gather himself. He knew that what was happening here was good. Joshua was now ready to face those hidden memories.

'That image of Mum never changes. It made me hate anything soft and vulnerable. But I got it all wrong, Michael.' Joshua's face, pale in the lamplight, looked emotionally drained. 'I'm so sorry for the way I treated you.'

Michael smiled kindly. 'I was a link with the tragedy,' he said.

The brothers sat quietly, a pot of coffee now cold on the low table in front of them.

'Your house is nice,' said Joshua, looking around him. 'How long have you been married?'

Michael nodded towards the framed wedding photograph on the sideboard. 'Fifteen years. We met on a bus travelling to Greece on an overland holiday. Those are my two girls,' Michael pointed proudly at a photograph of a pair of twins, two pretty, dark-haired girls with vivid blue eyes. 'They were six when that was taken. They're teenagers now.'

'You've made a success of your life, Michael, despite the start,' Joshua observed. 'I've just made one mess after another. I left my first wife Emma when she told me she was pregnant; I couldn't face the idea of her pregnancy because of …'

'… what happened to Mum?' asked Michael.

Joshua said nothing, just looked up at his brother.

'Did you explain that to her?'

'No. No one knows about *that*. I never told anyone about it, or even about you.'

'You kept my Christmas cards though?' Michael had followed his brother's career with pride, sending Christmas cards to his office, giving him his address and telephone number, hoping that one day he would reach out and find him. 'Did Emma have the baby?' he asked.

'Yes. She had a girl,' Joshua's face lit up at the thought of his daughter. 'Amelia.'

Michael remembered a happier afternoon, long ago, sitting with his brother and mother in the kitchen, choosing names for the baby. Joshua had wanted Thor for a boy and Amelia for a girl. They had just watched a documentary on Amelia Earhart and both boys thought her 'cool'.

'I'm happy for you. Amelia is a beautiful name. How old is she?'

'She's three now. And she is very beautiful, just like her mother.' Joshua paused and cleared his throat. 'I tried to take her away from Emma.'

Michael said nothing. He sat silently, watching the visible pain as Joshua continued.

'I waited and then I tried to claim she was physically and mentally unfit to care for her daughter.'

'Was that true?'

Joshua's face crumpled as he shook his head.

But Michael understood; he too had experienced dark periods in his life when he'd lashed out. It was only because someone had given him the time and compassion he needed that he had made it through his own personal journey. Now, in his role as a grief counsellor, he gave back that time and understanding to others.

'Bad things happened to us, Joshua. Pretending they didn't doesn't help.'

'I have to pretend, I'm too damaged deep down.'

'The little Josh of five was damaged; you are remembering the pain through the eyes of a small, frightened child. But if you can talk about things, you'll start to see what happened through the eyes of an adult. The facts won't change, but they will alter in their intensity. You're here now. That's a start.'

There was a lengthy pause as Michael allowed his brother to grieve in silence.

'Have you forgiven him?' Joshua asked.

'Who?'

'Our father.'

'Yes.'

'God, you're so noble,' spat Joshua.

'No, I'm just further on than you.'

Joshua gave his brother an apologetic look as he closed his eyes and dropped his shoulders.

'Hungry?' Michael asked, not giving Joshua time to respond. 'I am. Let's get something to eat, we have a lifetime to catch up on.'

And they did. They talked into the night and well into the following morning. When Elizabeth took the children to college the following day, the two brothers were both stretched out on the settees. She'd never met Joshua before, but as she looked at his face, she thought she glimpsed the missing part of Michael's soul in his sleeping expression. Brothers reunited at last.

Chapter 20

Amelia was excited and ready for her trip to meet Simon's parents, having carefully packed her most treasured possessions inside her small teddy bear bag herself. As she sat expectantly in the back of Simon's four-wheel drive, she asked for her beloved Buddy. Simon checked her car seat straps, then leaned over and pulled out the rabbit, dislodging a yellow and blue rubber ring as he did so.

'What's this for, Amelia?' he asked, wondering whether he had told Emma or Amelia about the lake at his parents' home.

'It's for Charlie,' she stated in her matter-of-fact voice. 'He can't swim.'

'Ok then,' Simon replied, exchanging a bemused look with her mother, while Amelia, tucking Buddy into her seat, folded her hands on her lap and sat quietly waiting for the vehicle to start.

As the car pulled away from the cottage, Emma turned around to smile at her daughter. The call from Joshua the previous evening, although thin on an explanation, had given her a sense of hope for them all.

The journey down was easy. Amelia slept most of the way and the toilet stops were few. For a man without children, Simon displayed an easy understanding of their needs.

'We're here,' said Simon, announcing their arrival. They approached the house through two stone pillars with ball finials and drove onto a gravel driveway. Comprising of three floors, the handsome, red-brick house displayed elegant white-sashed windows, a grey slate roof and an impressive porch. It was large by any standards and surrounded by extensive lawns that sloped to the right side of the property. A small lake nestled at the bottom and a pair of swans floated magnificently into view as Simon pulled up outside the main entrance. Amelia shrieked with amazement and pointed to the swans.

'Simon, I had no idea it was going to be so grand,' Emma whispered as she climbed out of the car, aware that Simon's parents were walking towards them.

'Remember, it's a listed building, so some of the very old bits can't be modernised easily – like the plumbing.'

'It's just so beautiful.'

'I know. I forget sometimes how lovely it is. Mother inherited the house from a great aunt. There's the most stunning and protected walled garden to the south-east of the house and a courtyard garden behind.'

'Who does all the work in the gardens? The lawns must take a day alone.'

'Oh that's Tom – he and his wife live in the converted stable block. Tom's wife helps Mother with the house a couple of days a week. Works well, apparently.'

Simon turned to greet his parents, wrapping his mother in a huge bear hug.

'Hello, my darling,' she said. 'Welcome home – and welcome also to your two young ladies.'

Camilla Leighton's eyes, the colour of cornflowers, were large and they shone as she kissed her son. Her abundant silver-grey hair was tied in a loose chignon that emphasised her delicate features, and she wore a pair of blue jeans and a white linen shirt. Around her neck hung a silver and turquoise necklace and on her wrist was a matching bracelet. Emma thought they looked Native American in design and made a mental note to ask her where she had found them.

Angus Leighton stood beside his wife. His thick hair, now iron grey, had been cut short for this weekend on Camilla's insistence, but it stuck up in places despite desperate attempts at grooming.

Simon ran his hand through his father's hair. 'I see Mother's still trying to modernise you, Dad,' he said and they both laughed.

Angus had put on a pair of well-worn green corduroy trousers, despite the heat, and wore an oatmeal-coloured cardigan with leather buttons, a checked shirt and a fawn knitted tie. 'She tries but I'm a lost cause, I'm afraid.'

Angus's manner and smile reminded Emma of Simon and she felt at ease as he propelled them all towards the house.

'Have you got fish?' Amelia asked, looking back at the lake.

'Yes, my darling,' Camilla answered softly. 'We've got a *huge* fish called Norman. He's an oversized carp that Angus has been trying to recatch for years. There are also swans and ducks to feed. We could go down to the lake after lunch – would you like that?'

Amelia nodded and, clutching her teddy bag tightly to her chest, stared up at the high moulded ceilings in the entrance hall. *Spectacular,* thought Emma, as she followed Simon through the doorway.

'Now, if you would follow me, ladies,' said Camilla, 'I'll show you to your room.' She led them up the stairs and into a brightly lit bedroom that looked out over the garden and surrounding fields. The walls were covered with pale cream and yellow striped wallpaper.

Through the open window Emma could smell the scent of freshly cut grass and hear the chirping of birds. 'How delightful!' she exclaimed.

'I've put you and Amelia in here together. I know the bed is large and high, but I assumed you could trap her beside you with lots of pillows. We have plenty of those, as you can see.'

Looking around, Emma noted the wide mahogany sleigh bed with crisp white linens, the matching furniture and the fresh white and lemon flowers placed in vases on the windowsill and bedside table. Amelia, happy with her surroundings, dropped her bag and wandered into the en-suite.

'Thank you, it's perfect. You have a beautiful home, Camilla, and it's very kind of you to have us for the weekend.'

'My pleasure, my dear. We don't get to see too much of Simon, what with his travels and lectures. The fact that he has brought you both is a bonus for me. Now make yourself at home and come down when you're ready. I've prepared a cold lunch, so there is no need to rush.'

Emma watched Camilla's agile form descend the stairs, then went to rescue Amelia. 'Well, young lady, what do you think?'

Amelia had lifted the lid of the toilet and stood on tiptoe, investigating the downward spiral of the floral decorations inside the porcelain pan. 'The flower pictures go all the way down the loo, Mummy! It's very pretty, isn't it? Will it wash off?'

'No,' Emma replied, removing a guest soap wrapper from Amelia's hands and encircling her daughter in her arms with a kiss.

Wriggling, Amelia snuggled her face into her mother's neck, 'Love you, Mummy.'

'Love you more!' Emma replied. 'Now, what did you do with the soap?'

Lunch was simple but delicious. Camilla had prepared sumptuous dishes and salads, served with baby potatoes and crunchy

French bread. Simon and his father deliberated over the meal on all subjects from golf to fishing to the state of the rectory and the world at large. Camilla held a serene position as referee, from the serving of the fresh poached salmon to the dessert. Angus, relaxed in his son's presence, drank a great deal of wine with the meal, followed by port and cheese.

'Looks like someone will need a rest this afternoon,' Camilla whispered to Emma, looking over in her husband's direction. 'Let's leave them here and join Amelia.'

The glass doors to the dining room led out to a walled garden. During the meal, Amelia had left the table on a number of occasions to explore. She now stood beside a large lavender bush, her sun-kissed skin flushed with excitement and the warmth of the day.

'Mummy – look what I've found: a fairy's wing!'

In Amelia's small hand rested the remains of a tiny leaf, a white skeleton of dainty veins being the only surviving part.

'It must have been a fairy princess, Mummy. Only a fairy princess could have wings this beautiful. See how they can still fly!' With that, she gently blew on the leaf and watched as it fluttered to the ground. 'She doesn't need that one any longer. She's probably all grown up now and needs bigger wings. She'll need the feather ones next. She'll get them from the birds, like the picture of the lady in the sitting room.'

Emma's expression made Camilla laugh. 'She's referring to the picture by the piano. It's a small oil painting of an angel with a pair of outstretched wings. Amelia must have seen it earlier. How clever of her to notice and what a lovely concept – a fairy growing into an angel.'

Yes, what a beautiful idea, thought Emma, smiling at her daughter's imagination.

The women sat on the old stone bench in the walled garden, their heads bent towards one another. Shaded by the overhanging wisteria, they talked easily about nothing in particular, while Amelia played around them, interrupting from time to time with her discoveries and explanations.

'Amelia has an imaginary friend called Charlie who tells her things,' Emma confided, by way of an explanation for her daughter's latest interpretation of the desiccated frog carcass that she had found in the bushes.

Camilla replied with a smile. 'I had one too.'

'Oh?'

'Yes, mine was a boy with wings. I lost touch with him when no one believed me. It's normal, Emma; pretend play is important to a child's development. Imaginary friends are an extension of pretend play. Does Charlie worry you?'

'No, he seems quite harmless, if a little too knowledgeable for my liking. Her father finds him worrying though.'

Camilla laughed. 'That's probably because he's a male. Limited imagination! She'll grow out of him as she begins to understand the difference between reality and fantasy. Sad to think that all that belief and imagination will just stop one day. Children can see so much more than we do.'

'Sometimes she sees too much …' Emma began, then thought better of it and lowered her eyes.

Camilla caught the fleeting expression on her face. She gently placed her hand on Emma's and they exchanged a look of trust. 'Please, go on. You were about to say something?'

'Just that Charlie can get Amelia into trouble sometimes. He appears to know about things that he … couldn't know about.'

'He appears to be a very clever Charlie indeed. How long has Amelia been talking about him?'

'Months, although I get the impression he's been around for longer.'

'Fascinating, I look forward to meeting him and hearing what he has to say.'

'Oh, you will. She never goes anywhere without him.'

'Simon tells me you've recently had past-life regression. Not from him, I gather.'

'No. I went for hypnotherapy, hoping to remove a memory block I'd built against bad dreams that frightened me. The past-life find was an accident.'

'Did it help with the bad dreams?'

'Not at the time, although that block has gone now. It's my past-life recall as someone called Charlotte that's demanding answers now. I asked Simon if I would have to keep returning with the same people every lifetime until I get it right. He couldn't answer me.'

'I'm not surprised. Simon finds it a lot less scary looking at it objectively through a scientific scope,' said Camilla, smiling wisely.

'So do you believe in a past life and the suggestion that we have the opportunity to live again?' Emma asked. 'Simon tells me you are the best person to answer these questions.'

Camilla laughed, her blue eyes twinkling. She knew her son. *Search and you will find,* she thought. Then, turning towards Emma, she answered, 'Yes, and I also believe the next life is of our making. All my instincts tell me I'm right and if I *have* lived before, I should listen to those feelings, as all the answers are within us, collected over many lifetimes.'

Emma lowered her eyes, quietly listening.

'I think your daughter is an amazing and charming little girl with a magical and free imagination. She is so young, yet so wise. I would refer to her as an *old soul.*'

Emma looked up at her hostess and, catching the sparkle of mirth in her eyes, returned the look.

'By the way, Emma, my boy with the wings came back to me … later in my life.'

Emma's eyes registered the meaning.

'Now, no one can chase him away again.' Camilla smiled at the thought before leaning her head back against the wall, allowing her eyes to close.

Emma drew Amelia away from the bench, putting her finger to her lips in acknowledgment of Camilla's need for a moment of tranquillity. Looking back at her, she watched the breeze play gently with the wisps of her silver-grey hair, noting the way her relaxed mouth still held a smile. A small bird dropped down onto the pavement to tease out an insect with its beak, unconcerned by the close proximity of the sleeping woman's feet.

Emma found Simon and Angus on the side lawn, attempting to play croquet. Bursting free from her mother, Amelia threw herself centre stage into the game. She selected one of the heavy, faded wooden balls, bent over and proceeded to push it like an oversized marble across the grass.

'Well, that's one way to play,' said Angus in good humour.

'Sorry,' Emma called as she ran to catch up with her offspring.

Angus relinquished his lead in the game and joined Amelia on the ground in an attempt to roll the wooden balls along the grass while Simon, resting on his croquet mallet, looked on, amused.

'Where's Camilla?' he asked.

'Resting,' Emma replied, nodding her head in the direction

of the house. 'I left her in the walled garden.'

'Why don't you two go off for a few minutes?' Angus asked. 'I can look after Amelia. In fact, I think she is quite capable of looking after me!'

Angus asked his small opponent whether she would be happy to continue playing with him if her mother and Simon left them for a short while. Her agreement was clear in her response: 'You can have the yellow ball.'

Simon looked at Emma, who nodded.

'Now off with you both. I'm sure Camilla will join me shortly. Enjoy some time to yourselves.'

Taking each other's hands, their heads bent towards one another, Simon and Emma walked quickly down towards the lake.

'This is so perfect, Simon. Thank you for bringing me here.'

'My pleasure. I'm very happy to have you with me,' he said, and raised her hand to his lips and kissed it. 'Come, I want to show you something.'

The house disappeared from view as Simon led the way through a dense pocket of trees and out again, alongside the lake and on to a wooden summerhouse.

'I used to read in here for hours as a child and later as a young student. Perfect place for thinking.'

The spectacular scenery around the old wooden shelter delighted Emma. Closing her eyes, she tilted her face to the sun and drank in the silence. The sound of a fish jumping drew her back to the present.

They made love on the long, soft grass and for Emma it was exquisite. As she lay beside Simon on the crushed undergrowth, she looked up at the clouds above them and shivered.

'Cold?'

'No, just a feeling that something's changed, forever. Perhaps the laying of a ghost.'

'Mmm, on the subject of *laying* …'

'Simon,' she giggled as he moved his body back over hers.

They found Amelia playing 'dress up' on the lawn to the front of the house. Camilla had put her in one of her own short cotton nightdresses and entwined a crown of grasses and garden flowers into her long hair. Barefoot, and with the nightdress tied up with cream ribbons and draped around her tiny frame, she resembled a Botticelli nymph. They watched as Amelia spun and danced, oblivious to her audience; then, noting the arrival of her mother and Simon, she pirouetted towards the group. 'Charlie's gone!' she announced breathlessly.

Camilla raised her eyebrows and looked in Emma's direction.

'Gone where?' Emma called out as Amelia spun once more and rushed off across the grass.

'Don't know,' she shouted back over her shoulder, her hair swinging as she swayed to the imaginary music. Then, pausing in mid-dance, she looked back at the group watching her and added, 'He said he'd be back again … soon.'

Chapter 21

With Amelia safely tucked up in bed and the men enjoying their limited time together, Emma found herself alone with Camilla in the drawing room.

Taking Emma's arm, Camilla drew her towards her study. 'Come; come with me while the men are occupied. We can have our coffee in here. Much more cosy.'

Emma looked around with appreciation. 'How exquisite,' she exclaimed, noting the soft cream and honey colours, the delicate antique furniture, the rug in front of the white marble fireplace and the thick drapes, spun with flecks of burnished gold, framing the oversized windows.

An ornate desk almost trembled under the weight of an old computer and printer, its spaghetti nest of cables and wires spewing onto the carpet below. As Emma's eyes scanned the old technology among the antiquities, Camilla laughed: 'I know, incongruous, isn't it? I need to have a small and thin laptop – Simon is always trying to update me, but as I always sit in here, it makes little sense to change what works.'

On the walls hung a number of pictures of different sizes, depicting delicate sprites, tiny fairies and beautiful winged angels set among a backdrop of woodlands, water and gardens. Drawn towards one in particular, Emma gasped as she took in the detail of the cherub's small wings, his chubby, childlike body and the expression on his face. 'I recognise this,' she said. 'I sent Christmas cards one year with this angel on them. I had no idea he came from a print.' Then her voice trailed off in embarrassment as she realised the pictures hanging on the walls were not prints but original paintings. She looked for the artist's signature and, not recognising it, she continued to wander around the study admiring the artwork.

'These paintings are wonderfully evocative. It is as if the artist was privy to some secret world within our own. I love them. Have you been collecting them for long?'

'Yes, a while now,' Camilla replied. 'It's my love of ethereal beauty, nature and wings, I'm afraid.' She stood beside Emma, her fingers gently following the outline of a sleeping fairy. 'These images allow me to detach from the brash brutality of the modern world and step inside a far gentler place.'

Emma nodded her head in agreement, continuing to marvel at the detail. 'So beautiful …'

Camilla smiled. 'I'll bring in the coffee. Won't be long. Feel free to browse.'

On the edge of the desk lay a hardcover book called *Spiritual Labyrinths*. Emma noted the name of the author and picked it up. As Camilla returned with the coffees, Emma turned towards her. 'C. M. White. That's the name on your paintings.'

Camilla nodded and placed the tray down on the coffee table. Emma, book in hand, moved over to the shelf, her finger stroking the spines, counting the different titles that bore the same author's name.

'Would you like to look at that one?' Camilla asked, referring to the copy of *Spiritual Labyrin*ths still in Emma's hand. 'I think it may be of particular interest to you – it has a chapter on past life.'

Emma paused and, turning the book over, read the blurb on the back: '… threads the reader through the maze of mythology, spiritual and religious concepts, covering reincarnation, third dimensions, higher consciousness and angelic realms, linking the entanglement theory to a continuous existence … science and spiritual collision … worth a read.'

Emma looked at Camilla. 'Entanglement theory?'

'Ah! The entanglement theory. It's pure quantum mechanics, Emma, and relates to the behaviour of "particles" that have been previously entangled or linked to one another. The theory is that any action performed on one of the "separated particles" will result in a simultaneous response from the "disconnected particle".'

Camilla watched Emma's expression. 'Putting it simply,' she continued, 'once two or more particles become entwined, they are then connected for all eternity throughout time and space despite their separation.'

Emma raised her eyebrows and Camilla chuckled. 'I know: Einstein called it "spooky action at a distance". I like that. Rather like the concept of emotional cords, linking the individual to their current lifetime connections, or souls linking in past or future lifetimes.'

'You mean once connected, always connected?' asked Emma.

'Yes, all deeds done now and in the future, continually affecting others, for this lifetime and possibly another. Helps with the concepts of soul groups, karma, telepathy and déjà vu.' Camilla paused and looked at Emma who stood quietly watching her, allowing the heavy book to twist in her hands. 'Have I lost you?' she asked.

'No, please carry on.'

Camilla sighed and sat down on one of the small, button-back chairs. 'We all experience the effects from "lifetime cords",' she continued. 'The cords of unresolved issues, where all our damaged loves, angry thoughts and grudges, our disappointments, our failures, our hurt, envy and jealousy will have created tiny connecting threads that attach themselves permanently to others. These connecting cords influence our future life or even subsequent lifetimes by creating behaviour patterns and forcing us to replay issues we have not understood or resolved. Cords that can bind us forever. Forgiveness and understanding can detach damaging cords.'

Emma thought back to her regression session. 'But what if you can't find it within yourself to forgive something that someone has done to you?' asked Emma. 'How can you cut the cords in that case?'

'Time is a great healer. It allows for understanding. When you understand, you can forgive. With forgiveness you don't have to agree that what was done to you or said to you was acceptable. It just allows you to let go of the hurt and anger and move on. Who was it that said, "If you can let go of the anger, it will allow you to take the hands from around the other person's throat, so that you can both breathe again."? Says it all, really.'

Emma stood quietly, taking in all she had heard. 'What's so strange,' she began, 'is that three months back, all of this would have been too far outside of my parochial Sunday-school teachings. But now ...' Twisting the book over in her hands, she opened it, noticing for the first time the author's photograph inside the dust cover. Lifting her head quickly, she fired a look at Camilla. 'It's you ... C. M. White is you!'

Camilla laughed at Emma's open surprise. 'Yes, another one of my many passions: writing. It's also proved quite lucrative over the years. My books allow me to communicate with words and my paintings allow me to express visually. I use my maiden name and yes, I'm afraid some of my angels have made it onto the commercial Christmas card route. Needed the roof patched up and I mustn't be selfish with my angels. Cream, milk or black coffee?'

'Cream please,' Emma replied, watching spellbound as Camilla broke from her conversation and poured, passing the cup and saucer over.

'In fact,' Camilla continued, 'I've just been commissioned to do a stained-glass window for the local church. That's where my childhood "winged boy" will be immortalised for all to see.' She paused. 'I haven't put sugar in it. Did you want some?'

Still astonished by the realisation that Camilla was both the author and painter, Emma shook her head in response, and the two women sat silently for a moment drinking their coffee.

On the wall opposite Emma hung a painting of a young woman sitting under a white blossom tree and watching two plump cherubs. Her face shone with a look of pure rapture as she smiled up at the angelic duo frolicking amid the heavy blossom-covered boughs. 'I take it that's one of yours too?'

'Yes. I call that *Contentment*. Could never part with that painting – too personal. The faces on the cherubs are those of my two boys when they were small. That feeling of unconditional love and wonderment for my boys never leaves me.'

'I'm amazed you've found the time to do any of this.'

'When you love something, you always make time, Emma.'

As Simon kissed Emma goodnight outside the guest bedroom later that evening, she put one hand gently around his neck and whispered wickedly as the other playfully measured his behind, 'Saw a painting of you as a cherub. A little chubbier then than now, but the bottom is still as round and as gorgeous.'

'Naughty!' he replied. 'Now, do you want me to wait and

turn the lights out for you?'

They both looked back towards the soft glow of the bedside lights that lit the sleeping face of Amelia.

'No thanks,' said Emma. 'I'm going to read your mother's book for a while.'

Simon blew her a final kiss before gently closing the door behind him.

Settling into the plumped pillows, Emma looked down at Amelia and watched the way her small fingers rhythmically tugged at Buddy's ribbon as she slept. 'Contentment,' she whispered to her sleeping daughter, understanding the emotions expressed by Camilla in her painting of the woman with the cherubs.

Chapter 22

The morning sunlight trickled through the partially drawn curtains and woke Emma. On the table next to the bed lay Camilla's book. She had read more than half of it before reluctantly putting it down in the early hours.

Camilla, Camilla, what an extraordinary woman you are, thought Emma as she tiptoed across to the bathroom. The creak from a loose board woke Amelia, who sat bolt upright in bewilderment, looking around her. Instinctively, Emma peered around the bathroom door, toothbrush in mouth.

'Hello, Mummy. Your mouth's frothing,' said Amelia, giggling as she climbed out from under the duvet and stood upright among the pillows. As Emma moved towards her, toothpaste dripping down her chin, Amelia grinned and began to bounce. 'Can we look for Norman, can we look for Norman?' she chanted.

After a large cooked breakfast the two men took an excited Amelia out fishing, leaving the women to clear and prepare for the next meal in peace. As Emma peeled the potatoes at the kitchen table, they shared stories regarding their families, siblings and loved ones. Camilla listened quietly as Emma told her about her short marriage to Joshua and the threats for custody of Amelia.

'Although Joshua said in our latest conversation that he's dismissed his lawyers, I can't help feeling worried. I don't understand why the sudden change. It was only a few weeks back that he was looking for a way to alter the custody arrangements.'

'On what grounds?'

'Anything that pointed to me being incapable, and unfortunately there have been a number of embarrassing incidents that could have played into his hands.'

Camilla paused in her pea shelling, turned towards Emma and raised an eyebrow. 'Embarrassing?'

'Oh yes,' Emma responded sheepishly. 'Very.'

'Seriously embarrassing?' Camilla probed with humour.

'Oh, you know …' Emma began flippantly. 'The normal everyday occurrences like nightmares that deprive you of sleep and cause you to rearrange your bedding, but never allow you to remember what it was that frightened you so much. Then there was the very public near-drowning experience in the local pool in front of my own daughter, followed by my reluctance to regain consciousness, which got everyone jumping. Oh, and I mustn't forget the embarrassing collapse in front of Joshua and his new wife, while still in my pyjamas!'

'Colour?' asked Camilla, taking her lead from Emma's tone and dry humour.

'Pink, of course!'

'Nice touch.'

'Then there's my latest claim of a past-life recollection – although I don't think Joshua knows about that one just yet.'

'You have been busy. Tell me more,' Camilla encouraged.

So she did. She told Camilla about her emotional struggles when Joshua left during her pregnancy, her business, the difficulties of bringing up a child on her own, the confused emotions on learning of Joshua's marriage to Annette, the devastation she felt when she thought she might lose custody of Amelia and Joshua's most recent strange behaviour. She spoke with an unguarded honesty, holding little back.

Camilla looked fondly at Emma. 'At least you still have a sense of humour; keep that always. With regard to your nightmares and near-drowning experience, yes, it's possible that they are a validation of your past life as Charlotte.' She paused again from her shelling. 'Or it might simply be that you are a seriously delusional and cranky woman!'

Emma laughed and allowed Camilla to refill her coffee cup.

'It's important to keep laughing, Emma. That will allow you to put it all into perspective. Of course, I don't think you are delusional or cranky – just someone looking for answers, which I find healthy.'

Emma sat back and eyed Camilla with a look of amused respect. 'I read your chapter on past-life recollections. Like Simon, you have a way of making me look at my own "memories" without feeling like a fool or a fraud. I understand the need to acknowledge false memories, no matter how real they feel at the time, but the question remains: could I have created them to fit my personal life?'

Camilla put her coffee cup down carefully on the table, brushing away an imaginary crumb as she thought. 'Well, that's a question I haven't got the answer to. What do you think?' she said, turning the question back to Emma. 'Do you think your memories from a past life led to the trauma in the pool? Or do you think it was the other way round?'

Emma groaned in response.

'I know,' Camilla said apologetically. 'Simon has to ask that question each time he researches a case. But whatever the explanation, Emma, whatever we experience during a past-life recollection, whether real or not, it *does* have a purpose, if only to reinforce issues that we need to resolve. Were you able to validate anything?'

'Possibly, although loosely.'

'What was that?'

'There was a woman I saw on the boat in my life as Charlotte. She was very beautiful and appeared to be interested in my father. Simon encouraged me to put on paper everything I remembered, and this woman's face haunted me, so I sketched her. I got down as much detail as I could – the way she held her head and how she wore her hair. She could have been a figment of my imagination, only Simon bought me an old second-hand book about American swimwear in the 1900s and in it I found a photograph of a woman with the caption "Unknown actress" – she resembled the woman in my sketch exactly. It could just be coincidence, but I think the woman on the boat could have been that American actress.'

'Don't dismiss it completely; trust in your own intuition. "Intelligence from the heart" is what I call it. Whatever you feel, feels right. After all, it's your memory,' said Camilla.

'Do you really believe we can be reborn into another life as a different person?' Emma asked.

'Like to think so,' Camilla answered with a twinkle in her eye. 'For me it's a comforting concept. We've been asking questions regarding our purpose and what happens to us when we die throughout the centuries. I simply work with my heart intelligence. Over the years it's served me well, allowing me to listen and to respect others' views.' Camilla leaned back in her chair and popped a shelled pea in her mouth.

'But is the claim of a reincarnation just another spiritual theory? Was it created as an escape from the nothingness of death?' Emma asked.

'You mean like Heaven, the Afterlife, Life after Death, the Hereafter, Valhalla and Paradise? Sometimes death is almost glamorised by promising rewards. Perhaps it's only human to try and escape from the nothingness of death.'

'So whose version is the right one?' asked Emma.

'Ah, the *atheist* wants credible and factual evidence proving the existence of God or an afterlife; the *agnostic* believes it's impossible to prove either way. I think the agnostic's hedging his bets,' chuckled Camilla, then she closed her eyes for a moment as if recalling something personal and private before adding, 'I don't need proof of an afterlife, Emma, but that's my personal belief. Everyone has the right to believe what they feel is right for them.'

'I do think it's possible I've lived before,' Emma quietly admitted.

'Does that thought frighten you?'

'It did. But not now.'

'When I was a newly qualified young paediatrician, before I had my own babies, I witnessed the death of a baby girl, which upset me very much. We were taught during training not to become involved, but I did with this family. I was asked to the funeral …'

Camilla shook her head gently and continued. 'I'll never forget it. The tiny white coffin draped with garlands of pink roses. I don't think anyone could hold back the tears that morning. So much love and promise trapped in that little white box. When the distraught mother told me she'd wrapped her baby's body in the silk shawl she'd worn on her wedding day and put a tiny pink knitted kitten beside her for company, I'm afraid I lost it. I can still see the look of anguish and disbelief in the father's eyes when he made reference to their baby cutting her first tooth before she died. It was as if he expected me to give him an explanation; I couldn't find the words to make the pain go away, Emma.

'Some years later the couple had another baby – a baby girl. I was lucky enough to be there at the birth and I felt so happy for them. The mother told me that this new child was her lost baby, returned back to her. She even showed me a photo of the baby who'd died. The resemblance was uncanny, but then siblings do look alike. She then showed me the tooth in her baby's tiny mouth, reminding me that when her first child had died she'd had a tooth in exactly the same place. To the mother this was proof that her baby had come back to them.'

'Did you think that?' asked Emma.

Camilla paused in reflection. 'I admit that at the time I found the idea of a reincarnation beautiful and comforting. But it was only some years later that I made up my own mind ...' A smile crept into Camilla's eyes then, as if she was remembering something private and special. 'As the little girl grew, she began to make reference to a pink knitted kitten. When she could communicate better, she thanked her mother for wrapping her in the "special shawl" and for putting the pink kitten beside her. The mother told me this story when her daughter was about three. She said *she'd* always known it was her lost daughter come back to them, but she thought *I* needed proof.'

Emma sat, momentarily speechless, before saying, 'But if that is the case, why did she die in the first place, only to be reborn again later?'

'The baby was sick, Emma; her death was inevitable. I could understand that.'

'So if our lives are meant for us to learn lessons, what lessons does a newborn baby who dies suddenly learn?'

Camilla looked at Emma, aware she was working her hard. 'Well, one theory is that those babies have no lessons to learn in this life. Instead, they've agreed to come back for a brief time to teach others something.'

'So why, in the case of your couple, was the same baby's rebirth so soon after?'

'Oh, I think that was different. I believe her parents needed her, so she came back, whole and perfect.'

Emma pushed her cup of cold coffee to one side. 'If we've lived before, is there a simple code we should try and live to in our current life?'

'Yes, I think the secret is simple: to love and forgive. View everyone as you view yourself, faults and all. We have always been and will always be connected.'

'Entanglement!' the two women uttered in unison, smiling at one another.

'Understand the weakness of man and the power of forgiveness – forgiveness brings understanding. Love is the answer,' Emma said, remembering yet again the words she had spoken to Dr Warner during her regression.

'Yes. Try it on Joshua and see the change in his attitude. It may not work instantly, but you will disarm him and your love and forgiveness will be like a beacon attracting more love and forgiveness back to you. Works for me,' Camilla said as she got up from the table. 'Now enough. We need to lighten up the conversation and I need to put the potatoes in with the meat. There is a bottle of white in the fridge – why don't you open it and take it out into the courtyard. I've got some nibbles I'll bring out. We can have a well-deserved treat before the troops come back.'

The sound of small running feet and laughter signalled the arrival of Amelia with the men in tow. Emma opened her arms to her daughter as she rushed towards her.

'Mummy, Mummy, we looked for Norman, saw him in the

water – *sooo* big. Angus said he's very old and wise, that's why he's got so big. Will I get big when I get wise?'

'Think you are quite wise enough at the moment, young lady,' Emma said, pushing back her daughter's wayward fringe. 'And I think we'd better leave the shrubbery in the garden, don't you?' she added, pulling a leaf out of Amelia's skirt pocket as she claimed her seat at the courtyard table, helping herself to the oatcake nibbles.

Chapter 23

Joshua and Michael opened the old oak 'kissing gate' which lead into St Bartholomew's churchyard. Beneath the wooden tiled porch stood two sturdy benches, their weathered oak polished smooth by scrambling children's knees and parishioners' bottoms.

'Why do you always find a pub close to a church?' mused Joshua, glancing over to where they'd parked the car. 'Do you think they do it on purpose? One house for ale and debauchery, the other for the Lord and absolution.'

'I think the Church has always had its own fair share of debauchery. Perhaps absolution requires a follow-up drink?' Michael suggested.

Joshua snorted.

'Are you ready for this?' Michael asked, looking at his brother.

Joshua nodded, 'Lead the way.'

A number of the older gravestones, some intact, others damaged, had been removed from their uneven and sinking mounds and now stood against the church wall like a row of jagged, decaying teeth.

A pale grey stone cross marked the final resting place of their mother. The simple plaque read, 'Claire Hart and infant daughter. Much loved.' Joshua placed his yellow roses on the grass in front of the gravestone. 'She loved yellow flowers, didn't she?'

'Yes, I remember cowslips were her favourites,' Michael reminded him. 'Do you remember the holidays we went on? Just Mum and us. We stayed in a house surrounded by fields filled with cowslips – we would collect them by the armful.'

'Vaguely. Didn't our room have sloping floors and dark beams?'

'Yes … Do you remember the lady with the horse?'

'I think so. I do remember a white horse with huge, feathery white hooves.'

Michael smiled at the image. 'I have a few of Mum's photos; she put them in an old biscuit tin. When you're ready, we'll go through them. There's one of us outside that holiday home. Would you like me to find it?'

Joshua nodded, 'Yes please. I'd really like to see that. Sometimes I can't remember what she looked like.'

'They were happy times, Josh.'

Joshua's dark blue eyes shone with unshed tears. 'Do you think she knows we're here?'

'What do you think?' asked Michael.

'I need to believe she does.'

'Then she sees us both. Together again. I know that's something she would have wanted – and something I've been waiting for, too, for a very long time.'

'I couldn't have done it sooner,' said Joshua, his voice low and strained with controlled emotions.

'I know,' Michael told him softly. 'She understands too.'

Joshua shuffled his feet and cleared his throat. 'I think I'd like to say a few words to her in private, if you don't mind.'

'Go ahead, I'll wait for you in the car.'

Joshua watched Michael walk down the pathway and out of the gate. A light breeze caught a cluster of small, white feathers and blew them gently over his mother's grave. Closing his eyes, Joshua clasped his hands together and lowered his head.

'I'm not very good at this, you know that … but I think I've been given another chance, Mum. I don't know why. I know I don't deserve it. But I won't waste it, I promise.'

There was a sound of rustling beside him. Joshua opened his eyes and turned quickly, but there was no one there. Then a particular gravestone caught his eye. Mottled with green mould and lichen, it stood tall and proud, shaped like an arched gothic door among the other stones. Joshua crouched down to read the old inscription: 'Behold a gateway to a better world. Beware those that follow lightly, reverence the only path.' Joshua shivered uncomfortably and moved away quickly. As he did so, a small gust of wind picked up the white feathers again and gently deposited them at his feet. Bending down, he picked one up, marvelling at its fragility between his thumb and forefinger.

'Pure white down,' he muttered. 'Amelia would say you came from an angel.' Then, blowing onto the feather, he watched it flutter softly as he held it. 'Have you been watching me?' he asked, still unnerved by the tombstone inscription, as he tucked the small feather into his top pocket. 'Well, today I like that idea!'

Chapter 24

It was late and dark when they arrived back at the cottage. Simon carefully lifted Amelia out of the car, managing not to wake her. Hetty had left the outside lights on and the night moths dipped and danced in the soft glow. Thomas, uncannily aware of their arrival, had woken from his curled slumber and padded out to greet them.

'Hello Thomas, have you missed us?' whispered Emma as she bent to rub his chin. The cat responded with a soft mew. Scrabbling for her keys, she unlocked the door, allowing Simon to carry the sleeping bundle upstairs.

Once in bed beside a slumbering Simon, Emma reflected on the weekend, realising that the last few days spent as a family had been happier than her entire marriage to Joshua. *Have I changed,* she asked herself, *or did I only think I was in love and happy with Joshua?*

Carefully, so as not to wake Simon, she slipped further under the duvet. Turning gently, she wriggled down the bed, nestling her cold bottom into his thighs for warmth, and as her face sank into the pillows she murmured goodnight. Registering her chill, Simon pulled her tighter towards him.

Feeling safe in his arms, Emma drifted, recalling images of her life as Charlotte at sea. As the detailed scenes replayed in her mind, she now saw Henry through the detached eyes of an observer. Although he only bore a slight physical resemblance to Joshua, it was their eyes that linked them – they were the same intense dark blue, their colour deep enough to hide their darkest fears and saddest moments. Her heart filled with compassion at Henry's wretchedness, so obvious were his guilt and fear at the end; also his deep love for his children. And she'd seen that look of love in Joshua's eyes when he held Amelia too. *Love is the answer,* she reminded herself.

Skipping forward to her last memories of Charlotte, she watched and felt the emotions as a fulfilled and loved old lady, safe and warm in her bed, ready and willing to leave that lifetime. *Peace,* she thought, wiping away the tears from her eyes. *Time for me to let you go.*

As if sensing Emma's emotions, Simon stirred and pulled her closer. Feeling his arms around her, she knew that all the damaging cords that once linked her to Henry and Joshua were now gone forever. Smiling at the realisation, she fell asleep in his embrace.

Simon woke early the next morning. Conscious that Emma was still asleep, he carefully stretched one arm over her body and reached for the small clock on her bedside table. There was a muffled thud as he knocked it onto the floor. He groaned in frustration and Emma grunted in response, tucking the duvet more firmly around herself.

'Sorry,' he whispered.

'Mm ... I'm awake now.'

'What's the time?'

Emma lifted her head from the pillows, opening one eye to look up at the space where her alarm clock should have been. 'Don't know; someone's stolen the alarm clock!'

'Sorry, that was me. I knocked it over.'

'Well,' Emma whispered, turning her body towards his, her voice now heavy with suggestion. 'As we are both awake, now ... if we are quiet, we can make up for the time we lost over the weekend in separate beds.'

'Naughty!' Simon replied, reaching for Emma's pyjama-free form under the covers.

Emma giggled. 'I intend to be!'

Chapter 25

Joshua and Michael hugged each other goodbye beside the hired Volkswagen Golf. On the passenger seat sat a smart brown leather holdall bag, a gift from Michael.

'Let me know how it goes with Emma?'

'Will do.'

'And remember, there's always a job and a bed here for you, any time.'

Joshua felt his raw emotions rising to the surface again as he reluctantly let go of Michael. 'Thanks, but I need to extract myself from Annette and the business concerns my end first. I'm surprised I haven't had a phone call or read about my supposed illegal dealings in a tabloid newspaper yet. God help the company and me should Annette decide to play clever with journalists. I'm hoping she just wants to cut and run while she can.'

'Perhaps she's found a way to hide her involvement,' suggested Michael.

'She managed once before. Who knows? I just want out, Michael. Out from all the slime and dirt that I associate with her and that life.'

'Are you going straight to your flat in London?'

'No. I have to see my lawyers first today. There may be some fast untangling required. Currently I'm on sick leave from Barrett's, but it can't stay as vague as that. I need to officially resign and I don't know the implications. Then I need to see Emma; I have some explaining to do there.'

'Will you tell her about Annette and Mum?' asked Michael.

Joshua took time before replying. 'Not Mum. That's still too difficult to share. But she needs to know about Annette – after all, I'm potentially jobless.'

'Never. Like I said, there's always a job with me if you want,' Michael reminded him. 'I'm so proud to have you back, Josh. You have no idea how much I prayed for this day.'

'I know,' Joshua replied softly, glancing up towards the sky. 'Your man moves in mysterious ways. If it wasn't for Annette's sickening revelations and my accident, it might never have happened.'

'All the same, drive safely,' said Michael, patting Joshua on the back. 'He's good, but don't deliberately test him.'

Joshua grinned, the newly healed scar rippling on his unshaven cheek. 'You bet – this isn't even my car.'

Pulling away from Michael's house, Joshua felt a new mix of emotions. Annette's admissions and her sudden departure made him recognise how he too had been guilty of deceit and duplicity, and with this came a strong sense of remorse. But what he found most interesting was that he wasn't even sorry to see her go. Also, Joshua intended to retire from the Barrett organisation, whatever the outcome, and while the decision, he knew, would have financial consequences, he was surprised to discover he didn't care about that any longer either. Any wealth associated with that organisation felt tainted; even the thought of walking through the company's main glass doors again made him shudder. *I wonder if you still walk those corridors,* he thought, his mind flashing back to images of Max and to Annette's appalling disclosure. *You must be so ashamed of our behaviour.*

The decision to resign gave Joshua a huge sense of relief. He would use the time to repair his damaged life where possible. He wanted to become involved with something that benefited others, a project with real long-term gains and a purpose, not just financial reward or instant gratification. He had responsibilities to face up to, and a future, including a daughter and a wronged ex-wife. He smiled, catching a glimpse of his face in the mirror as he checked the traffic behind him. 'Well, I might not be an angel, Mum, but I'm a changed demon,' he said, patting the small white feather in his jacket pocket. 'Now I need to know why I've been given a second chance.'

The road through the Surrey Hills took Joshua past the scene of his accident. Slowing down, he pulled the Volkswagen over into a layby and stepped out of the car. From here he could see the manicured golf course below. A gaping tear through one of the hedges and tyre marks bore witness to his near-fatal accident. As he retraced the route his car took down the grass bank, he passed an old oak tree with a hastily made wooden cross nailed to its base. A number of small faded bouquets, each wrapped in cellophane and tied with various shades of now bleached ribbon, lay in a semicircle in front of the cross. Joshua's heart missed a beat as he dropped to his knees to examine the shrine. *An animal or a person,* he wondered. Casting his mind back to the mysterious cyclist from the evening of his accident, then recognising that he didn't want to know the answer, he hastily stood up again, brushed the grass off his knees and retraced his steps.

His walk down the bank had unnerved him. Joshua knew that whatever had really happened down there on the golf course could never be explained, but it had changed his life forever. He shivered at the image of his wrecked vehicle and the ghostly cyclist, and he started the engine. Despite the warmth of the day, he turned off the air conditioning and wound up the windows, tuning into the loudest rock radio station he could find.

Chapter 26

The day of Emma's meeting with Joshua had arrived and the weather was warm and sunny.

'Well, at least it's not raining,' Emma mumbled as she anxiously wandered around the bedroom. Gabby had arranged time off to babysit Amelia and the two of them now both lounged on Emma's bed among a pile of discarded clothes and watched her furtive movements.

'Think you should wear this,' said Gabby, picking up a sheer silk shirt dress.

'That? No, I don't think that's suitable – it's too see-through.'

'I know, but it shows him what he's missing.'

'That's not the purpose of this meeting.'

Amelia looked at Gabby, who lifted her hands and feigned disinterest.

'Pink! Mummy should wear pink.' Amelia had found a pink and yellow flowered shirt among the pile of clothing and held it up to her mother. Emma smiled and shook her head as she put on a trusted fitted beige jacket, which today felt constricted over her bust.

'Looks a bit tight, Em,' observed Gabby. 'Change the bra.'

'I don't think that's going to help. Nothing seems to fit properly any more,' Emma whimpered. 'Gabby, have I put on weight?'

'Not that I've noticed. But your bust is definitely bigger than that jacket can handle,' Gabby said with a laugh. She knew that today's meeting with Joshua was not going to be easy for Emma.

'Come on, Amelia, we're getting in the way here. Mummy needs some peace and space. We'll go out for some fresh air.'

As the two left for the open fields, Emma changed into a much-loved loose turquoise shirt, hastily brushed her hair off her face, and reapplied her lip gloss.

'Much better. More me,' she told her reflection.

They had agreed to meet for afternoon tea at a small hotel in town. As she walked into the reception area and saw Joshua, Emma noted how his face looked leaner than she remembered and there was a scar, fresh and obviously newly healed, across one side of his face. His clothes, once tailored to fit his broad shoulders and toned body, now hung loosely on his frame. He looked fragile.

Greeting her with a peck on the cheek, Joshua ushered Emma into the conservatory area. On reaching a table, he removed his jacket and hung it over the back of his chair. As he turned, she noticed how his belt was notched in, gathering in the waistband to hold his trousers up.

'Tea or coffee? Or would you prefer something stronger?' he asked. His hands trembled slightly as they sat down.

'Tea please,' she replied, increasingly aware of a vulnerability she had never seen in him before.

Joshua ordered the tea with a request for a selection of cakes. Sitting upright in his chair, he said, 'Starving, I'm afraid.' Then, looking at Emma, he added, 'You look well.'

She did look well. Her face glowed with the promise of new love. 'Thank you,' she replied.

'We need to talk,' he started. 'I'm so sorry Emma …' he mumbled, breaking off and giving her a sad smile.

As she sat back in her chair she held his gaze for a moment. The dark blue eyes that once flashed so dangerously now looked dull and filled with pain. Even his faint smile sat on pale lips. 'What happened to your face?' she asked.

Joshua lifted his hand and touched the scar. 'I had a car accident; no other cars involved, just mine. I lost control on a blind bend and wrote off the Mercedes.'

'Were you alone?' she asked with concern.

No, I wasn't, thought Joshua. *But I can't tell you that, you wouldn't believe me ...* 'Yes, I was alone. I was lucky; two travelling Aussie students found me and called for help. I was taken to hospital with concussion and a few nasty cuts and bruises.'

'Your face looks very ... sore.'

'Still a bit fresh, that's all.'

'Are you sure you're all right?' Emma asked. 'You really don't look ... yourself.'

Joshua looked at her. *Please don't be kind to me, Emma,* he thought, wrestling with his emotions. *I really don't deserve your compassion.* Then, steeling himself, he said, 'I'm fine, but thanks for your concern. I know I look dreadful, but that's because I'm finding it difficult to eat or sleep properly. Things have happened to me over the last month that have made me look at my own life and I don't like what I see.' He paused, and as Emma attempted to interject, he held up his hand. 'Please. Let me finish. I need to tell you this. I've been cruel and selfish and I've done so many heartless things and I don't know how to undo them. I have no excuses, Emma.' Joshua looked down at his hands clasped tightly on his knees. He raised both hands to his face and lowered his head, his shoulders shaking as he sobbed.

Emma remained perfectly still, uncertain how to react to the scene playing out in front of her. Camilla had told her that to forgive someone else you needed to forgive yourself first, then try to understand what it was that made that person behave the way they did towards you. She had told her to question their motives and ask herself what it is they are afraid of. Leaning forward now, she gently pulled Joshua's hands away from his face and asked him, 'What is it you want me to say to you, Joshua?'

Joshua looked up at Emma, his eyes filled with unmistakable anguish.

She continued, 'That I forgive you for all the hurt you caused me? That your behaviour towards me and your daughter was acceptable?' Emma's beautiful green eyes searched his for the answer. Joshua held her gaze for a moment too long. Memories from the past threatened to undo him. How he would have loved to tell her everything, the dark secrets he'd buried. Perhaps then she might understand and forgive him. Her eyes, so strong now, shone with such hope for a new future; he knew he had no right to burden her further.

'You need say nothing, Emma. It's me that needs to say so much, but I don't know how to start.'

Never had Emma seen Joshua lost for words, and as she watched the man responsible for so much of her past pain struggling with his emotions, she knew she'd finally let him go. What she saw sitting in front of her now was just a man – a flawed man – and as she saw him for what he was, she began to understand.

'How about we start with Amelia,' she suggested. 'It's obvious you love her and want to spend time with her.'

'Oh, I do. I really do,' Joshua said, a smile appearing again on his gaunt face. 'She is the most important thing in my life, Emma,' he added more quietly. 'She is *now* the most important person in my life.'

'Now?' asked Emma, registering his remark. 'What about Annette?'

'Annette and I have separated ...' There was a pause as

Joshua shuffled uncomfortably in his seat. 'You may hear some unpleasant rumours from the City regarding illegal dealings, and I could be implicated together with Annette and a number of others. An internal investigation is already being carried out. But it's important you know that I was not involved in or even aware of these dealings.'

'Was Annette?'

'It appears so. Others too. Unfortunately, my reputation has been tarnished through association, so I have resigned my position within the company. There's a can of worms about to be opened and some may well stick to me. Until the investigations are completed I will need to keep a low profile.'

'What will you do?'

'Clear my name and take some time out to re-evaluate my life. I'm going to be working in a soup kitchen in Reading,' he told her.

Joshua had already agreed to spend time with his brother working for a local charity. 'It will give you a chance to see real people surviving against adversity, Joshua,' Michael had told him. 'It might make you feel less sorry for yourself.'

Emma looked hard at Joshua. 'A soup kitchen?' she asked incredulously.

'Yes. I'm looking forward to it in an obscure way. Nothing like other people's problems to take your mind off your own!'

Emma reached out and gently touched his hand. 'I'm sorry it's all come to this,' she told him.

'Don't be. I deserve it. Too busy chasing the wrong things. But regarding Amelia, I'm now back in my London flat, which you know has only one bedroom. I'm willing to sleep on the sofa if necessary. Can we come to some arrangement so I can still see her on my days off?'

'How about we ask Amelia what she wants. I know she loves spending time with you and I'm happy with that. I've always encouraged it. That's why I still can't understand why you threatened to take her away from me.' Emma shook her head, frowning in disbelief.

'Oh Emma, I'm so sorry. I got it all wrong. I know that now. You have no idea how sorry I am for everything. I've treated you both so badly and neither of you deserved it.'

'No we didn't,' she replied, her eyes flashing for a moment in defiance. Joshua lowered his head but not before Emma had glimpsed something deeper behind his eyes. 'But that was back then, and this is now,' she said. 'If you really mean what you're saying, we need to work this out for the sake of our daughter.'

'Thank you,' was all Joshua could manage as he hastily cleared his throat.

'No more lawyers, then?' she asked, her head on one side looking closely at Joshua.

'No more lawyers.'

'No more claims that I'm an unfit mother?'

Joshua, crushed, shook his head. 'I know, I know, it all got out of hand, including that business with Simon. Are you serious about him?'

'Very.'

'I'm pleased, he seems nice. What about you? Do they know what caused your blackouts?'

Like Joshua, Emma had secrets, secrets she chose to keep from him.

'Stress and overtiredness,' Emma replied, oversimplifying the answer. 'I'm fine now.'

'My behaviour towards you didn't help, did it?' asked Joshua.

'No – it didn't.'

There was an awkward silence.

'Can we start again?' he asked.

Emma looked over at the broken man in front of her and nodded, then calmly poured the tea.

Back at the cottage, a more relaxed Emma told Simon and Gabby about the conversation she'd had with Joshua.

'It sounds as if his accident may have shaken some sense into him,' Gabby suggested. 'Pity it didn't happen earlier.'

Simon smiled wisely, 'I know it sounds harsh, but it helps to remember that everything that happens in life, good or bad, has its purpose.'

'I'm just glad we can now talk to one another like rational human beings. Strange, but I still can't shake off the feeling that he was going to tell me something more but changed his mind,' Emma said looking at Simon.

Joshua rang his brother as soon as he got back to London. Michael could tell from his voice that the meeting had gone well.

'She's happy for me to see Amelia,' Joshua told him. 'Despite what I've done, she's happy for me to see Amelia.'

Michael was relieved. 'Good – I knew you'd both work it out. See, a little faith does wonders.'

'We talked, Michael – really talked for the first time.'

'That's a good start.'

'But I couldn't tell her about … what happened.'

'Perhaps not the time or place. You'll get there one day, though. It will help her understand a lot, Joshua.'

'I know. I'm still coming to terms with it all myself. Such a sad mess.'

'As I told you, I'm a good sponge for mopping up.'

'I know. Oh, and thanks for the photo, by the way. Nice surprise. Found it in the post when I got back.'

'I thought you'd like to have it.'

Joshua's finger gently traced the image of his mother standing within a small group in the sun against a backdrop of blue sky, outside the front door of an old period house.

'I'll bring Amelia down to see you guys one weekend.'

'We'd love that.'

Ending the call, Joshua took the precious photograph over to his desk and reread the inscription on the reverse: 'Pepper Hill Farmhouse – the happiest place on earth.' Joshua took one more look at the group captured in the sunshine and then tucked the picture under the small white feather in his desk jotter.

Chapter 27

Joshua bought a small, two-bedroom house in Sussex with the money he made from the sale of his penthouse flat. Having seen and approved of the property, Emma agreed that Joshua could have access to Amelia one weekend a month and on individual days or holidays at her discretion.

In September, Amelia returned to her local nursery school, giving Emma time during the day to catch up on her design work. Simon now divided his working and private life between his home and the cottage. This happy and effortless arrangement worked seamlessly, allowing everyone time and space to themselves. Simon began to share the responsibilities of cooking when Emma was tied up and even helped with the nursery school drop-off. On the weekends that Amelia stayed with Joshua, Simon and Emma would take full advantage of her absence, eating out, lying in late and falling into bed whenever they wanted.

Joshua too had become an accepted visitor to the cottage, and on the days and weekends he had Amelia, he would bring her home early and join them all for dinner. It was as if a page had been turned in everyone's lives, enabling them to read one another differently and allowing a close and special friendship to develop between Emma and Joshua. For Simon, Joshua's presence had never been an issue; he enjoyed the male interaction, especially at the dinner table when Gabby and Emma got together. In the beginning Gabby had been the most difficult to convince, but even she found she was warming to the 'new Joshua'.

Emma could no longer pretend her body shape wasn't changing. She purchased two predictor tests from a chemist out of town and she and Gabby huddled like two conspirators in the upstairs toilet.

'Well?' Emma asked, unable to look herself.

'Definitely!'

'Definitely yes or definitely no?'

'Yes.'

'Oh my God! Are you sure?' Emma grabbed the stick from Gabby's hands.

'Shall I do the other one to make sure? It could be faulty.'

Gabby raised one eyebrow and looked at her flustered friend. 'It's not faulty, Em. It's brand new.'

Ripping off the cellophane, Emma opened the second test nonetheless. 'Let's just make sure.'

So they did. And the result came back the same.

'And you're sure?' an excited Simon asked. 'A playmate for Amelia?'

'Yes, I did two tests this morning. It seems we are having a baby, Simon Leighton. How do you feel?'

'Overwhelmed. And very happy. Any idea of when?'

'No, we'll have to leave that to the doctor to establish.'

According to its size, baby Leighton had been conceived around the time of their trip to Simon's parents.

'It was obviously our passionate encounter on the grass,' Simon told Emma.

'Don't admit that to my father,' she laughed as he pulled her closer.

'Have you told anyone else?' Simon asked, stroking the top of her head.

'Only Gabs knows.'

'Good, because I want to keep this little secret between us, for a while longer, if you'll let me.'

Emma looked up at him and nodded. Her life at that moment was pure happiness.

That weekend, Simon returned to the cottage to find Emma sorting the washing in the conservatory.

'You're back early. I didn't expect you until later.' She hastily switched off the iron and placed the pile of freshly pressed clothes into the washing basket.

'Here, I'll carry that for you. Do you want it upstairs?' Simon asked.

'Please. Oh, hold on, there's a rogue sock.' Emma bent to pick it up, and dropped it with its partner onto the ironed clothes. As she did so, she noticed a small, dark blue box among the washing. 'Wait. What's that?' she asked.

Simon chuckled and lifted the washing up into the air. 'What's what?' he teased.

'The box, the blue box,' Emma giggled as she held onto one side of the washing basket and pulled it towards her like an inquisitive child.

Simon lowered it back down onto the table, allowing Emma to retrieve the box and open it. She took a deep breath. Inside was nestled a perfect emerald-cut diamond, flanked on each side by four brilliant-cut diamonds, set in a white platinum band. It shone like a square of shattered sunlight. The tears in Emma's eyes shone brighter than the gems.

'It's beautiful, isn't it?' asked Simon 'Dazzling, complicated, perfect and reflects the light, just like you. Marry me, Emma?'

Her answering smile and kiss said it all.

Emma wandered around the cottage in a state of contentment, unconsciously twisting the ring on her left hand from time to time. The sound of the phone made her jump.

'Hello Emma, has Simon left for the day?' asked a familiar voice.

'Yes, just a few moments ago, Camilla. Did you want to speak to him?'

'No, actually I wanted to talk to you.'

Both sets of parents had been delighted at the news of the engagement, and now Emma waited, expecting the inevitable awkward questions regarding venues and dates.

'I just wanted to tell you how happy Angus and I are with your news. We can't think of a more perfect woman for our Simon.'

Emma felt her eyes water. 'Thank you, Camilla.'

'I really believe you two were meant for each other. It's what I like to call "divine timing", both finding one another after periods of disappointment and hurt. This is your time together now. Enjoy it. Remember, forget the past, never compare and always appreciate what you've both been given.'

'Oh I will,' Emma answered, absentmindedly rubbing her stomach.

'I'm very proud of my son, Emma. He's not perfect, but he's a good man. Make the most of every day you have together – the good moments and the bad. They all bring lessons and will have been given to you for a purpose.'

'I'll try to remember that, Camilla.'

'I know you will. That's why you are so right for Simon. Oh, by the way, has Amelia mentioned Charlie of late?'

'No. Why do you ask?'

'No matter, just curiosity.'

Camilla had been intrigued by Charlie's abrupt departure on the weekend of their visit. Knowing how important he had been to Amelia, she had wondered why he suddenly left then.

'No, she's made no further mention of him. She relies on Simon now for answers to the trickier questions; that's after she's discussed matters with Thomas, of course!'

'Isn't that the cat?' Camilla asked.

'Yes, and a very special member of the household.'

Camilla laughed. 'Do send her our love. Tell her we think of her often.'

'I will,' promised Emma.

The following weeks flew by all too fast and the day of Simon and Emma's wedding arrived. Both sets of parents had accepted their invitations without comment, offering to assist where possible. In truth, behind closed doors they all shared their suspicions, each hoping they were correct.

As stipulated, the wedding was a small and personal affair. The civil ceremony was held in the local registry office in early December with Amelia as bridesmaid, and afterwards they all went back to the cottage for a reception lunch in the conservatory. Emma and Gabby had spent hours decorating to make it look like a winter wonderland. The huge green spruce tree that took centre stage trembled under the weight of hundreds of tiny silver and white crystal icicles. Twinkling white lights sparkled among its boughs, reflecting off the carefully positioned baubles and bouncing prisms of coloured lights onto the surrounding windows and walls. The chandelier, once the centrepiece because of its bohemian opulence and heavy white crystals, now paled into insignificance, while throughout the cottage the enchanting smell of white lilies mingled with that of the wood fire.

Emma wore a long, empire-line dress in a cream woollen crepe that skimmed the gentle swell of her stomach. A short, rust, embroidered jacket provided some colour. Amelia had insisted on wearing a ballet dress in silver and white netting with a seed-pearl crown perched on her head. Caroline had provided an angora wrap to keep her warm for the actual ceremony and she completed the outfit with her long, grey snow boots. To Simon, both girls looked beautiful; he felt he must be the luckiest man alive.

After the wedding celebrations, Emma's parents stayed on in the cottage to look after Amelia, giving the newlyweds a week away. They spent their short honeymoon in Tuscany, where Emma shopped for Italian maternity wear in an exclusive designer shop.

'Feels rather gauche to be shopping for maternity wear on my honeymoon,' she giggled.

'Not at all, I hear it's all the rage among the young nowadays. We'll remember it with pride when we are old and past it,' Simon told her.

'I'm still young, Simon, and I intend *never* to be past it.'

Emma was so enthralled by the style and materials of the Italian maternity wear that she bought up most of the shop.

'Are you going to wear all of these?' Simon asked her back at the hotel.

'You haven't needed to wear anything remotely stretchy so far.'

'I know, but I will eventually,' defended Emma. 'The truth is, I want to unpick the designs and look at the patterns. I have an idea for my next venture: an affordable maternity-wear line to complement Heart Seeds. I'm going to call it Bump-n-booty.'

'How about Fat-n-Sassy?' suggested Simon dodging the look Emma threw at him. 'Anyway, I thought you were designing a swimwear line?' he continued.

'That will have to wait,' replied Emma, patting her stomach. 'You can't get excited about something you can't wear.'

On their return home, Christmas was almost upon them. Amelia had finished pre-school and had painted a number of large and colourful masterpieces for her mother and Simon, which she insisted needed to be put up in the kitchen. One had been stuck on the fridge door, where it hung like a piece of rogue wallpaper. Painted in shades of greens and browns with flashes of red and yellow it resembled a military camouflage sheet.

'Do you think Amelia has any recollections of a past life involving jungle warfare?' asked Simon as he negotiated the oversized artwork to get himself a cold beer.

'Be careful, she may have been trained in hand-to-hand combat and still remember the moves. Best to just tell her it's wonderful.'

'Does that mean we'll get another?'

'Probably. You'll have to get used to this.'

'Can we persuade her to make them smaller in future?'

'Nope. She likes to be dramatic.'

'Like her mother,' he mumbled.

News of Emma's pregnancy had now been officially announced to the family, although most had already surmised it. It had been decided that the best plan for Christmas would be that both sets of parents, Gabby, and Emma's sister Helen join the new couple for Christmas Day and share the responsibility of the feast.

The conservatory was still decorated from the wedding

reception, so Emma only had the table to lay. Standing back, she admired her work. Each setting of silver cutlery had been polished until it sparkled, individual table gifts lay wrapped and labelled on the empty plates and the white napkins had been twisted to resemble white orchids, with a sprig of gold inserted to represent the stamens. Above them, green spruce boughs with white frosted berries were draped from one side of the conservatory to the other.

On Christmas Eve, an excited Amelia stood with her empty stocking in her hand and looked up at the tree with all its sparkling lights. 'So beautiful, Mummy. Can we always have it like this?'

On Christmas morning, as all the family and Gabby were opening gifts and milling around the cottage, there was a knock at the door.

'Father Christmas!' shrieked Amelia as Simon opened the front door. Joshua stood in the doorway, a tacky Santa Claus hat perched on his head and a collection of wrapped parcels in his arms. 'Daddy!'

'Hello, Amelia, Merry Christmas,' said Joshua, leaning down to kiss his daughter, who had wrapped herself around his legs and was smiling up at him. 'Merry Christmas, Simon. Sorry to barge in like this, but I'm on my way back to Reading and thought I'd drop Amelia's presents off en route. I hope you don't mind.'

'Not at all, come in, have a drink, you know most people here.'

Joshua followed Simon, with Amelia holding on tightly to his left hand, as Thomas bounced across their path wearing a collar of red tinsel.

'Hello, Thomas,' Joshua laughed, greeting the cat.

'Thomas has been looking for mouse pies,' Amelia proclaimed.

'Don't you mean mince pies?' Joshua asked.

'No. He doesn't like those.'

Any awkwardness for Joshua melted as soon as he saw Emma walk towards him with one of her beautiful smiles.

'Happy Christmas,' she announced and kissed him on the cheek.

'Thank you and a Happy Christmas to you. I've got a present for Amelia and a wedding present for you and Simon.'

'How kind,' Emma answered, taking the beautifully wrapped gift and placing it safely on the bureau.

As Simon poured Joshua a glass of mulled wine, Stephen and Caroline Stockwell watched with interest. Any misgivings began to evaporate as they witnessed the interchange between the two men, their daughter and granddaughter.

Joshua gave Amelia a pair of pale pink glitter shoes, a pink plastic magic wand and a set of fairy wings.

'Fairy shoes!' exclaimed Amelia putting them on her feet and standing on the settee.

'Not on the furniture,' said Emma as Amelia began to bounce.

Simon, acting quickly, swept Amelia up into the air, lifting her high above his head.

'I'm flying, Daddy. Look! My shoes are magic.'

'Time for me to fly too. I've got to go and see some people who don't have anywhere to stay this Christmas,' said Joshua.

'Why?' Amelia asked, as Simon deposited her back on the ground.

'Some of them don't have a home or family like you do.'

'Do they have presents?' a serious-looking Amelia wondered aloud, sparkling wand in her sticky hands.

'Not always. But this year they will. I've had a word with Father Christmas and he promised to make a rare and special trip tonight. I'm going now to make sure there's milk and cookies for the reindeer. Be good for Mummy and Simon, won't you?'

'Ok. Will you say hello to Rudolph for me?'

Squeezing his daughter tightly, Joshua laughed. 'I'll do one better. I'll give all his reindeer scrubbed carrots from you.'

Amelia clapped her hands and danced towards her mother.

'Bye Joshua – and thank you. Have a good Christmas,' Emma called out as he left.

Camilla looked out of the window and saw the lonely figure of a man wearing a Santa Claus hat walking back towards his car, shoulders hunched and head bent.

Chapter 28

The New Year came and went, winter surrendered to spring and by the end of April, Emma looked enormous and longed for the baby's birth. The size of her stomach now prevented her from climbing over the wooden stiles, so she walked those paths and fields that offered latch gates, drinking in the fresh smells of spring and talking privately to her bump. Emma had been told it was a boy, but as Simon wanted it to be a surprise she hugged that information to herself.

'You do realise that when you come out, I'm not going to be able to have these deep and meaningful conversations with you again. You'll be too busy getting on with your own life,' Emma told her son.

Simon loved every stage of Emma's pregnancy and the way her body changed. Seeing her returning from a walk across the fields one afternoon, her dark hair blowing across her face and the swell of her abdomen pushing against the thin fabric of her maternity dress, he took a number of photos and sent them to his mother. Camilla loved them and agreed to reproduce the image on canvas for them both as a gift. As she looked closely at one of the photos she noticed the interesting cloud formation behind Emma. Obscured slightly by her flowing hair was a shape in the clouds that resembled a ship.

'Ooh, how I long to see my feet again,' Emma moaned as Simon helped her into the bath one evening.

'Are you sure you wouldn't be better using the shower tonight?' he asked.

'No,' Emma groaned. 'My back aches and I need to relax; the water helps support my weight and the baby loves it.'

Simon laughed. 'Oh no. Not another water baby. What with you and Amelia, let's hope this is a boy or I'll never get into the bathroom.'

'Would you like a boy?' Emma prompted as she lay back onto the inflatable bath pillow, murmuring in pleasure.

'I don't mind, Emma. I'm just so thrilled to have found you and Amelia. The baby just makes it even more perfect.'

'Oh no,' gasped Emma clutching the side of the bath.

'What is it?' asked Simon, a look of concern on his face.

'I've dropped the soap.'

Simon laughed. 'I don't think I can get to it. There's not much room in this bath. You'll have to hurry up and have this baby. Any bigger and we'll have to hose you down outside.'

'Don't think there's much more stretch left in this body either,' she mused.

Emma went into labour that night. Their son was born at three-thirty in the afternoon of 7 May, and Emma wept as he was finally placed in her arms. His tiny body, his smell, the touch of his skin – all felt familiar. When he opened his eyes and gazed back at her, she trembled and held him closer, as if remembering him from a lifetime ago.

They had agreed on the name Rupert James, but as the baby lay in his small hospital cot, both Emma and Simon questioned their choice.

'He doesn't look like a Rupert,' Emma whispered, watching the way her son's eyelids flickered as he slept.

'I know,' answered Simon quietly. 'Nor a James. We'll have to rethink.'

When Amelia arrived to meet her baby brother, the question of a name resolved itself. As Simon lifted Amelia up to see her baby brother, they heard a soft sigh escape from her lips as she stretched her small hand out to touch him. As if aware of her presence, the baby stirred, and his bright blue eyes shone back at her.

'Hello, Charlie.'

Chapter 29

Emma brought Charlie back from the hospital wearing one of her favourite Heart Seeds designs. Hetty and Gabby arrived to welcome the 'new man' of the family into his home, both remarking on how gorgeous he looked in his outfit. Within minutes, however, Emma had to whisk him away to his bedroom for a complete change.

Amelia stood beside her mother and watched in disbelief. 'Yuck … it's everywhere.'

Emma laughed as she wiped Charlie's bottom and threw the wipes and dirty nappy into the plastic nappy sack Amelia had been clutching.

'Did I do that when I was a baby?' she asked earnestly, holding the bag as far away from her body as she could manage.

'I'm afraid so,' Emma replied, watching Amelia's face as she gingerly walked towards the bin to dispatch the offending package.

'Not nice,' she exclaimed, wiping her small hands on her pinafore dress and calling out for Simon.

'What's wrong?' he asked Amelia, who stood on the landing holding her nose.

'Charlie's done a stinker. Can I come down with you?'

Simon took a quick look into Charlie's bedroom to check on Emma and the baby before opening the stair gate, tossing Amelia over his shoulder and carrying her down.

Later that night, as Emma put Amelia to bed, Thomas jumped up onto her coverlet. Mewing and rubbing his face into the covers, he chased his tail for a number of circuits before collapsing down beside Amelia and purring with happiness.

'Thomas is smiling. Look.'

The cat lay on his back, displaying his white underbelly, while four ginger and white paws flopped contentedly in mid-air and his whiskers twitched above his wide, stretched mouth. He appeared to shake with happiness.

'Thomas's motor's running,' said Emma, stroking the cat. 'Are we leaving him here for a bit?'

'Yes please. He's very happy with me. We're happy Charlie's come back,' Amelia said. 'I told you he was coming back, didn't I?'

Emma looked down at her daughter's serious face. 'Yes, you did. Now it's bedtime – snuggle down.' She kissed Amelia goodnight, partially closed the bedroom door, allowing a gap for Thomas to leave, then paused for a moment on the landing. She thought back to that special weekend at Simon's family home, where she'd met Angus and Camilla for the first time, and smiled at the memory. That was when Amelia had chosen to let go of her Charlie. It was also, allegedly, when her son was conceived.

I wonder ... she thought, remembering Simon's passionate lovemaking in the grass. *Could it be ... but does it sound nonsensical? Who knows?* Descending the stairs, she made a mental note to speak to Camilla. If anyone could make the ridiculous sound probable, it would be her.

Charlie settled into the cottage with the minimum of fuss. Amelia fell happily into the role of older sister, protecting and fussing over her baby brother. On the days she went to pre-school, she drew or created gifts for Charlie, all of which had to be displayed around the cottage.

When Joshua arrived to collect Amelia for his weekend access, she proudly took him upstairs to meet her brother. Joshua had never been keen on small babies, and tiptoeing up to the cot, he expected to see just another newborn. The emotional punch that hit him was unexpected.

'Look – he's awake, Daddy.'

As Joshua looked into Charlie's blue eyes, he felt both weak and dizzy with delight. Strange emotions flooded through his body and he looked back at Emma questioningly.

He feels the connection too, she thought.

'Isn't he beautiful, Daddy?'

Amelia's voice tugged Joshua back to reality. He watched as she placed her small finger into the palm of Charlie's tiny hand.

'Look,' she whispered, as Charlie's pink fingers curled around hers. 'He knows it's me.'

Joshua reached down and picked up his daughter. 'He is very beautiful. He's a lucky boy to have a sister like you,' he told her, blowing a kiss into her warm neck in an attempt to anchor his spiralling emotions.

When he dropped Amelia back home that Sunday night, they invited him to join them for supper. Gabby had arrived earlier and was helping herself to wine in the kitchen. As Emma put Amelia to bed, the two men stretched out on the settee.

'Parenthood is exhausting,' Simon said with a wry grin.

'Yup. I'm beginning to find that out too,' replied Joshua. 'Does Amelia have an off button?' he asked.

Simon opened one eye to look at Joshua's reclining form. 'Not that I've ever found.'

The sound of Charlie on the baby monitor cut through the

relaxing silence. 'No rest for the wicked,' said Simon. 'This one's my feed.'

Emma wandered through to the sitting room to remind Simon, who stretched his agile frame and leaped towards the stairs. 'On my way. Express time.'

Emma warmed the milk while Simon changed Charlie's nappy and brought him back down to feed. 'Here, put your fingertip into his mouth,' Simon whispered, placing the blanket-wrapped baby into Joshua's arms. 'I know it's not the most hygienic thing to do, but it works for me – stalling procedure while the bottle cools. Only don't tell Emma. This feed's normally mine; gives Emma's breasts a rest and he's a hungry and impatient man.'

Charlie had stopped crying and raised his eyes to look up at Joshua. His tiny rosebud mouth pulled and sucked on the finger, an inquiring expression on his upturned face. Mesmerised by the trust in the baby's eyes, Joshua felt two fat tears collect in the corner of his eyes, the salty liquid distorting his image of the baby. For a moment, he felt he was looking at Charlie through a veil of water and instinctively drew him closer to his hammering heart.

When Simon asked Joshua if he'd like to feed Charlie, he unknowingly began the exorcism process for that tragic day in his past. As he watched Charlie feed, content and safe in his arms, Joshua felt the heavy chains of self-denial, self-blame and guilt drop away, link by link.

Later that night, in the warmth and safety of the cottage, Joshua finally told Emma, Simon and Gabby about his lost childhood and the death of his mother. There wasn't a dry eye in the house.

Chapter 30

Simon's property sold more quickly than expected, and although he put most of the contents into storage, the few essential things he did bring made the cottage feel small and cluttered. He and Emma danced around one another in a vain attempt to give each other space. His books spilled out of the overfilled bookcases and stood in precarious piles on the floor in the conservatory, which now served as their living room, playroom and a workplace for Emma. During the day it buzzed with the sound of sewing machines, children's television programmes and laughter, its large table now covered in swatches, tailor pins and patterns.

On the days when Amelia went to pre-school and Emma took Charlie out, Simon could write without interruption, but when the family were around, he lost his concentration. Their living and working arrangements quickly became impractical.

It was Emma who cracked first. 'Simon, we need to find somewhere bigger. I can't cope with all the mess,' she announced at breakfast one day as she crammed the washed frying pan into an already overcrowded drawer. 'Nothing is where it should be any more,' she groaned as she pulled a small pink doll's arm out of the sugar bowl.

'That's mine!' Amelia cried, grabbing the severed limb and using it to spread the butter on her toast.

'Amelia, put that in the sink now.'

Simon paused and looked up over his newspaper at his wife who was still dressed in her bright pink nightshirt, her hair hurriedly scraped back into a ponytail and a piece of toast clenched tightly between her teeth. She moved purposefully towards her daughter who surrendered the doll's arm.

'It's yucky, Mummy.'

Emma casually threw the plastic limb onto the pile of washing up with one hand and simultaneously grabbed the coffee percolator with the other. She filled up Simon's cup then wiped the crumbs off her chair and retrieved the flopping toast from between her teeth.

'How do you do all of that at the same time?' he asked with admiration.

Emma glared back at him and he hid behind his paper. Then, folding the top down an inch, he ventured a quick glance in her direction. 'By the way,' he said, 'you've got butter on your chin.'

Meanwhile, seemingly aware of the commotion, Thomas stealthily pushed the cat-flap open with his head. In his mouth he held an oversized grey pigeon.

'Thomas!' yelled Amelia, clambering down from her breakfast chair and crawling under the table towards the back door. 'Bird, Mummy … Thomas has a bird in his mouth!'

'Quick, Simon,' panicked Emma. 'Grab him before he gets upstairs.'

Now halfway through the cat-flap, Thomas realised his mistake. With his mouth full of bird, and with no way to back out, he punched his body through the small perspex flap, and, dodging Simon's arms, he dived under the table.

'He's here with me,' Amelia announced, now down on all fours and staring menacingly into Thomas's eyes. 'Thomas looks cross, Mummy, and the bird's eyes are blinking at me.'

'Oh no, Simon …' Emma cried. 'Do something. It must still be alive.'

With his reading glasses perched on top of his head, Simon dropped down to Amelia's level where he attempted, unsuccessfully, to negotiate the bird's release.

'Drop it, Thomas,' he tried again.

Thomas gave a muffled growl of indignation, his mouth full of heaving feathers.

'Oh, let me,' said an exasperated Emma, falling to her knees to join them under the table. Grabbing the loose fur behind Thomas's head, she forced him to open his jaws. There was a flurry of feathers and a violent flapping as the pigeon taxied across the kitchen floor before making an ungraceful flight onto the top of the fridge.

The sound of a baby's cry froze the group crouching under the table.

'Was that Charlie?' Emma whispered.

Three faces all looked towards the kitchen door. For a moment the crying stopped, and then it resumed as a high-pitched wail.

'Yup, that's Charlie,' announced Amelia, returning to her toast.

Emma rubbed her face with the dishcloth and wiped her fingers on it before playfully throwing it at Simon. 'Bird. Cat. Amelia. I'll sort your son out.'

'I know, I know,' he responded, taking off his glasses and gathering the scattered pages of his newspaper. He watched as Emma rushed out of the room and up the stairs. 'He's your son too,' he shouted after her.

'Don't I know it?' she called back. 'And this weekend we're looking for a larger home.'

Simon chuckled under his breath.

Just then, arriving unannounced amid the mayhem, Joshua

nervously peered through the open kitchen door. 'Hello?' he said. 'Knock, knock – is it safe to come in?'

Simon, now standing on a kitchen chair, a large flapping pigeon in his hands, smiled at the visitor.

'Joshua. Great, you can help me get this albatross back into the wild. I've been hunting him around the kitchen for hours.'

Amelia screamed with laughter. 'It's Thomas's pigeon, Daddy. Simon's just being silly.'

Joshua laughed at the chaos. Part of him ached with envy at the easy relationship between Emma, Simon and his daughter. Life with Annette would have never worked for Amelia. She needed this – this happy world of love and disorder –not designer bedrooms and boarding schools.

'Were you having Amelia today?' Simon asked as he launched the bird back into the open.

They all watched as the pigeon took flight, landing on the bough of a large oak tree in the adjoining field.

'No, I'm off to Reading today. Michael needs my help in the centre for the next few weeks. I was hoping I could have Amelia to stay with me when I get back though.'

'You'll have to check with Emma – she's the diary queen.'

'Can I swim in the paddling pool today?' asked Amelia, throwing the last of the feathers into the bin.

'Go find Mummy and clean your teeth first,' said Simon, picking a small feather from her dishevelled hair before she darted towards the stairs, shouting for her mother.

'I need my swimming costume,' she called.

Simon looked at Joshua with a meaningful expression. 'Life was very different a short while back.'

Outside in the garden, Charlie lay in his pram beneath the shade of the weeping willow tree. The blue and yellow paddling pool had been filled with fresh water, and Amelia, wearing a poppy red and black spotted bikini, was splashing around happily.

Emma still managed to find pockets of time to design clothes for both her labels, more aware now that practicality was as important as high fashion. Having recovered her figure after Charlie's birth, she was already mentally designing her swimwear range that included costumes for children. The prototype Amelia wore today in the paddling pool was one of Emma's few disasters. Based on the concept of a ladybird in flight, the gossamer straps that represented the wings had slipped under Amelia's armpits, and the costume was riding up between the cheeks of her tiny bottom. *Not a good look,* thought Emma as she gently removed the restricting garment.

'Not happy with it?' asked Simon knowingly, winking at Joshua as he passed him a beer.

'No. I think this particular ladybird swimsuit will never fly home,' she admitted. 'Talking of which, we're off for a drive tomorrow to see if we can find any suitable properties for sale locally.'

'It could be an interesting drive,' Simon quipped. 'We're looking for a bigger house, with enough space for all of us and the two businesses. Emma needs a warehouse now for her outfits,' he chuckled.

'Is it that bad?' Joshua asked, looking first at Emma and then Simon, whose nod spoke volumes.

'Our problem is we want to stay in the same area for schools and things and I've been spoiled with the cottage. I'm looking for something like this, but bigger,' explained Emma.

'I'm surprised you can't find anything like that around here?

There are farmhouses and cottages everywhere,' said Joshua.

'Yes, but with too much land, not for sale, or *not* in our price range,' explained Simon.

'Hetty thinks she knows of a property whose owner could be looking for a private sale,' said Emma, hacking at a large piece of cheese for Amelia. 'It's so frustrating. I know that what I'm searching for is out there, I just can't find it.'

'Yoo-hoo!' sang Hetty, right on cue, smiling at the group as she joined them in the garden.

Amelia danced her way out of her towel and ran towards Hetty. 'Hello, Auntie Hetty. Look at me – I'm a rudey-nudey!'

Hetty dropped down to her level with open arms.

'Amelia, you're still wet,' laughed Emma, chasing her with the damp towel.

Hetty's blue eyes sparkled with mirth as she took the towel from Emma and wiped Amelia's damp hair back from her face.

'Look at you. You look like last week's wet washing. You do remind me of someone, I just can't place who at the moment,' Hetty said, shaking her head as she wrapped up the giggling child.

'Emma thinks you might know of a property that would suit us?' Simon asked.

'Yes, I do. It's the old black and white farmhouse, behind Whitaker Copse. Wasn't sure whether it was available yet, but I've been given the go ahead now to tell you about it.'

'Whitaker Copse?' queried Simon, looking at Emma, who seemed equally baffled.

'Up towards the Horse and Hounds Pub,' Hetty told them. 'It's not easy to find – can't be seen from the road because of the copse. It's set back in the fields and surrounded by hedges.'

'Do you know the owner?' asked Simon.

'Oh, very well; and the property. It belonged to the Browne

family. My mother worked for them before and after the war. Sad family – both father and son were killed in the war. The surviving daughter, Beatrice, took to wearing breeches and riding boots the day she heard about their deaths. I can well remember her running around the farm in her chosen outfit. She grew from a striking girl into a handsome woman. Always wore her dark hair short and swept back from her face; but despite the haircut and her masculine clothing, there was no hiding the fact that Beatrice was a stunner. I always envied the way she looked. Of course, I was a lot younger than her ...' Hetty giggled. 'She could be seen riding around the estate on one of her mares; loved her horses, did Beatrice ... Back straight as a broom handle, no hat. Highly polished riding boots and a leather cane with a silver top. Never used a whip on her horses – famed for that.'

'Sounds like my sort of woman,' Simon said as he helped himself to a large pork pie.

'She ran the farm when her mother was alive and inherited it after her death. Strong woman was Beatrice; managed the estate as well as any man could. She would be out there in all weathers with her workers. Gave up a lot for that farm. We lived in one of the estate cottages back then, but that was eventually sold,' Hetty said wistfully. 'The farmhouse and its backfield are all that remain of the estate now.'

'How sad. Didn't Beatrice have her own family?' Emma asked.

'She never married. People used to suggest she wasn't interested in men, but that was probably because no man could get the better of her. She had a lot of men on the estate happily working for her though.

'She did adopt a young man in his early teens. Rumour said it was a relative from America, although she never confirmed that.

He was a good-looking young man: tall, slim set with tawny brown hair and rich brown eyes. His name was Peter Ballantyne-Browne and he used to call her Mother Bee. Bit of a gent, he was. "Peter Ballantyne-Browne at your service," he used to say with a trace of an American drawl. Anyway, he left the farm one day suddenly and was never seen again. Some suggest he went back off to America with someone he met at the farm; they used to take in paying guests for a time. Well, whatever happened to him, it broke Beatrice's heart.'

'That's terrible. How old was he when he left?' asked Emma.

'Must have been in his late twenties or early thirties. Always been a mystery around here, he was said to be the sole heir to Beatrice's estate. After he left, she continued to run the farm with help. Took in more paying guests and ran part of it as a riding school – that had been Peter's idea. She bred some Arab horses for a period too; she had some real beauties – magnificent beasts. That business was closed down a long, long time ago.

'Beatrice stayed in the farmhouse for most of her life. She had a housekeeper first, then a full-time carer. She eventually moved into a bungalow nearby and got her solicitors to manage the property.'

'Is the place empty?' asked Emma.

'Yes, the farmhouse is empty now; did have a live-in tenant for a while, but they left recently. There are a few pieces of furniture in there, but most of the good stuff has been sold off. The surrounding fields were bought by the local dairy farmer who uses them for cattle in the spring and summer. He keeps the fields cut and the hedges and ditches maintained. Mark and Sue Johnson look after the house and gardens for Beatrice at the moment. Mark's father and grandfather also used to work for her.'

'Loyalty still?' remarked Joshua, feeling a sense of admiration for the woman.

'Oh, Beatrice commanded respect. She didn't suffer fools gladly, but she was a fair master. And she still has her finger on the pulse. She wants to see the property sold to the right type of person. She's given strict instructions to her solicitors to handle it privately once the suitability of the purchaser has been established.'

'Oh dear – are we to be vetted, then?' asked Emma.

'It's all right, I gave her a rundown on you both. She was *very* interested in hearing about you.'

'Do you think the farmhouse would be suitable for us?' asked Emma.

'Oh yes, perfect.'

'So when could we go and have a look?' asked Emma.

'It's empty, so you can see it any time. I'll just need to let Mark Johnson know when you're coming and get some keys for the main property and the outbuildings.'

'Outbuildings! Oh Simon, it sounds perfect. Perhaps we could see it today?'

Simon looked at Emma's flushed face and bright eyes and grimaced. 'This could be a very expensive weekend. I've got to meet my agent this afternoon, but I could join you later. Why doesn't Joshua go with you? That's if he's free today?'

'I'm free all day, en route to Michael's later this evening.'

Emma clapped her hands. 'Perfect!'

'Does it need a lot of work?' asked Simon, a twitching eyebrow betraying his apprehension.

Hetty smiled wistfully. 'I haven't been there for years. It's "sound", according to Mark, but needs updating throughout. The gardens are a bit overgrown and the flower beds long gone, but the grass is cut and the trees pruned in the winter. They still get a lot of apples off the ones in the orchard. Think most get thrown away, sadly. Beatrice used to have an apple press and made cider – potent stuff and a bit cloudy, but very easy to drink. She would hand it out to the workers and their families.'

'Maybe we should look at the idea of making cider,' suggested Emma.

Simon raised an eyebrow in her direction. 'Keep her calm, Joshua, won't you?'

'What's the property called?' Emma asked.

'Pepper Hill Farmhouse,' replied Hetty.

Hearing this, Joshua lowered the can of beer from his mouth. The liquid suddenly tasted bitter.

Chapter 31

They drove over to the farmhouse separately. Emma drove ahead of Joshua, her car bursting with pushchairs, car seats and sticky children.

As he passed the familiar landmarks and hedgerows, Joshua frowned in thought. 'Pepper Hill Farmhouse' was written on the back of that precious photograph, now tucked into his desk jotter. The photo, the worse for wear, was of two women and two small boys. According to Michael, one of the women was their mother when she was in her mid-twenties. Pretty and smiling, in a floral summer dress, Claire Hart held the hand of her son Michael, while Joshua held tightly to the hem of her dress and scowled at the camera. A tall woman with short dark hair stood behind his mother, one hand resting on her shoulder, the other on Michael's. There was a sense of natural ease between the women, as if they were close friends. Michael had told Joshua that the photo was taken on one of their summer holidays. Joshua's eyes pricked as he recalled the image of his beautiful mother. *I'm going to see if this is the place that made you smile, Mum. I need to know if this Pepper Hill Farmhouse is the place you called 'the happiest place on earth'.* Just then, a squawk from a hedgerow brought him rudely back to the present, and turning the steering wheel, he just avoided a road-running pheasant.

They found the farmhouse as Hetty described, tucked up a long track through surrounding fields and sheltered by a copse. A picturesque building with a slate grey roof, whitewashed brickwork and seams of dark weathered oak, it sat proudly on top of the rise. Steep, crumbling stone steps led up to its terrace and forgotten flower beds, and sheltered by a twisted rose- and clematis-wrapped porch stood a solid dark oak door. Chunks of loose stone and crumbling plaster lay against the skirt of the building, and a network of spiders' webs competed with the climbing ivy roots. 'I'm waiting …' it seemed to call.

Emma had driven along the main connecting road on numerous occasions, unaware of the farmhouse's existence. She now scanned the surrounding garden, where despite the more recent neglect, she could still trace the owner's horticultural designs: the overspilling bushes of Michaelmas daisies, the woody lavenders and towering lupines marking the once thriving flower beds.

With the keys to the house and outbuildings firmly in her hands, Emma breathed in the afternoon air. 'What a beautiful place!' she exhaled. 'A hidden treasure.'

Joshua said nothing, aware of the fast thumping in his chest as he silently compared the house in front of him to the image in his jotter.

'Think of all the lives that must have lived, loved and died here,' Emma continued. 'I know it sounds strange, but it feels as if the house has been expecting us.'

A distant memory whispered faintly to Joshua as ghostly fingers beckoned to him, wrapping themselves around his heart and filling him with a sense at once of wholeness and sadness. Clearing his throat, he followed Emma away from the front door as Amelia tugged at his hand.

'Can't we go in?' she asked, her eyes wide with anticipation.

'In a moment, sweetie,' said Emma. 'We're going to do the outside buildings first, then we'll have a look inside the house when it's time for Charlie to have a feed. Are you ok with that, Joshua? Not sure I want to feed him in the back barn.'

Needing time to manage his own reactions, Joshua nodded and pulled Amelia towards him. 'Ok with us,' he said, inclining his head and nodding towards his daughter.

'Ok with me, Mummy,' she mimicked.

At the far end of the garden stood a large, dark barn, and to the rear of that, adjoining a smaller field, was a converted stable block. As they wandered around the overgrown grass, a flock of Canada geese flew noisily over the farmhouse and landed in one of the surrounding fields. Their combined call startled Charlie and made Amelia jump.

Emma watched the birds goose-stepping noisily across the grass, like a small grey army, marching in formation. 'Just silly, noisy geese,' she said, reassuring her children.

Strapped securely in his papoose across Emma's chest, Charlie closed his eyes as Emma patted his bottom, pulling him closer. Holding tightly to Amelia's hand, she walked the overgrown garden, ducking under the bough of an old split cherry tree. 'Well the garden's not bad, considering. Would love to have seen what it looked like before.'

Most of the flower beds had been left to their own devices and were now home to an assortment of weeds and wild flowers. Although the grass had been cut recently, the ground beneath their feet was uneven in places where tunnelling moles had disturbed the surface. Emma moved Amelia away from a large clump of knotted grass, where she had stopped to poke at a fat orange and beige slug.

'Look at all the cowslips in that field,' Emma pointed to the paddock as she brushed past an overgrown and woody lavender bush. 'A sea of yellow.'

Mum's favourite flower, thought Joshua.

Stopping her slug patrol, Amelia picked a fragrant lavender

head and held it to her nose. 'Smells like Auntie Hetty,' she told them.

Lost in thought, Joshua said very little as he followed Emma towards the stable block. Crossing the overgrown garden, he began to feel his melancholy lift.

'This garden has such an amazing smell,' said Emma, stopping to sniff the air. 'It smells … energised.'

Amelia lifted her face up to the sky and took in a noisy snort through her nose.

'You try, Daddy. Sniff like this.' Amelia made a noise like a piglet then dissolved into contagious laughter.

'Shush, you two,' giggled Emma. 'You'll wake Charlie up.'

Joshua looked down at Charlie's sleeping face pushed up against Emma's body. 'Not a chance,' he grinned, shaking his head.

Fumbling with the keys, Emma opened the door to the stable block and gasped. Cleverly converted, with large arched windows to the rear offering views of the neighbouring countryside, it boasted two main rooms with high ceilings and wooden floors, a small kitchenette and a tiny bathroom. Emma listened; there was no noise apart from the sound of Amelia's boots scraping on the wooden floors.

'Stand quietly, darling,' said Emma, her finger on her lips. Amelia remained still momentarily, one leg lifted out in front of her and a wide smile stretched across her face.

'It's so beautiful and quiet in here; perfect for writing. Look at the views. Simon will love it.'

The noise of small boots on the wood floor started again.

'Well, it *was* quiet,' Joshua quipped.

'I'm doing the goose walk, Mummy. Look.'

'Very clever, now don't kick the walls,' Emma said, measuring them with her arms and imagining the positioning of Simon's desk and bookshelves. 'Do you think Beatrice used this for paying guests?'

'Maybe, or perhaps her "son" Peter lived here?'

Wandering around the dusty rooms, Joshua ran his hands down the old beam supports, pausing as his fingers felt shapes cut into the wood. 'Think someone's engraved their initials here.'

Emma moved closer to see. 'Where? Oh yes, looks like a shaky "P". What do you think? P for Peter?'

Joshua ran his fingers over the engraving. 'Don't think it's just a "P". There's a straight line here and a curve under the blunt cut. Could be two initials laid one on top of the other. Sort of thing we used to do as children.'

'What? Cut initials into wood?'

'Wood, walls, trees, desks. It's a boy thing, I suppose. Territory marking.'

'Well, my Charlie's not going to be encouraged to engrave his initials on the woodwork,' Emma said, her eyes wide in mock horror. 'Perhaps the initials belonged to lovers?' she went on to suggest. 'Peter and a local farm girl. Or one of the guests staying here.'

'We'll never know,' said Joshua.

'Sad to think he just disappeared like he did. Perhaps there was a happy and romantic twist to the tale.'

'Let's hope it wasn't a sad love,' Joshua added, a small frown above his dark eyes.

Emma paused, looking at Joshua for an explanation.

'Love has two sides: great happiness and great sadness,' he told her.

'Not always sadness, surely?' said Emma.

Joshua's smile was tinged with melancholy. 'We all lose

someone we've loved – one day in our lives.'

Emma stood silently, her arms protectively around Charlie's small frame. Having learned how Joshua's mother died, there was no suitable answer. Emma's eyes lowered with a mixture of sadness and embarrassment.

'Come on, let's go and explore the barn next,' said Joshua, his voice filled with forced joviality.

'Ooh, yes … let's,' cooed Amelia.

'I think Simon will love this stable block. All he needs is a pen knife,' said Joshua, laughing as he scooped Amelia under one arm and marched towards the barn.

Once lovingly painted with black creosote, the barn now looked patchy and brown in areas. Numerous black lacquer-painted bolts and stainless steel padlocks secured the doors.

'Think opening this might be your job,' said Emma, fumbling with all the keys.

Joshua took over and opened the doors. The old barn was in good condition inside. The concrete floor was dry, albeit covered in a layer of dust. Above, in the high rafters, the spiders had made ambitious homes, their fine threads spun into a grey thatching that stretched like a circus marquee from beam to beam.

Emma shivered. 'Glad I'm not feeding Charlie in here.'

'Spiders like the dry and this place is evidently dry,' said Joshua, looking up. 'They're up too high to worry you down here.'

'Well, I'm very glad they like the dry. Let's hope they don't decide to drop in to meet us.'

'Is it a museum, Mummy?' Amelia asked, looking around in amazement while pointing to the piles of ornate picture frames leaning against one of the timber walls, their images obscured by sacking.

'A defunct Tate Gallery. Or Beatrice's family gallery,' Joshua suggested, walking over and lifting a corner of hessian. 'Look at this one.' Joshua carefully moved the framed portrait from its shadowy resting place. '*Woman with Horse*,' he announced and then paused as he looked closely.

'Beatrice?' questioned Emma.

Joshua stared reverentially at the portrait of a tall, dark-haired woman beside a magnificent white horse. Wiping the dust from the glass, he stared at the woman in the picture. Her short, dark hair framed her face like a perfect cloche hat, emphasising her high cheekbones and large, dark eyes. Wearing light-coloured jodhpurs, short black riding boots and a crisp white shirt, she rested one arm against her horse, unbridled and groomed to perfection, while her other hand, wearing a gold signet ring on a long, slender finger, reached over to gently stroke her mare's muzzle. Joshua peered closer still.

'Do you think that's Beatrice?' asked Emma again.

Joshua remained silent. The woman in the painting he held in his hands was the same woman who stood behind his mother in that summer holiday photo. 'I don't know,' he said, eventually, 'but if this is Beatrice, then I've been here as a child.'

'To Pepper Hill Farmhouse?'

'Yes.'

Emma looked at Joshua in disbelief. 'You never said you knew the place, let alone spent time here.'

'I know. I wasn't sure until just now.' Joshua went on to explain to Emma about the photo Michael had given him.

'Oh Joshua, how lovely if it's true. How old would you have been?'

'Michael thinks I was about two or three in the photo; he was older than me and remembers cowslips in a field and a lady with a horse. If this picture is of Beatrice, then we *did* come here in the past. Happier days, I think.'

Emma looked at Joshua, who gently returned the picture to its place against the wall. *I hope so,* she thought.

'I wonder what happens to all of these things after the sale?' Joshua asked, walking around the ancient mechanical farm equipment. 'She obviously didn't want to part with any of these old faithfuls.'

'Maybe they sold the good stuff,' suggested Emma. 'That lawnmower and tractor look as if they've come out of the Ark.'

Joshua touched the Suffolk Punch's dented grass catcher, his hand tracing the scratched and damaged logo against the original green painted metal, now pockmarked with rust. 'Hasn't been used in a long while, probably still works though,' he answered.

Emma coughed as she lifted a dustsheet. 'There are a lot of wooden crates and containers left in here. They're piled high, back there.'

'If there are valuables in them, will they be yours at point of sale or the estate's?'

'Joshua … how could you?'

'Well, there's sentimental and auctionable,' he added.

'And rubbish. Look at this,' said Emma, picking up an old metal watering can with a broken handle and no spout. 'Why keep this?'

Joshua laughed. 'That's a sentimental one!'

'Look, Mummy.' Amelia had crawled into the pile of crates and retrieved an old hat box. Dirty grey in colour, it had obviously been lying in the back of the barn for many years. Struggling with its awkward shape, Amelia half pushed, half dragged it onto the barn floor, tripping over its carrying cord and knocking off its top.

'Oops!' cried Joshua, rushing to Amelia's assistance.

Emma watched and laughed as Joshua untangled Amelia's foot from the cord. As she laughed, her eye caught the greenish shimmer of dark feathers poking out from under the tissue paper inside the hat box.

'Ooh,' said Amelia, ripping away the wrapping and cramming the exotic hat on her head. 'Look at me!'

It was as if time stood still. Emma remained frozen, watching as Amelia twirled to imaginary music, the colours of the raven feathers changing in the dappled light as she danced.

'Emma,' Joshua called. 'Are you all right?'

The colour in Emma's face had drained. The image she saw was no longer of her daughter; it was of a woman walking on the deck of a ship, her gloved hand tucked into the arm of a man, the sea breeze fluttering through the feathers on her hat. In the distance she could hear someone calling.

'Mummy ... Mummy!'

Emma snapped back to see the worried faces of both Amelia and Joshua looking at her. 'Creepy hat, darling,' she said, with a forced laugh, shaking her head and stamping her feet in the dust. *Grounding,* she told herself. *Ground yourself, and quickly.*

Amelia laughed at her mother's shuffling on the dusty floor and sneezed.

'Bless you,' said Joshua, removing the hat from Amelia's head and retrieving its box. 'The label on here is interesting – it's from a hatter in New York. I wonder who wore this, it looks like it could be Edwardian?' Joshua turned the hat around in his hands, admiring its design. 'It's quite beautiful in a grotesque way, isn't it?' he said, passing the hat in Emma's direction. 'See how the hues of green and blue on the feathers change depending on the light.'

Emma's legs trembled as she felt the barn floor tilt and drop away. Flustered, she pulled Charlie closer and began her stamping again. 'I think Charlie must be due a feed. Can you look after Amelia?' she hastily suggested.

'Sure,' answered a bemused Joshua. 'We'll meet you up at the house in a while.'

Left to her own devices, Amelia had climbed onto a pile of sacking and sat cross-legged, patiently surveying the half-uncovered hoard of objects. Unable to resist, Joshua took a photo of her sitting there.

'Did you know the lady with the horse, Daddy?' she asked.

'Yes, I think so … a long time ago when I was about your age. I think her name was Beatrice and she used to live here.'

'Then she needs to come back into the house,' said Amelia with the innocent conviction of a child. Joshua looked down at his small daughter and smiled.

'I think she'd like that. Shall we take her, then?'

'Yes.'

The two of them walked back towards the farmhouse together, the portrait of Beatrice and her beloved horse carefully wrapped in its sacking, tucked under Joshua's arm.

Emma pulled the front door open before Joshua could knock.

'There you both are,' she said, putting her finger to her mouth and gesturing at Charlie's pushchair in the hallway.

'All fed and watered?' Joshua whispered, tiptoeing onto the hallway floor.

'Yes and sleeping. Amelia, tiptoes please.'

'That's *all* Charlie ever does now,' whispered Amelia, raising her palms dramatically to the ceiling. 'I can't wait till he's talking again.'

'Again?' Joshua looked at Emma for clarification.

Emma chuckled quietly. 'She's convinced our Charlie is the return of her "invisible" Charlie. Only Charlie number two is not so ... chatty.'

'Ah,' he nodded, pretending to understand.

Standing on the wooden parquet floor, which was scratched and dulled by years of wear, Joshua gazed around the entrance hall. The bare walls, painted white at one time, were now faded to a shade of creamy yellow. He noted the line of picture hooks alongside the carpeted staircase and the brighter shades of paint-work that marked where pictures had previously hung.

'That large space there at the top of the stairs must be where Beatrice's portrait hung,' Joshua said, pointing to the top of the first flight. 'She could have seen everyone arriving and leaving from that position.'

Joshua ventured up the staircase, carrying his precious wrapped cargo.

'We're putting Beatrice back in her home, Mummy.'

Joshua paused, looking back at Emma. 'Do you mind? It seems wrong to just leave her in the barn.'

'Joshua. You are an old softy. Let's hope it is Beatrice and not some random relative she didn't like.'

Joshua carefully hung the picture back in its place on the wall and rejoined Emma and Amelia at the foot of the stairs. 'No, it's her,' he said. 'And she fits perfectly there. That's her place.'

'Look, she's happy now,' Amelia said, clapping her hands.

And Beatrice did indeed appear to be smiling down onto the assembled group.

'Can we see something else now?' asked an impatient Amelia, dodging Charlie's pushchair and running into the kitchen.

Amelia's excited cries echoed around the empty kitchen as she pounced upon a large house spider in the base of the deep porcelain sink. Joshua watched with interest as she persuaded the leggy creature to leave via the open plughole.

'What is it with Amelia and her need to fight all small wild-life?' Joshua asked.

'Oh, she's not fighting them, she's "gently" removing them.'

'With a stick?' asked Joshua dubiously, eyebrows raised.

The kitchen boasted a large cast-iron Aga which had been set into the fireplace recess. Emma opened its door. There was a clunking and scraping of metal. Wiping her hands together, she shook off the sticky burned remains.

'Do you think it still works?' Joshua asked, as she crouched down and looked inside.

'Needs a good clean, whatever. Think of all the porridge that must have been cooked on here,' she said, running her fingers over the dull metal top. 'And all the animals that must have nestled down beside its heat at night. Thomas would love this.'

Joshua looked sideways at Emma. 'Remember Simon's instructions: don't get carried away with romantic ideas.'

'You can talk. We've already put Beatrice and her horse back in the house because of you.'

Joshua smiled. 'Yes, a silly notion, I know. But Amelia and I felt it was appropriate.'

'On the subject of silly notions,' Emma replied with a mocking nod of her head, 'I don't know about you, but I think this farmhouse wants us to be here. Like I said before – it's as if it's been waiting for us to arrive.'

Joshua looked around the kitchen. A long scrubbed pine table with two rows of old church pews had been left to one side of the room, and he ran his hand wistfully over its surface. There was something so tantalisingly familiar about the place. He too felt an emotion he couldn't explain. 'Not sure Simon will go for that one as a reason to buy,' he said eventually. 'But I like the sentiment.'

'Do you still think this is the house your mother brought you and Michael to?'

'Yes. I can't be sure, but it feels like it is.' Just then, a text message on Joshua's mobile bleeped. 'It's Michael. He's reminded me about the bedroom high up in the house with dark beams and a sloping ceiling. According to him, that's where we slept. I do have a vague memory of a room like that.'

'Was it just you boys and your mother who visited here?'

'You mean, did my father come too?'

Emma winced, wishing she hadn't asked the question.

'I don't remember him with us. He's not in the photo. He may have taken it, of course, or ...'

'Or what?' asked Emma.

Joshua's mouth set straight. 'He could have been away on one of his trips.'

'What did he do?' Emma asked, aware that she knew nothing about Joshua's family background.

'He worked on cargo vessels at sea; or that's what they told us.'

'So he was away a lot?'

'Yes. Short trips mostly. But he always made sure he made up for lost time when he returned.' Joshua remembered the leather belt and buckle that crashed down on the back of his legs on the bad nights.

Leaving Charlie to sleep in the kitchen, they explored the downstairs.

'Needs some modernisation,' said Emma, tapping the walls. 'I could create one large kitchen and living area, with an informal dining area overlooking the garden terrace. Wouldn't that be perfect?' she said, twirling with excitement.

237

Joshua saw the look in her eyes. 'Remember what Simon said …'

Emma laughed and moved into the sitting room. 'This room's perfect. Love the fireplace. Nothing much to change in here. Oh look, it has a connecting door.' The door led into another smaller room with a large, central window. 'Light and private, this would make a perfect study. Some nice drapes and a large desk under the window …'

'Thought you were putting Simon in the stables,' Joshua said.

'Oh yes, but this would be for me,' replied Emma, pulling at the existing drapes, wary of spiders.

'Where's my room?' asked Amelia.

'Upstairs,' Joshua and Emma chorused.

They climbed the staircase to the next floor, acknowledging Beatrice and her white horse as they passed her.

'She's wearing a magnificent ring on her finger; rather masculine though. Looks like that could be a family crest,' Emma said.

Joshua examined the picture more closely. 'I think it's a phoenix.'

'The bird of resurrection,' said Emma, steering Amelia up the stairs.

'What's resurrection?' asked Amelia.

Emma and Joshua smiled at one another.

'Ask Simon. He's the best person to explain that one,' suggested Joshua.

'Ok,' she replied, satisfied with the answer.

'Ah, modernisation,' announced Joshua as he pushed open the bathroom door and saw the colour of the suite. 'Why is it always avocado?'

Emma sniggered. 'That was "classic chic" in the eighties,' she reminded him. Stepping over the beige carpeted floor she lifted back a grubby net curtain. 'Beautiful view from here,' she said.

'Don't estate agents get lower prices on the houses with avocado-coloured bathroom suites?' asked Joshua.

Emma laughed indulgently. 'Then it could work in my favour.'

There was a shriek of delight as Amelia burst into the room and sat down on the bidet.

'This is a funny toilet.'

'Oh, darling – that's not a loo. It's a bidet. Do you need to go?'

'No,' was the indignant reply.

Joshua stood in the doorway, his arms crossed.

'What's it for?' Amelia asked, standing up and fiddling with the taps.

Emma scooped her daughter away from the bidet. 'It's for washing bottoms,' she started, and before she could add anything else, Amelia had wriggled free to look for more bidets.

'No botty washer in here,' she shouted, finding an en-suite with a pale pink toilet and matching basin and bath. The wallpaper, lifting in places, had a flower design with repeating bunches of pink and mauve flowers. Following Amelia, Joshua found himself staring at the flower pattern on the wallpaper as snippets of disjointed memories drifted in and out of his head.

'Familiar?' Emma asked.

'Something's gelling.'

Amelia bent down to collect an old blue toothbrush from under the radiator, its scant bristles grey with accumulated dust and cobwebs.

'Mummy, look.'

'Not nice, darling. Put it back where you found it.'

There were four large bedrooms on that level, two with en-suite facilities while the others shared a good-sized bathroom with double windows overlooking the grounds to the back of the house.

Joshua stood beside Emma, making a mental calculation of the number of bidets they'd seen while smiling at the familiar colour of the bathroom suite. 'Still interested?' he asked, looking at Emma's beaming face.

'Oh yes, providing the price is right.'

'You could always run it as a bed and breakfast; I hear avocado bidets are all the rage.'

'Very funny,' Emma retorted.

Climbing up to the next level, Emma opened a door that led to a smaller bedroom in the eaves. A thick, central pillar in the middle of the floor supported an overhead oak beam that ran the width of the room and disappeared into the plasterwork of the sloping ceiling.

'Dark beams and a sloping ceiling. Familiar?'

It did feel familiar to Joshua. 'Looks so much smaller, but yes, it could have been the room Michael and I stayed in.' Joshua walked around the room. 'Perfect for small people,' he added. 'I'll take a photo and send it to Michael.'

On one wall there was a small Victorian fireplace painted gloss black with surrounding ornate tiles depicting thistles in shades of grey, green and mauve. Emma bent down to pick up a hatpin that had become lodged in a crack between the floorboards.

'What's that, Mummy?'

Emma turned the delicate pin around in her hands. It was light and about two inches in length, its head roughly the size of a large almond, smooth and black, set with a sparkling gem. 'It's a hatpin.'

'Why does a hat need a pin?'

'I think it must be old, darling. The ladies used these to keep their hats and veils attached to their heads.' The vision of Beatrice with her riding breeches and boots suddenly didn't fit the description she just gave to Amelia.

'Probably belonged to the lady who wore that bird hat,' suggested Joshua.

Emma shuddered and carefully placed the hatpin on the narrow shelf above the fire.

Disinterested, Amelia walked under the sweeping beam and around her mother, crouching to look up inside the chimney. 'It's blocked. How does Father Christmas get down it?'

'Your turn,' said Emma, looking at Joshua.

'He doesn't need to. He uses the main one in the sitting room.'

Emma smiled and nodded at Joshua's answer.

There was a small, painted door that opened into a deep recess lined with dusty shelves that had obviously been overlooked during the house clearance and still had a number of boxes and cartons tucked inside. Joshua shivered; there was a smell – part dust, part damp – and it evoked a momentary sense of sadness.

'The scent of the past and forgotten lives,' said Emma, pulling him back to the present. 'Would we be nosy if we looked at some of this stuff in here?'

Joshua watched as Emma crouched to see better. 'No, I don't think so. Someone will have to clear it out at some stage, if only to throw it away. I'm sure no one will mind,' he said, passing out a box.

'Phew, bit musty,' Emma remarked, lowering it to the floor.

'It's all yucky rubbish, Mummy,' Amelia declared.

''Tis a bit,' she replied looking at the contents.

Among the boxes they found tennis rackets, a bald teddy bear, a box of lead soldiers, numerous *Boy's Own* annuals and an assortment of riding boots, cricket pads and battered cigarette cards tied with rubber bands.

'Peter's things?' asked Emma.

'Or staying guests'?' said Joshua, examining a grey and red painted lead soldier.

There was another buzz from Joshua's mobile. 'It's Michael. He says he remembers playing with toy soldiers on the bedroom floor.'

'You'd better tell him we've found one of them,' said Emma.

The sound of a car hooting drew their attention away from the memorabilia.

'Must be Simon,' Emma said, answering her ringing phone. 'You're here! Isn't it the most incredible place you've ever seen? Just perfect ... needs some work, but oh, the possibilities,' Emma cooed down the phone.

'Thought that might be the case. Do I have to work nights?' Simon asked, good-humouredly.

'We're on our way down. Joshua has to leave shortly, so I'll finish the tour with you. It's definitely worth an offer, Simon. Just wait till you see it all. You'll love the stable block.'

'Stable block? How big is this place?'

'Just the right size,' Emma laughed. 'I'm about to check on Charlie, so I'll be in the kitchen.'

'No ghosts or spooks then?' asked Simon as he gingerly entered through the open door. There was a pause as Emma thought about telling him of her experience in the barn with the old hat. Then, deciding better of it, she launched into Joshua's latest revelations.

'So you've been here before?' Simon asked.

Joshua raised his eyebrows. 'Appears so. Now I need to fill in some gaps.'

'Filling in family gaps can be tricky,' said Simon with a smirk. 'Trickier still when the people are alive though; they fiercely guard their secrets.'

Joshua grimaced. 'I know. I've been guilty of that. Anyway,

I'm off to Reading now; hopefully Michael may remember more. Nice to think this is the place my mother loved so much.'

'You mean Amelia's grandmother loved so much,' Emma reminded them all.

'I'll walk you out to the car,' said Simon, smiling and shaking his head.

'Think she's already made up her mind,' warned Joshua.

'I knew that, as soon as I drove over the ridge.'

'What will you do?'

'Put in an offer, then leave the rest to the powers that be.'

'And these particular powers are?' asked Joshua, expecting a reference to some divine influence or other.

'The lawyers and the bank,' Simon replied.

'Ah, *those* deities,' said Joshua wryly.

'When are you getting your new wheels?' Simon asked as Joshua climbed back into the hire car.

'Next few weeks. Getting used to this one though – wondering if I really need another Mercedes. Might keep the new one for six months then trade down.'

'By the way,' Simon started, 'I read an article in the financial papers that implied Annette was under investigation? Does that affect you?'

'Yes and no. I'm cleared of any intentional involvement. However, my relationship with her makes any existing or future position within associated companies untenable.'

'Sorry. What's happened to her?'

'In hiding.'

'Any idea where?'

'According to her lawyers, she's somewhere in South America.'

'Is that lawyer speak for "You can't touch her now"?' asked Simon.

Joshua smirked. 'She's still legally under investigation and "on the run". She can't leave South America without someone arresting her. They've frozen her assets here in the UK. The authorities aren't stupid; they know she didn't act alone. That's why they interrogated my finances and role within the organisation. It's their belief she's protecting someone. As they can't get to her, they want the other person.'

'Do you know who it is?'

Joshua grinned knowingly. 'I can't possibly comment. I think the financial press have an inkling. The newspapers have a way of forcing the worms out of the cans. The question is, can this particular worm be prosecuted? I'm sickened by the lot of them; as long as I can close that chapter forever, I'll be happy.'

'You're being very understanding over all of this. She's run out on you, ruined your career and left you to face the music.'

'Funnily enough, it's the best thing ever to happen to me,' said Joshua. 'Taught me something about my life that I would have never known. I'm enjoying working with Michael, putting something back, instead of taking.'

Simon patted the roof of the car, thinking that Joshua looked more relaxed than he'd ever seen him. 'Thanks for looking after Emma and co.,' he said.

'My pleasure, always. The co. are pretty special.'

'I think so,' replied Simon.

'I don't talk about my accident, Simon, but by rights, I should have been killed. I've been given another chance – a chance to put things right. Not many people are given that opportunity. I'm not going to waste it.'

Simon looked into Joshua's eyes and saw the look of wounded honesty.

'Well, you're doing well, Joshua. I admire you. You're able to see Emma and Amelia without any malice towards me. A lot of lesser men wouldn't be able to do that.'

'A lot of lesser men wouldn't have made the mess I made of my life and relationships in the first place,' Joshua replied. 'I don't think Emma was really meant for me. You are a much better man for her, Simon. She looks happier now than I've ever known her to be. As for me, well I'm not sure I want anyone else now, except Amelia, of course. I'm a better person on my own.'

Simon shook his head as Joshua strapped his seatbelt and started the car.

'One day, Joshua, when you're least expecting it, you'll find that person who will finally make your life complete.'

Joshua smiled and gave Simon a dismissive wave as he drove off. Simon stood and watched the car disappear down the long drive.

One day, Joshua, thought Simon.

Chapter 32

Joshua sat in his brother's sitting room, his mother's biscuit box empty beside him, its contents sprawled out across the carpet. Among them was a stained envelope addressed to Claire Hart with a Surrey postmark. It contained loose photos.

'I found the tin in the house after she died. I've kept it as she left it. I just took out the photo of Mum at Pepper Hill Farmhouse because I remembered staying there and I liked the inscription on the back. The rest just stayed where they were.'

'Is this me as a baby?' asked Joshua, pulling out a photo of a group in the sun against a backdrop of fields, blue sky and a barn.

'I think so, what does it say on the back?'

'"My boys with Peter. Sunny days, Pepper Hill Farmhouse,"' Joshua read.

'So we must have visited the farm more than once, then,' said Joshua, looking at his brother. Michael nodded. Joshua looked down again at the photo in his hands; his mother looked relaxed and happy, gazing at the baby in her arms. Michael, who appeared to be scowling at the camera, stood beside a handsome young man with wavy light brown hair and a soft smile.

'And this one?' Joshua passed over a photo showing the same young man. Tall and slim, he was laughing into the camera and held out one of his arms as if reaching for someone. The words 'My love forever' had been written on the back.

'You're sure this isn't Dad when he was young?' asked Joshua, feeling they were uncovering something they would regret.

'No. He didn't look like that, even when he was young – too

slim and tall to be Dad. And the hair's wrong.'

Joshua picked up another photo and read the writing on the back again.

'So who is it?' Michael asked.

'Just a "P". Think that's the mysterious Peter again.'

'He seems to be in most of them,' remarked Michael.

'I know. Were there any other photos in the house when they cleared it out?' Joshua asked.

'No idea. Everything got removed and sold to pay for funeral costs.'

Joshua nodded sadly. 'And all that's left of her lifetime is this – a handful of pictures. She looks so happy in them though. Do you think she and Peter were more than friends?'

Michael nodded. 'I think that's possible.'

Joshua pored over the photos, looking at each one carefully. 'There's something else here, isn't there?' he asked, his dark blue eyes searching those of his brother, afraid of what he might hear.

'Yes.' Michael swallowed, his eyes dropping to the floor. 'I saw Dad in prison before he died.'

Joshua narrowed his eyes in disbelief.

'I couldn't tell you, I'm sorry. He told me things on that day that I didn't believe. Couldn't believe. I promised myself that if I never repeated them, they wouldn't be true.'

'What did he tell you?'

Michael shuffled uncomfortably on the sofa avoiding Joshua's interrogating eyes.

'What did he tell you?'

'Firstly, that you ... weren't his son.'

Joshua sucked in his breath.

'And secondly ... that he killed a man,' Michael struggled with the words.

'Who? When? And who was my father, then?'

'He didn't tell me his name. I didn't ask. He just said that the man was going to take us away from him.'

Joshua remained still, his mind battling with this latest revelation. 'So Mum was finally leaving him. Do you think it could have been for this man in the photo?'

'Yes, I do now,' whispered Michael.

Joshua closed his eyes, his face draining of colour as the enormity of Michael's words sank in.

'Did he kill him before or after he killed Mum?'

'Before.'

'How do you know for sure?'

'He told me.'

'Same day?'

'He didn't say. I didn't ask.'

'So what did he do with the body?' Joshua asked, not wanting to know the answer.

'He said "friends" dropped him out at sea. Said the fishes took him long ago.'

'Did you believe him?'

'Yes, I did. I didn't want to, but I knew he wasn't lying.'

'So why didn't you tell anyone what he told you?'

'He was dying. He told me he'd deny it if questioned. He said there was no proof. He wanted me to know why he killed our mother.' Michael lowered his head.

'Did he want your forgiveness?' Joshua asked.

'No. He was still filled with hatred. There was no remorse there at all.'

Joshua shivered at the thought of his beautiful, gentle mother and his vengeful father. 'Do you think she knew he'd killed the man?'

'Yes,' Michael replied, scanning his brother's face for a reaction. 'He said he told her what he'd done before he hit her.'

'Cold bastard. So who was the baby's father, Michael?' Joshua's anguished face searched his brother's for the answers.

'We'll never know.'

'Why did she stay with him if there was someone else?'

'I don't know. Mum tried so hard to protect us. Perhaps she was frightened of what he might do to us, to her and to the man she loved.'

'She was right, then, wasn't she?'

Michael quietly nodded.

Joshua thought back to the violent rages, the table thumping, the nights he cowered under his bed, waiting for the noises downstairs to go away, remembering how his mother would deliberately put herself between him and his father's fists. 'I still hate him, Michael. It never goes away.'

'I know. But hate eats us alive, Josh. You need to let it go.'

'Do you think Dad was mistaken about me not being his son?'

'I've thought about those claims he made in the prison hospital. You've always looked like Mum, so I could never see any other resemblance. But now,' Michael paused, 'I'm not so sure.'

'Why now?' Joshua asked, his face twisted with anxiety.

'Look at this photo. Who does *she* remind you of?' Michael passed over the picture on his phone of Amelia, taken in the barn at Pepper Hill Farmhouse. 'Look at Amelia's delicate features, how she holds her head as she laughs. Even her fringe falls the same way.'

Joshua held the image of his daughter in his hands. 'What are you saying?'

'Look at the photo, Joshua.'

Joshua looked again. The resemblance to the 'Peter' in his

mother's photo collection was uncanny.

'Is that just coincidence?' Michael asked.

Joshua shook his head and shut his eyes, the possible truth too awful to acknowledge.

'Joshua,' Michael prompted.

Joshua lifted his head. 'I know what it is you're saying. If the Peter in these photos is Peter Ballantyne-Browne, then he is the man who disappeared from Pepper Hill Farmhouse. That means he could be the man Dad killed.' He allowed the words to float over him.

'It also means,' Michael added, haltingly, 'that you might have been his biological son.'

There was a pause as Joshua looked back through the photos. The gene pool was evident.

'We can't prove anything now, though, can we? Just a few photos, a dying man's confession and a supposition that serves little purpose,' said Joshua.

Michael nodded again sadly.

'Then let's pretend we never saw these photos, you never heard Dad's confession ... we never had this conversation.'

Michael looked at the worried expression on his brother's face. 'Can you live with that, Joshua?' he asked.

'You did. What's the purpose of raking up the past now?'

Michael hesitated; he knew what Joshua was trying to do. 'Ok, I agree.'

'Do we need to keep these?' Joshua asked, pointing to the photos on the floor. 'Have you shown them to anyone else?' he asked.

Michael saw the pain in his brother's face. 'No,' he replied. 'As you say, it's all speculation, anyway. I'll keep the ones of us and Mum though.'

'Thank you,' said Joshua with relief, visibly shaken by their discovery. His mother's tragic death had been difficult enough for him to come to terms with; the rest ... it was unthinkable.

Aware of his brother's reluctance to accept any evidence linking them to Peter Ballantyne, Michael collected up the photographs after Joshua left and placed them in a drawer he kept locked. Destroying the pictures might make Joshua feel better now, but he could regret it later. The truth always had a way of surfacing. And for now, nobody would find them.

Chapter 33

'Our offer to buy Pepper Hill Farmhouse has been accepted,' a beaming Simon told Emma.

Emma's green eyes flashed a look of pure joy as she threw her arms around him. 'I can't believe it. It's ours. I always knew it would be. Did they haggle on the price?'

'No,' Simon replied. 'Surprisingly, they didn't. Just asked if we could complete within the next few weeks.'

Emma face dropped. 'Can we do that? We haven't even put the cottage on the market yet,' she said, her voice now filled with disappointment.

Simon smiled at Emma. 'Come here. There's nothing to worry about,' he told her, giving her a big hug. 'We can still do it. It's tight, but there's the money from my house sale.'

'So we can afford it, then?' asked Emma, bewildered but ecstatic.

'Yes, it drains my bank account, but we don't need a mortgage or a top-up. I'm still very surprised they accepted my first offer. I went in very low expecting them to quibble.'

'Perhaps Beatrice likes the sound of us, as a family,' suggested Emma flippantly, looking at Simon's serious face. 'What is it I'm missing?' she asked, her heart lurching suddenly.

Simon shook his head. 'No, nothing. If Beatrice wants us to have it at that price, I'm not arguing,' he laughed. 'One interesting thing though. Her lawyer was very interested in the name Hart. I explained it was your business name and your previous married name.'

'And?'

'He wanted to know if there was any connection to a Claire Hart?'

'Did he know her, then?'

'I didn't ask. I just told him your ex-husband was her son.'

'Have you told Joshua about the conversation?'

'Yes. I also told him Beatrice wanted to meet him again. She remembers him from when he was a little boy.'

'Well, I think that's lovely. What did Joshua say?'

'He said he'd think about it.'

Hetty was delighted when Emma told her about their offer being accepted. 'It'll be nice to have some youth again at Pepper Hill Farmhouse,' she said.

Emma nodded back. 'Beatrice has asked to meet up with Joshua. She remembers his mother bringing him to stay with her as a child and wants to see him again.'

Hetty raised an eyebrow. 'Well, I never. What does he think about that? Does he remember her?'

'Vaguely. He remembers the house though. He asked me to check with you to see if she's *compos mentis* before he agrees to see her?'

Hetty laughed. 'Oh yes, sharp as a knife. It's only her limbs that have let her down. Has an electric wheelchair that she drives like Boadicea, but it's the getting in and out of the chair that causes the issues. Seems an odd request to want to see him after all these years, but then that's the luxury of old age. If you call yourself "eccentric", you can get away with most things.'

Later that evening Emma rang Joshua. 'Hetty says Beatrice is completely with it. You will see her, won't you?'

'I'll give it some thought,' he replied, worried that someone was connecting the dots.

'Good. I'd like to meet her myself. Perhaps after you've been to see her I can introduce her to Amelia and Charlie.'

Joshua felt instantly nauseous at Emma's suggestion.

'Are you still taking Amelia next weekend?' she continued.

'Yes, if that's still ok with you guys.'

'Please. We've got so much to sort out with the cottage. Did I tell you Gabby wants to buy it?'

'No, you didn't. Easy sale though.'

'Yes, I know. She's always loved it here. She's also happy to wait until we've got the farm habitable. We'll move Simon's office and all of his books into the stable block as soon as we've completed. That way he can work in peace, but be there for the contractors if necessary.'

'When are you completing?'

'Imminently. There's no chain, and we have the cash from Simon's house sale, so as soon as legally acceptable, I suppose. I can't wait to finalise everything; it really feels as if we're supposed to move into Pepper Hill Farmhouse. I'm terrified something could happen to jeopardise it.'

'I'm sure it won't. What does Amelia think?'

'She's over the moon; she says it's the "happiest place on earth".'

Joshua remembered the writing on the back of his mother's photograph and shivered.

'Well, what do you think?' Emma asked as they wandered around Pepper Hill Farmhouse the following day.

'This is quite an amazing place,' said Gabby. Then, pointing at the large picture above the staircase, she asked, 'Who's she?'

'That's Beatrice Browne – and before you say anything, she's still very much alive,' said Emma. 'Unless she falls from her hanging place and hits us going up the stairs, she can't do us any harm.'

'What about her horse?' Gabby whispered. 'Does it walk the backfield at dusk?'

'It's a mare, and no. Don't put ideas into Amelia's head,' implored Emma.

'What ideas?' asked Amelia, joining them.

'Oh, Auntie Gabby is just being silly about Beatrice's horse.'

Amelia looked up at the picture of Beatrice with her magnificent white mare.

'I've seen her Spirit in the field,' she told them.

'Don't be silly, darling,' Emma hastily corrected her daughter, giving Gabby an unimpressed 'I-told-you-so' look.

'But I have,' whined Amelia, clambering down the stairs and rushing outside to the garden. 'She's there now, I'll show you.'

'Amelia,' Emma called, running out of the house after her.

'She's up there in the field, Mummy.' Amelia pointed towards the stable block. 'Simon and I found her there the other day.'

Emma and Gabby exchanged looks. 'Why don't you show us where?' suggested Gabby.

The two women followed Amelia's lead to where a small, white headstone had been placed to one side of the entrance to the backfield.

'Simon says it's here 'cos it's a secret.'

Crouching down, Gabby moved the grass away from the inscription and read it aloud: 'Here lies my Spirit, my much loved friend. I wait to hear the sound of your hoofbeats again.'

'How lovely and how sad,' said Emma.

'Simon said that must be the name of her horse in the

picture.' Amelia told them.

'But why a secret plot?' Gabby asked.

'Large animals shouldn't be buried on farm property,' Emma told her. 'That's if it is buried here. Could just be a monument to her horse.'

'Whatever – it seems we were both wrong, Emma. There *is* a "Spirit" up in the backfield.'

'I told you her Spirit was up here, didn't I?' said Amelia. 'I don't tell fibs.'

Emma collected her daughter into her arms. 'My mistake, darling. Simon should have told me about the headstone. Let's go back to the main house now ... And speaking of Simon, Gabs, when are you going to allow him to regress you?' Emma teased. 'He'll be based here shortly, so it should be easy to arrange.'

'Never,' Gabby smirked.

'So you're no longer interested in discovering your links to Cleopatra, then?'

Gabby grinned in embarrassment. 'No, silly idea.'

'Pity, always thought you might be the asp in the basket,' said Emma, fielding a swipe from her friend. Then, linking their arms together, the two of them walked back to the farmhouse with Amelia running ahead.

Chapter 34

Beatrice Browne moved slowly. Aided by two carers in matching blue uniforms, she allowed herself to be helped into her electric wheelchair.

'Thank you, my dears. Sorry to be such a nuisance.'

'You're not,' the younger and prettier of the two told her. 'What time is your guest calling?'

'Three o'clock.'

'Then we'll make sure you're comfortable before he arrives.'

Beatrice smiled and nodded. 'Thank you. Such a stupid bother. Sadly, I've come to that age when my bladder is more active than my limbs,' said Beatrice.

When she recognised she could no longer walk unaided up or down the stairs, Beatrice had moved herself and her two faithful carers into a bungalow close to Pepper Hill Farmhouse. 'Down but not out!' she had told Richard Taylor, her solicitor – her oldest and most trusted friend. 'It's not where I want to be, but at least I can enjoy the views in a place of my own choice and on my own terms.'

A Danish architect had designed what was now Beatrice's home back in the seventies. It was a one-level house created out of glass and wood that blended sympathetically with the surrounding countryside and offered magnificent views out across the farmland. There was a small copse to the rear that provided protection from the winds and a private access road ensuring seclusion. The property had been named 'Tranquil House', which had appealed to Beatrice, although she felt 'Woodland

Folly' was more appropriate. The property boasted three large bedrooms with en-suite facilities and underfloor heating, adequate for Beatrice and her live-in carers. The kitchen was well equipped, the living area open-plan and spacious and designed around a central fireplace, while the glass-framed conservatory, a window cleaner's dream, provided stunning views and fresh country air with protection from the seasonal elements.

All the suggested modifications to the house for assisting in Beatrice's care met with her full co-operation – that was until her young and newly appointed doctor had recommended the creation of a wet room to help with washing her. 'A wet room? Never!' she had firmly announced to the assembled company. 'If I can't manage to get into the bath myself, then I'll get a hoist with a special chair installed to load me in and out. When a horse breaks its legs we get them in and out of swimming pools for exercise without any fuss. Hoisting *me* into a bath will be far easier.' Then, raising her finger to silence the doctor's interruption, she added, 'I will not give up my bath. It's one of my few remaining luxuries.'

'But the hoisting might make you feel undignified,' the young doctor had bravely suggested.

It took Beatrice fewer than six seconds to respond (Richard Taylor had been counting in amusement). Using the arms of her wheelchair, she had raised herself up onto both legs and, although shaky and ignoring her carers' pleas, stood up, matching the young doctor in height.

'Beatrice Browne will never be called "undignified",' she had informed him. 'Whatever is done to me, for me, or with me will be done because *I* allow it. That's how I will retain my dignity.'

The young doctor had stubbornly continued along the wet room route, much to Beatrice's irritation. 'But some carers have difficulties with their patients' weight,' he had added. 'A wet room might be the more practical solution for all,' he had told her, looking around for support. Both carers had ducked their heads at Beatrice's outburst and her solicitor had merely smiled – he was enjoying the exchange. He'd known Beatrice for most of his working life and realised that the young GP was not going to win this argument.

Dropping back into her seat, Beatrice had expelled her breath noisily, giving the doctor a weary stare over the rim of her reading glasses. 'The solution is simple. There will be no wet room. As for any weight issues, I'll watch my food intake and, if necessary, hire stronger carers,' she retorted. Then, turning to one of her staff, she said, 'Now, please show the doctor the way out.'

There was a flurry of activity as the young man was ushered from the premises while Richard Taylor looked on with veiled admiration at his client.

'As I said, Dicky, I might be down, but I'm not out. Kindly ensure that man does not come near me again.'

A bath hoist was duly installed at Woodland Folly, alongside the large, deep bath Beatrice insisted on keeping. When she finally took up residence in the bungalow, the young, opinionated doctor was discreetly replaced with a more mature GP.

'Joshua Hart is here to see you, Beatrice,' the younger carer announced. Beatrice looked up from her novel, the slight shaking of the pages the only evidence of her apprehension.

'Thank you, Carrie. Please show him into the courtyard – I'll join him there.'

Joshua stood in the partially shaded enclosure where slithers of light from the afternoon sun cut through the surrounding greenery and flickered across his face. Beatrice looked up from her wheelchair and gasped as the sparkling sunlight danced around his head like a golden halo. *My Angel of Retribution,* she thought as his intense blue eyes fused with her own grey ones.

Joshua smiled. Somewhere in his psyche he remembered her. 'Hello, Beatrice.'

'You remind me of your mother,' she whispered, her arthritic hands clawing momentarily at the tartan rug on her lap. Then, lifting one hand, she beckoned him.

'Your mother was so beautiful, so kind.'

Joshua moved slowly towards Beatrice.

'Please, sit close by, there's something I need to tell you.'

Joshua sat on the wicker chair beside her, his emotions a mixture of apprehension and confusion.

Beatrice leaned back in her wheelchair and closed her eyes, allowing long hidden memories to rise and collect. Frailty was not an image Beatrice wanted to project, but at that moment in time, as Joshua sat beside her, she felt fragile. Opening her eyes, she turned her face towards him. 'You never forget your first love or your first lie, Joshua. Sometimes the two are connected,' she started, her voice touched with sadness. 'When love is tarnished with deceit, it damages all it touches.'

Joshua edged himself closer to hear.

'There's so much to tell you, so little time to make amends,' Beatrice said, offering her hand. 'This is not easy for me, Joshua. I've never spoken of these things before and I'm frightened of the pain these truths may cause us.'

'I understand, I'm listening,' he answered, looking into her sad eyes, feeling his own guilt. Gently he took her hand in his.

Beatrice, returning his gaze, looked deeply into his eyes. *Oh, my warrior angel, why have you taken so long to come to me?* she thought, the tears gathering in her eyes threatening to overflow.

'A long time ago I fell in love,' Beatrice began. 'A young girl's love, full of intensity and romance, with never a thought that actions have consequences, nor for the secret I would live with for so long.' Her face was now damp from her unchecked tears, but she carried on. 'I was eighteen when he died and eighteen when I discovered I was pregnant; he never knew about the baby. To avoid a family scandal I travelled out to visit a distant cousin of my mother's in America – an Emily Ballantyne. My son, Peter, was born out there. As arranged, I returned home without him, leaving him to be brought up by Emily in America – a decision I always regretted. When Peter was thirteen, Emily died. As I was the last remaining relative, my own mother having passed away earlier, I inherited Emily's estate and became Peter's legal guardian. I brought him back home to England. My secret was still safe. I told people that Peter was a distant relative from America, and nobody questioned anything. First love always bites deep, Joshua – the more impossible the love, the more exquisite the pain. I never stopped loving Peter's father. I never stopped loving my son.'

Beatrice's face softened as she spoke those tragic words, and a vision of one of his mother's torn photographs of a young, smiling man flashed into Joshua's head.

'My Peter loved England; he loved Pepper Hill Farmhouse. He loved everything about the countryside and the horses. And in time, he grew to love me too. He called me Mother Bee or Mrs Bee. Never Beatrice.' Her grey eyes shone bright with the memories.

'He also fell in love ... with Claire, your mother.'

Joshua's heart hammered in his suddenly tight chest, dreading what he thought he might hear, but knowing he needed to hear it. Beatrice's eyes watched his for a reaction.

'Your mother stayed with us when she could – we were her refuge when your father was away. We all knew about his temper

261

and promised to keep Pepper Hill Farmhouse a safe place for you all to visit. No letters, she used to say, no phone calls, just in case. But love is always worth the risk and Claire and Peter took risks. When I heard about Claire's death, I knew who had killed her. I didn't know about the baby though.'

Joshua watched as more fat tears squeezed out from Beatrice's closed eyes and slipped silently down her face, catching in the lines etched around her mouth.

'We both lost so much on that day, Joshua; so much. I always suspected Peter had gone to find your mother and that's why he never came home.'

Joshua remembered the envelope with the Surrey postmark. Perhaps Peter had written to his mother despite her warnings, telling her how he intended to take them all away, and his father had intercepted this letter.

Beatrice lowered her head and withdrew her hand from Joshua's grasp. Clasping her hands together and dropping them onto her lap, she sat silently, the only movement coming from her weaving thumbs and fingers.

'I told people that Peter had just left one night. Suggested he'd gone back to America. I never indicated a link with Claire's death, nobody questioned his disappearance and his body was never found. I even said he would return when he was ready. I hoped in my heart he was still alive, somewhere, protecting someone. But deep down, I knew he was dead too. Peter would have come back to me and Pepper Hill Farmhouse, if he was still alive.'

Joshua lowered his head as a vice of sickening guilt squeezed his own heart. 'I'm sorry Beatrice. I think I might be to blame.'

Beatrice's age-spotted hands fluttered like a wounded bird, grappling for his sleeve. 'No, Joshua. You were *not* to blame.'

Joshua looked down at the intense blue veins raised in frustration on her fragile hands.

'Yes, I may have been,' he insisted, his voice thick with emotion. 'My father believed I wasn't his son. If Peter had shown an interest in my mother, he may have assumed I was Peter's child and not his own.'

Beatrice could clearly see the raw despair stamped on Joshua's face. 'No,' she said again, her voice stronger and firmer as she dug her fingers into his arm.

'You were never to blame.'

'But my father told my brother Michael, just before he died, that he'd killed the man who was coming to take us away with him. That must have been your Peter.'

Visibly distraught, Joshua pulled his arm away, wiping his hands through his hair. 'I only learned that recently and I intended to *never* tell you. I even asked my brother to destroy the photos. What does that say about me, Beatrice?' Joshua asked.

'That you, like me, were frightened. We are only human,' said Beatrice, her tone now calm and gentle. 'The truth often hurts, Joshua. I too did wrong. I should have brought you two boys back with me as soon as I found out about Claire's murder. But I didn't. I convinced myself in the beginning that her death had nothing to do with Peter's disappearance. When I finally accepted the truth and enquired after you both, I was told you'd gone through the system and been fostered separately. They told me they weren't interested in anyone who wasn't family.'

Joshua's eyes met hers, the unspoken truth hovering between them.

'That was my greatest mistake. I've lived with that guilt for a lifetime. Perhaps you can help me find some peace now.' Beatrice paused, grappling with her handkerchief and blowing her nose noisily. Looking back at Joshua she continued. 'It took me many years before I was able to visit your mother's grave. After seeing her pitiful marker, I commissioned the white granite cross in memory of her and the baby. As I couldn't bury my Peter, I marked his passing with hers. If you look carefully, at the base of her cross you'll see two initials entwined: a C and a P – hers and his.' Beatrice's frail body began to tremble. 'I let you down, Joshua. I'm so sorry. Can you ever forgive me?' she asked.

Joshua looked into Beatrice's uplifted face, her beseeching eyes so filled with remorse and guilt. Kneeling down in front of her chair, he leaned forward and gently kissed her forehead. A loud cry tore from her chest, and one of the uniformed carers, rushing in to check, witnessed a sobbing Beatrice, holding Joshua's tear-stained face gently between her trembling hands. Nodding to herself, she discreetly tiptoed from the room.

Joshua liked Beatrice. He found her funny and wise. When she asked him to tell her all about his life, he found it easy – no pretence, just the truth. She listened with interest, never interrupting or commenting, quietly patting his hand in encouragement from time to time. When she asked to see a photograph of Amelia, he showed her the one taken at Pepper Hill Farmhouse in the barn. Beatrice, glasses perched on her nose, drank in the image of the little girl.

'She does remind me of Peter,' she told him, a faraway look in her eyes. 'Take care of this little one, Joshua. She is our past and our future.'

They both knew what she was alluding to.

When Joshua got up to leave, Beatrice removed her gold signet ring from her finger. 'A present from someone who made mistakes,' she told him, pushing it into his palm. 'The symbol of a rebirth: a phoenix rising from the ashes. A new life from a death ... Now it's your responsibility to repair the past, if you can.'

As Joshua walked away, the ring with all its associations felt heavy in his hand.

Chapter 35

With the purchase of the farmhouse, Simon now had an alternative place to work. It had been Emma's suggestion that they take his furniture out of storage and utilise the barn and stable block ahead of the move into the main house. Beatrice's team had cleared the barn of all her unwanted effects, including the hat that worried Emma so much. Joshua had asked that the picture of Beatrice and her white horse, Spirit, be allowed to remain in the farmhouse – a request Beatrice was only too happy to grant.

As soon as the sale was complete, Simon and Emma, armed with pots of white emulsion, painted the inside of the stable block. When they'd finished, they both stood back to admire their handiwork.

'I'm amazed there was so little that needed to be done in here,' Simon said.

'I know,' acknowledged Emma, looking at the high ceilings and wooden floor. 'Perhaps this was an area she used for letting … would make a perfect love nest. Talking of which, have you noticed the letters carved into the beam?' she asked.

'No,' Simon replied, walking over for a closer look.

'They're here, see? It's a P and a squiggle underneath. Can they be sanded off?'

Simon ran his fingers over the initials. 'I think that squiggle is a C. They're cut too deep to sand out. Let's leave them; could be a testimonial to undying love.'

'Should we carve ours here too?'

'Emma Leighton. You vandal.'

'Well, if we can't "etch" our undying love here, how about we just practise it instead?'

'Practise?' asked Simon, smirking as he replaced the lid on the paint tin. 'I'd have thought we were quite proficient by now,' he said, lifting Emma and pushing her gently backwards over the painting table.

That evening they returned back to the cottage later than expected, both flushed and covered in paint.

'What have you two been up to?' asked a giggling Hetty. 'You look like you've been rolling in the stuff.'

Simon and Emma exchanged a wry smile.

'I've been looking through my albums and look what I've found,' Hetty went on, excitedly passing over a photograph for Emma to see. 'It's a photo of Beatrice and Peter.'

Emma wiped her hands on her jeans before taking the grainy photo from Hetty. She looked closely at the image, her wide eyes darting between Hetty and Simon, as if looking for an acceptable explanation. Simon took the photo from her outstretched hand.

'Who does Peter remind you of?' Hetty asked.

Simon examined the image and looked back up at Emma before replying: 'Amelia.'

'That's right,' said Hetty, taking the photo back and holding it to her breast. 'I knew she reminded me of someone.'

October was wet and dreary. As the leaves collected in the drains and gutters of the cottage, the warmth of the long summer seemed far away. A team of gardeners had brought the grounds of Pepper Hill back into general repair and Amelia and Emma had planted bulbs, hoping for bursts of colour the following spring. By November the rain had come with a vengeance, and even when it stopped, the air felt damp.

Work on the farmhouse was well under way. The walls between the dining room and kitchen had been removed to create one large open-plan living area. Emma had chosen a grey slate floor to complement the kitchen furniture, which still remained under plastic sheeting, lined up against the walls.

Sadly, Beatrice Browne never got to see the changes to Pepper Hill Farmhouse; she caught a simple cold that November that led to pneumonia. Joshua spent her last few days sitting at her bedside, replaying one of Simon's throwaway remarks to him: 'One day ... you'll find that person who will finally make your life complete.' Looking at Beatrice now, her fine hair fanned out on her pillow, he realised that this had happened. Over the weeks they'd had together, they'd created a deep relationship fashioned from mutual trust, admiration and love; their belief that the same shared blood coursed through their veins only strengthened their bond. Joshua had wanted to provide DNA evidence on himself and Amelia, but Beatrice had waved his suggestion away. 'No need,' she'd said. 'Kin recognises kin!'

He sat listening to her much-loved mantle clock record the passing seconds. With each 'tick' he felt her slipping away from him. Raising her frail fingers, he kissed her hand and held onto it tightly, as if his love could halt her departure. She stirred and opened her eyes, searching for his face. Seeing him there, she smiled and gently squeezed his hand.

'I'm ready to leave now,' she told him.

Joshua's face, wet with unrestrained tears, crumpled in anguish.

Beatrice looked at him and smiled again weakly. 'Come closer, Joshua. Can you hear that?'

Wiping away the tears, he leaned closer. 'What am I listening to?' he asked, stroking back the hair from her forehead.

'There! Can't you hear it?' she asked. Her face was alert now, listening to something only audible to her. 'It's the sound of hooves. My Spirit has come to fetch me.'

Broken, Joshua dropped his face into the cover beside Beatrice's frail body and sobbed.

'It's fine, Joshua. I'm not leaving you, just taking a long ride with Spirit. We'll meet again when it's time. Look after my Amelia ... so like my Peter. You have made me so happy again.'

Joshua lifted his head and looked into her grateful, tear-filled eyes.

'I need to close my eyes now, Joshua. Stay with me. Richard knows what I want. No secrets any more. Remember, I love you, always.'

'I love you,' he replied, grasping her cool, bony hand in his.

Beatrice died peacefully in Joshua's arms. Having just found her, Beatrice's death was, for him, a vicious blow. She had been the missing jigsaw piece in his fractured life. With her, he had managed to understand his past and embrace his future. Now she had gone, he felt something vital had slipped away again. Through Beatrice he had learned the power of forgiveness and the richness of sacrifice. Meeting her had given him closure, and her loss affected him greatly.

Beatrice knew Joshua didn't want her money, so she had recognised her great-grandchild, Amelia, in her death instead. Her considerable estate was tied up in a trust, part of which could be used for educational purposes, should Richard Taylor believe appropriate, but the bulk of which would not pass to her until she reached the age of twenty-five. The terms of the trust also necessitated that Amelia should not be made aware of the money outside that used for her education until she reached the appropriate age.

'She must make her mark in life for herself,' Beatrice had whispered to the solicitor, her chest tight with the effort.

'Agreed. I shall see to it for you,' he'd replied.

Beatrice's funeral took place in the local parish church. Joshua gave an emotional reading to the small congregation. All eyes were on his solitary figure as he escorted the coffin towards its final resting place.

Huddled together under an umbrella, Emma and Simon looked up as forked lightning lit the grey sky and a huge thunderclap boomed.

'Only Beatrice could do that,' said Richard Taylor, dabbing his sparkling eyes.

As the small group collected by the graveside, partially hidden by brollies, the rain stopped as suddenly as it had started. Emma looked up again to see the sun break through the clouds and a large rainbow arch over the churchyard.

'As I said ... only Beatrice could do that,' Richard mumbled as the umbrellas collapsed around him and the vicar continued with his sermon.

'Ride fast and free, Beatrice. I will never forget you,' Joshua told the lowering coffin.

Chapter 36

Emma's parents were interested in the developing stages of Pepper Hill Farmhouse and, happy to camp on the sofa bed in the conservatory, they invited themselves over to the cottage to stay. Desperate to feel useful and be involved, they offered babysitting and cooking services, allowing Emma time to sort through her business and private clutter.

The cottage heaved with activity and extra bodies, making Emma all the more determined to speed up the move to their new home. With the final move set for early January, she had already transported some of the non-essential items to store in the finished rooms at the farmhouse, and Simon had installed his office and reference books into the newly decorated stable block, as planned.

Early one morning Simon escaped the madness in the cottage by taking Emma's car over there; he was desperate for some quiet writing time as his deadline was fast approaching. Sitting at his lovingly polished desk, a hot cup of coffee by his side, he could just make out the pair of majestic oaks in the backfield, set against the darkening sky. Leaning over, he turned up the thermostat on his heater and shivered. Then, lifting his coffee mug, he drank in some warmth as the wind whistled around the stable block.

A loud crack suddenly drew him from his writing. 'What the hell!' he exclaimed, pushing back his chair and opening the door to the wind and elements. A handful of leaves wove around the door frame, spinning as they dropped onto the wooden floor. Simon stepped outside, the pounding rain now soaking his face and body, but unable to see anything obviously wrong, he returned to the warmth of his study. *Must have been a tree up in the backfield,* he thought, resuming his writing.

As it was Joshua's weekend to have Amelia, Emma had invited him to join them all for an early dinner that evening, the idea being that he would take her back with him afterwards. In the meantime, Emma was taking Amelia to a birthday party in the village.

'Shall I look after Charlie for you?' asked Caroline, watching her daughter bundle her belongings together.

'No thanks, Mum, he's grumpy. I'll keep him or you'll never be able to get on with anything.' As Charlie had been fretful all morning, Emma hoped the car journey would get him off to sleep. From birth he'd liked the movement of the car and she needed no excuse to take him with her.

Caroline nodded. She had offered to prepare the meal for that evening and knew that small, agitated babies required a lot of attention.

Amelia was overexcited; she loved dressing up and she loved parties, especially the birthday cake. Today she was dressed as a 'fairy princess', complete with a pair of tiny sequinned wings, which Emma had lovingly sewn onto the back of her dress, and the pink plastic wand Joshua had given her for Christmas. Pressing the button on her magic wand, Amelia checked it glowed sufficiently.

'I need fairy dust in my hair, Mummy,' she said.

Already holding Charlie, her oversized bag and a birthday present, Emma had no hands free. She looked at Amelia. 'I'm out of fairy dust, darling,' she replied in frustration, feeling a pang of guilt for the dismissive way in which she'd spoken to her daughter.

Caroline came to the rescue. 'I have some,' she told her

granddaughter, and retrieving her blue leather handbag, she produced a bottle of scented hair mist. 'It's super fairy dust, Amelia. You can't see it, but you can smell it,' Caroline explained, spraying a little over her hair.

'Thank you, Fairy Grandma. Now, are you ready for the ball?' Emma asked.

On Amelia's nod, they all moved towards the car. 'I should be back by about five-thirty, Mum. Simon will be home around then too.'

'What time is Joshua arriving?' asked Caroline.

'He's usually here about six. I'll make sure I'm back before he arrives.'

The rain was coming down heavily now. Protected by her mother's umbrella, Emma secured Charlie into the car.

'Ok, my darlings. Please drive carefully – it's not nice out here.'

'I know.'

A gust of wind turned the umbrella inside out, and a number of spokes tore away from the material.

'Quick, Mum, go inside. I'll make sure I'm not too late. The party won't last that long, but I did offer to stay back and clear up. See you later,' Emma shouted, as she pulled away in Simon's silver four-wheel drive, the windscreen wipers on full speed.

Emma carefully negotiated the wet roads and bends as she drove back to the cottage, mindful of her precious cargo. The birthday party had been a great success, and baby Charlie, tired from all the handling and fussing, slept peacefully in his car seat now, despite the stormy weather. Amelia sat strapped securely in the back of the car, still dressed in her fairy princess party clothes, the tell-tale remains of her chocolate feast around her mouth and across the back of her right hand.

It was later than Emma had realised and her mobile had run out of battery. *Poor Joshua*, she thought, *he's still a bit uncomfortable with my parents; I hope he doesn't arrive early.* Her mind raced as she negotiated a tricky bend in the road, mentally mapping out the positions of the familiar potholes, now covered with grey surface water. As she drove, the windscreen wipers battled to clear the glass from the force of the oncoming rain.

The last week the rain had fallen continually. The river level had risen and burst over its banks in many places, spilling out over the low-lying fields, filling ditches and spreading onto parts of the surrounding roads. Although it happened often, it still made for uncomfortable driving. All the roads around the bridges had flood alerts and the villagers drove to their daily business through a constant veil of water. This evening, on top of the heavy rain, the wind had picked up to gale force, tearing at the vegetation and tossing loose or decayed shrubbery across the neighbouring countryside. Emma had noted the strewn branches on her way to the party and secretly wished that she had not committed to stay late and help with the event. The car's heater was on full and Emma turned up the radio in an attempt to block out the sound of the wind and rain.

'Nearly there, Amelia, not far to go,' Emma said in a sing-song voice to keep the tension out of her words.

The road out of the village was now pitch black. Lined with trees and high scrub hedges, it seemed unfamiliar in the dark. Along this stretch, houses were few and Emma counted the beats of the wipers as she waited to pass West Gate House. The walled and gated property was a comforting sight, indicating that the local pub, The Fox, would be her next landmark.

The road became increasingly more hazardous as she took

the next bend, but through the frenzied movement of her windscreen wipers, the lights from the pub came into view and even as she remembered stories of past flooding, when its cellars filled with river water, she felt reassured nonetheless.

'Nearly there,' she sang again as Charlie stirred. Just then a small branch blew into the side window, scraping like fingernails against the glass. 'Only an old stick, Amelia,' said Emma; her voice had lost the singsong tone and the words sounded tense to her own ears. Passing the pub, she could just make out the warning sign: 'Road liable to flood'.

In her rear-view mirror Emma watched the glow from the pub lights disappear as she turned into the next bend. Headlights on full beam, she could see the ominous stretch of dark water across the road. Slowing down, she mentally gauged the level of water, confident that Simon's car would get through it on either side of the bridge, as it had done earlier.

The West Gate Bridge was an old brick humpback and had been raised in the past because of flooding. When the river was high it was the crossing favoured by the locals. Alarmed at how quickly conditions had deteriorated since she'd set out for the party, Emma selected the lowest gear and drove slowly through the water, taking comfort in the knowledge that her vehicle was high off the ground and heavy. 'Take it easy and don't stall the car; create a gentle bow wave,' she mumbled to herself.

As if aware of the tension, Amelia remained silent. To the right the river had swamped the lower fields and the trees stood like giant colossi in the fast-flowing torrent. The surrounding vegetation, trapped by its waterlogged roots, appeared to wave the car forward in a frenzy of movements. As the wheels pushed through the dirty water up onto the bridge, Emma breathed a sigh of relief.

Pausing on the crest, the Toyota stood hunched like a large metal warrior, headlights on full beam, engine growling and wheels dripping weeds and mud onto the road. Ahead, Emma could make out a stretch of black water across the road. Tensing her body at the next sound of thunder, she took a deep breath and, dipping her full beam, rolled the car forward. A lightning fork lit the angry skies ahead, and through the furious movement of the windscreen wipers, she saw the tree bough falling towards them.

Emma reacted instinctively, throwing the steering wheel over to her right in an attempt to avoid the travelling bough. The impact was inevitable and swift. There was a loud thump and a noise like a small explosion as her windscreen shattered. She heard the shriek of disconnecting metal as the heavy bough bounced off the car, ripping away part of the left windscreen wiper and leaving a tortured stump to twitch pathetically alongside its mate.

Unable to see a thing through the windscreen now, Emma braked, her wheels locking as the Toyota found the opening between the bridge wall and the hedgerow. There was the sickening sound of scraping bodywork as the car scored its side along the end of the bridge before plunging down the short bank. In helpless horror Emma screamed, hitting the car horn as they lurched towards the black, swirling water.

A large old oak growing below the bridge and alongside the riverbank stopped the Toyota. One side of the bonnet had crumpled and the collision had taken out a headlight. The damaged vehicle sat among the moving water, corralled by the tree's complex system of raised roots. Out of her side window Emma could see nothing but darkness, but she heard the torrent of water all around them. Afraid to let go of the steering wheel, she locked her hands tightly onto it as her body shook and her head felt giddy.

Emma was brought back to her senses by the high-pitched cries of frightened children behind her, but, held firmly in place by her seat belt, she couldn't turn to see them. Charlie's shrill cry and Amelia's sobbing conjured up frightening images of tiny shattered bodies. In shock and shaking, Emma groped for the interior light and then, with one unnatural twist of her arm and torso, she managed to release the seat belt and dragged herself over the front-seat console to reach her children.

'It's all right, darling,' she reassured Amelia, whose small face looked pinched and white in the internal lights. 'It's going to be all right.'

Emma stroked her daughter's head as she watched her push her pink sticky fist into her mouth to stifle the sobs. 'It's all right, Charlie, Mummy's here,' she crooned to her baby son, still strapped tightly in his car seat. His small, tear-crumpled face relaxed at the sound of her voice and he calmed his frantic arm movement as he searched her eyes for encouragement.

All instincts told Emma she needed to get the children out of the car, but she knew that just six inches of moving water would be enough to knock her and them over. Still, the fear of being trapped made her test a window. Opening the nearest one, she felt the full force of the wind and rain as it flew into the car. She glanced back at the front windscreen; the laminated glass had shattered into a mass of spider-web cracks but still remained intact. *Small mercies,* thought Emma as she inched further into the back of the car and hastily shut the window again.

Amelia sobbed loudly now, her eyes dark with fear as she watched her mother. And sensing the unease and having been hit by the incoming rain, Charlie started to cry again too.

Charlie's papoose lay on the floor in the back footwell. Emma had forgotten to take it into the cottage after their last walk and now silently offered thanks for this oversight as she fastened it to her body. Releasing her son from his car seat, she positioned him facing her chest and strapped him tightly into the harness, uniting the two of them. His cries turned to soft whimpering as Emma then reached across to Amelia, taking her small hand and holding it tightly while surveying their options.

The light in Simon's office flickered. Feeling cold despite the heat from the radiators, he stood, stretching out his body and rubbing his arms for warmth. He felt uneasy, a primeval fear rising in his stomach. A flash of lightning followed by a loud clap of thunder added to his disquiet. Leaning towards the window, he looked more closely. The rain was falling relentlessly.

Simon grabbed his mobile and opened the stable block door, pushing against the angled stream of water. Slamming it shut behind him, he ran towards the car. There was no signal on his phone. He tossed it onto the passenger seat and drove out towards the main road. He needed to contact Emma – something didn't feel right.

Chapter 37

Joshua made his way towards the cottage in his new Mercedes. The rain was heavier now and the wind had increased in ferocity. *Foul night,* he thought, sitting forward in his seat and straining to see ahead of him in the dark. As he passed The Fox he remembered with a smile the warmth and friendliness of the customers and landlord. Then he turned into the bend and saw the flood warning sign.

'Damn!' said Joshua, thumping his fist on the steering wheel. Stopping the car, he reluctantly climbed out, torch in hand. The wind and rain pummelled his face mercilessly as he moved towards the flooded approach. He used his torch to scan the water level around the bridge. The surrounding road and immediate fields were under water, but the top of the bridge appeared clear. Using a stick he measured the depth of the water on the road. Confident with the level, he returned to his car, driving carefully up onto the bridge. From this position he would normally be able to see the other side of the crossing and the road ahead, but this evening a large tree branch stretched across the exit.

'Shit,' he mumbled, as he wound down the window and pointed his torch into the dark. The rain lashed into the car, soaking his arm and right thigh. A car hooted behind him. Joshua looked in his rear-view mirror and saw the lights of a stationary vehicle at the flooded approach.

'Hell, looks like I'm going to get wet again,' he told himself as he climbed out of the car. A farmhand from the neighbouring estate, impatient to be home in the dry, leaned out of his battered blue and silver Land Rover window and hooted again.

'Tree branch across the bridge!' Joshua yelled, his voice swallowed by the rain and wind. The Land Rover hooted yet again and flashed its lights. 'Blast!' shouted Joshua as he descended the bridge towards the flooded road, waving his torch and arms for attention.

The man, more suitably dressed than Joshua, climbed out of his vehicle and waded towards him in his wellingtons.

'There's a branch across the bridge,' Joshua yelled again, his hands cupping his mouth in an effort to project his words. The farmhand heard nothing but the sound of the rain and wind, but realising there was a problem ahead, he continued to wade towards Joshua, the muddy water now sloshing up and around his boots.

'Tree branch across the base of the bridge – doesn't look too large, think we could shift it,' Joshua shouted at the man who was now leaning close to catch his words.

'Have to!' the man yelled back. 'No other way over tonight. Got a mate in the back, he'll help. Failing that, we'll shift your car and bring the Land Rover up over the bridge and push or drag it.'

'Sounds good,' Joshua agreed, turning up the collar of his coat in a vain attempt to prevent the rainwater trickling down his neck. He watched the man wade back towards his vehicle and then turned and walked towards the fallen branch, squinting against the rain. His torch played across the bridge, picking up the surrounding brickwork and hedgerow. It was then that he saw the opening in the hedge. Training his torch through the gap, he just made out a large silver vehicle jammed against a tree on the flooded bank below. The water was already halfway up its wheels and he could see a figure moving about within its lit interior. Edging closer to the hole in the hedge, he pulled out his phone, dialling the emergency number. Something about the surreal image felt familiar. Having passed directions over to the emergency services, he carefully dropped down the bank towards the vehicle. He heard the faint sound of a car horn in the wind. The water around the vehicle looked dangerously fast flowing, and as Joshua watched, he thought he saw it lift in the current.

Emma felt the car rock and panicked. Terrified that its battery life would give out and leave them without light, or worse, trap them inside, she had opened two windows fully, allowing the rain to pour in. She knew she was delaying the inevitable and that she would soon have to leave the car and get them all to higher ground. Emma had no idea of the depth of water surrounding them, but she sensed it was rising fast. With her son strapped to her body and her daughter holding onto the hem of her jacket, she pressed the horn one final time.

Joshua couldn't shake off the feeling that there was something familiar about the scene below. He carefully descended the bank towards the car, his feet and ankles now submerged in wet mud and grass. Torch in hand, he played the light directly onto the vehicle as Emma, with Charlie strapped to her chest, opened the back door. Then he saw the child in the seat behind her, lit by the interior lights and dressed as a fairy.

Chapter 38

Emma's parents waited at the cottage for their daughter and grandchildren to return. Caroline had the dinner fully under control and the fire had been lit in the sitting room. The warmth from this and the dull drone of the television, which had been turned down low, had lulled Stephen to sleep.

Simon had just pulled into the driveway when his phone rang. 'Hello?' he shouted, not recognising the number, but relieved that he now had a signal. Leaping out of the car and into the rain, he pressed the mobile to his ear.

'Simon! It's Joshua!' the voice shouted. 'Emma's in trouble. She's driven off the West Gate Bridge … she's stuck on the flooded riverbank, cottage side. I've called the emergency services. Can you call the pub for assistance? I'm going to try and get them out of the car.'

As Simon burst through the back door, Caroline and Stephen both jumped. The look on his face sent shivers down Caroline's spine.

'Emma's stuck on the flooded riverbank near the West Gate Bridge. Joshua's called the emergency services and I've called the pub. The landlord is sending help from his end. We need to be quick.'

Frightened, they rushed out into the rain.

'How far?' Emma's father asked.

'Seven minutes, if we hurry.'

It would be the longest seven minutes of their lives.

Joshua continued further into the flood. Although shallow in parts, it had a strong current and he realised the dangers. Shining his torch into the dark water, he watched as it wrapped around his lower legs. He knew getting all three out of the car and across to high ground in one crossing was going to be difficult. Back above him, the two men from the Land Rover had returned to the bridge and were looking for him. One trained a torch on the activity below while the other returned to his vehicle for a rope and to call for assistance. Joshua knew that the emergency team were on their way, together with Simon and local help, but he couldn't wait for them. An emotion so powerful and overwhelming drove him; he needed to get to Emma and her children.

'Emma!' he shouted, competing with the sound of the wind, rain and rushing water. 'Emma can you hear me?' he yelled again into the wind, his face taut with tension as he waved his torch and waded towards the vehicle.

Emma turned her white face towards the approaching figure. His hair, like hers, was soaked and plastered to his face. She didn't recognise him. Amelia, now screaming in terror, refused to move from her car seat. The figure – half wading, half running – reached them.

'Emma!'

One hand under Charlie's bottom and the other scraping her wet hair out of her eyes, she stared at the man shouting at her. 'Joshua!' she cried out in disbelief. 'Thank God. Help me with Amelia, she's terrified and I can't get her to move. I've got Charlie,' she shouted to the wind.

Grappling with the swinging door, Joshua leaned in and collected his screaming daughter, tucking her close to his chest in an attempt to protect her from the elements. Amelia's cries changed to hysterical hiccups as she buried her face in his armpit.

'We need to get you all to higher ground, fast. Can you carry Charlie?' he shouted.

Emma looked at the churning water as a raft of terrors revisited her. She watched how it sucked and dragged the debris around the vehicle wheels. Shaking her head, she raised her frightened eyes to his. 'I'm afraid I'll slip. Take Amelia first and come back for us.'

Joshua saw the torch lights on the bridge. He knew that at least two men stood there above them. 'Ok. You stay here. I'll get Amelia to safety then come back for you. Do you hear me, Emma? I'm coming back for you and Charlie. Ok?'

'Ok,' Emma answered, nodding her head, as Joshua struggled through the water with their daughter. As she watched the torch light move further away from the car her legs began to tremble. She felt weak, as if someone had just removed a plug within her, draining all the strength from her body. Emotionally and physically exhausted, too frightened to close the door, she dropped to the far side of the vehicle. Avoiding the oncoming rain, her face pressed against the seat back, she cried, her lips silently forming the words, 'Please don't leave us, please come back.'

Knee deep in water, Joshua moved towards the lights on the bridge with Amelia tightly wrapped around his body. The younger of the two men there was secured by a rope and now made his way down the slope towards the returning figures. The trained torches lit enough of the bank for Joshua to realise help was close at hand. Still holding fast to a wailing Amelia, he felt two strong arms pull him out of the fast-flowing current.

Passing Amelia into the open arms of the older man, Joshua saw a string of torch lights in the distance weaving towards them.

'That's help coming from the direction of the pub,' the younger man told him.

'Good. Can you look after my daughter for me? I'm going back to get the others.'

'Wait, you'll need a rope,' the young man shouted as Joshua dropped back into the water.

The words were lost in the wind.

Chapter 39

As they reached the bridge, Simon and Emma's parents saw the lights moving down the bank. The fallen tree bough had been dragged to one side, and although the approach to the bridge was under a few feet of water, it was now accessible on both sides. The dim interior light from Joshua's car shone out like a weary beacon on the crest of the crossing.

Simon leaped from the car, running down onto the flooded bank, leaving Caroline and Stephen to wade through the deluge and up onto the bridge. Finding Amelia safe, Caroline climbed into Joshua's car and held her granddaughter tightly. Pushing back her wet hair, Caroline traced the contours of Amelia's face. 'Oh my baby girl, you're safe, Grandma's got you now,' she crooned.

Down below, a frightened Emma took Joshua's outstretched hand tightly as she dropped into the water. The water was now above her knees, and with Charlie still strapped to her chest, she fought hard to remain upright. As she lifted one leg the current pushed her sideways, breaking Joshua's hold. Her legs no longer supporting her, Emma was dragged like a stick by the current.

'No!' she screamed, as her body, together with Charlie's, spun under the water.

It took less than two seconds for Joshua to throw himself after her. 'I'm coming', he shouted. But both his cry and Emma's scream were lost in the sound of the rushing water and torrential rain.

Emma fought hard to keep Charlie's face above the water as the current dragged her down. Searching for something to anchor her, her hands felt the tangle of spongy tree roots and, grabbing these, she clung on in desperation. Her body twisted as the force of the water pushed her legs out from under her, spinning her in the direction of the river current. She lay, almost horizontal, sobbing on her back in the water while her bleeding fingers clung desperately to a mass of sinuous tree roots along the side of the riverbank.

Joshua's body winded Emma as he hit her. Grabbing for a root, he secured himself beside her, lacing his hands into hers and wrapping his other arm around her. Using his body, he secured them all against the base of the tree, pushing one of his feet through a nest of submerged roots. The muscles in his arms shook with the effort and he dug deeper into the wet wood to ensure the hold.

'Emma,' Joshua screamed into her ear. 'I'll trap you. Keep Charlie's face clear of the water.' He knew their hands and arms would only hold them temporarily and prayed that help was close by. 'Hold tight, Emma. I can see the torch lights working towards us. They're getting nearer. Don't let go now!'

Emma, lying twisted in the water, could see nothing in the dark. 'Please, please don't let Charlie drown!' she cried out. Her fingers hurt and her arms felt as if they were being torn from their sockets.

The roots that Joshua and Emma clung to belonged to a tree known locally as Drunken Duncan. Over the years erosion had exposed the roots and left the tree perched tenuously alongside the flowing water. Its thick, twisted trunk had grown upwards, despite its precarious position, with two of its branches outstretched like the limbs of a stumbling drunk. In the spring and summer the locals would sit among its root cradle and fish the river, sheltered by its low-growing foliage. Today, the roots of Drunken Duncan provided something much nobler – a handle to salvation.

The rescue chain was made up of volunteers, all of them familiar with the geography of the river. Keeping to the higher flooded ground they used ropes, trees and sheer manpower to secure one another on the flooded bank. A familiar voice shouted among the closing torch lights as Simon, secured with a rope around his waist, reached them.

Simon knew they needed to get the rope around Emma and under her arms to avoid Charlie being crushed from the tightening hemp. The difficulty would be lifting her out of the water without dragging her through the deluge. Drunken Duncan provided the leverage for a rope pulley, and in the torchlight everyone worked quickly to create a small crane on the riverbank. Joshua, still trapping Emma and Charlie to the tree roots, realised what they were doing and shouted at Simon. Both men had only one hand free, but together they managed to thread the rope under Emma's armpits, carefully avoiding trapping Charlie.

'They're secure. Pull them out first,' Joshua yelled, moving his body to one side to release them.

As they concentrated on lifting Emma and Charlie to safety, no one saw the large clump of wood and debris travelling along in the swirling current. Joshua made no sound as it hit him from behind, his unconscious body slipping silently into the flow, away from the torchlights and into the darkness.

Chapter 40

For two days the ferocious weather hampered any further search operation. The river was swollen and the banks treacherous.

The noise of the wind outside the cottage woke Emma. For a moment her memory had anaesthetised the tragic scenes on the riverbank. But the recollection waited, like a clawed animal, ready to tear into her consciousness, to tease out her terrors. And with the memory came the pain; it was unbearable.

Aching with grief, Emma swung her legs out of the security of her warm bed and went towards the window, opening the curtain a fraction. In the moonlight she saw Charlie in his carrycot. Moving softly towards him she watched the rise and fall of his chest.

'Safe,' whispered a voice.

Emma turned, looking around the room. Simon lay sleeping, Amelia tucked up beside him. Moving back to the window, Emma opened the catch to let in the night air. The wind had died down and the rain had stopped. Again, she thought she heard a voice – Joshua's voice – in the sounds of the dripping gutters.

'Joshua?' she whispered.

'I'm here,' the night answered.

Closing her eyes, she saw him in her mind's eye: the image of his face; he was smiling at her. A sense of peace, unlike anything she had ever experienced before, filled her whole being. With it came a sensation of joy, the emotions so strong and pure that she sank to her knees. Holding her hands to her heart she found herself smiling despite her pain. She tilted her face to the sky and whispered, 'Thank you. We will never forget you. We will always love you.'

Emma stayed there until the milky light of the morning crept across the sky, banishing the dark of the previous night and the days before it.

As Simon stirred, he realised Emma was no longer next to him and his heart missed a beat. He saw her silhouette against the dawn light and breathed more easily. Carefully, so as not to wake Amelia, he climbed out of bed and walked softly over to join her.

'It's cold, darling. Close the window and come back to bed.'

Emma looked up at Simon. Her pale face was bruised and scratched from the branches and debris in the river. The nails on one hand had been torn away when she clawed into the root system to save herself and Charlie, and she held it now tight against her chest.

'Simon,' her voice was low and he heard the tremor within it. 'My nightmares. They weren't memories of the past; they were predictions of the future – things to come. In my dreams the face-less man was not trying to hurt us; he was trying to save us. That man was Joshua. Had I realised, could I have changed anything?'

Simon, filled with mixed emotions on hearing the distress in Emma's voice, dropped to her level. He wrapped his arms tightly around her.

'No,' he answered. 'That was Joshua's choice of journey's end.'

'It's all so tragic, Simon – losing his mother like he did, then finding Beatrice, only to lose her too. Do you think they're together now? I'd like to think she was there for him.'

Memories crowded her head: her life as Charlotte, being

thrown from a sinking ship by her father, her life as Emma, her marriage to Joshua, Amelia's birth, the love, the sadness, the loss and finally the discovery of a new beginning with Simon and Charlie. Emma took a deep breath, then exhaled softly.

'I think I understand now. We're all entwined throughout eternity, destined to meet again and again, guided by those whispers of past memories to find one another, to learn from one another, to love one another and finally to leave one another. Joshua knew us in this lifetime and I believe in a past one. He's left us now, but I know we'll meet him again, whoever he will be … in that lifetime to come.'

Raising herself from her knees, Emma smiled and stretched out a hand to Simon. 'When that time comes … I'll know him.'

They recovered Joshua's body downstream later that morning. According to one of the search team, he had been found on the riverbank, not in the water. This, and the discovery of unexplained hoof prints close by, led to speculation as to what happened to Joshua in his final moments. But Emma and Amelia already knew.

Beatrice and Spirit had come back to collect Joshua.

Epilogue:
Henry's story

7 May 1915

There was a crack like the sound of thunder, followed by a second more muffled explosion that seemed to come from below the ship. It was lunchtime and Henry had been walking on the deck with his children, his son cradled in one of his strong arms and his small daughter eagerly grasping his free hand. He thought he could see the coast of Ireland despite the fog, and at that particular moment in time, just prior to the first explosion, he was more at peace with himself than he had ever been.

With the blast came shock and confusion, then the ship began to list rapidly towards starboard. Crew and passengers around him ran across the deck, scrambling for the lifeboats, most of which lay tantalisingly out of reach. Henry thought of his wife back in their stateroom. A woman threw herself overboard as a lifeboat was launched; she bounced off the edge of the boat and dropped into the sea, her screams lost among the noise. Shock had turned to fear and panic; chaos reigned.

Henry threw his young daughter Charlotte into the arms of a member of the crew who was installed in one of the few descending lifeboats. He heard her shout for him and watched in horror as the lifeboat spilled its precious cargo directly into the sea. In his arms he still held his son Charles, now terrified to let go of the small form.

As the magnificent ship began to drop its bow, its metal bulk screaming out in indignation, Henry scanned the water for his daughter. Wrung with grief now, parted from his wife and daughter, he held his son Charles ever closer to his chest. He stood, as best he could, on the uneven deck and cried out for some higher intervention. 'Save my son,' he begged, as he desperately searched for a lifeboat.

Henry knew that the ship's stern was at an ominous angle. The water below him churned with thrashing bodies. There was no one to pass Charles to. Sailors and passengers alike had leaped or been thrown over the side of the ship in an attempt to escape the fire and suction. They bobbed below in the black waters. The cries of the frightened and dying, merged with those of the failing ship, sent a final guilty chill through Henry's heart; it had been his selfish deeds that had brought them to this final day.

Still holding tightly onto Charles, Henry made a final plea for forgiveness. 'Allow me another chance to make amends for my actions. Let me save my children,' he screamed into the night.

When Henry jumped and succumbed to the churning water, he held his small son tightly to him for as long as he was able.

As the Lusitania's *bow dropped below the water, pulled inexorably towards the ocean bed, Henry's plea from that lifetime was recorded. It would whisper deep within his soul, until his next awakening, and his chance for atonement …*

Acknowledgements

Thank you to Debbie and David for their valuable feedback on my earliest drafts and to Suzy for pushing me towards publishing. Your warmth and encouragement has been amazing.

I owe a great deal to Anne Newman, whose editorial suggestions have been invaluable, and all the team at whitefox, without whom this book would have remained in a draft form and never seen the light of day.

Thank you.

Lightning Source UK Ltd.
Milton Keynes UK
UKOW01f0312121116
287437UK00002B/4/P